EXPERIENCING
DOMINION

EXPERIENCING DOMINION

Culture, Identity, and Power in the British Mediterranean

THOMAS W. GALLANT

University of Notre Dame Press
Notre Dame, Indiana

Manufactured in the United States of America

A record of the Library of Congress Cataloging-in-Publication Data
is available upon request from the Library of Congress

∞ *This book is printed on acid-free paper.*

CONTENTS

ACKNOWLEDGMENTS

This book is the result of many years' work, and some of the chapters have already appeared in print, albeit in a rather different form. I acknowledge and thank those who helped me with the previously published article versions of some of the chapters. I cannot thank enough the three people who have most shaped the way I study the past: Jeffrey S. Adler, Mary P. Gallant, and Michael Herzfeld. My deepest appreciation goes also to Barbara Hanrahan and the staff at the University of Notre Dame Press for their help with publishing the book. The following foundations provided the financial support for my researches: the National Science Foundation, the H. F. Guggenheim Foundation, and the Division of Sponsored Research at the University of Florida. Finally, I acknowledge the invaluable assistance of the archivists, librarians, and staff at the Topiko Istoriko Arheio tis Kefallenias in Argostoli, the Istoriko Arheio tis Kerkiras in Kerkira, the Gennadeion Library, the British School at Athens, and the Public Records Office, Kew Gardens.

A version of chapter 4 appeared originally as: Agency, Structure, and Explanation in Social History: The Case of the Foundling Home on Kephallenia, Greece, during the 1830s. *Social Science History* 15:4 (1991): 479–508; chapter 5 as: Turning the Horns: Cultural Metaphors, Material Conditions, and the Peasant Language of Resistance in Ionian Islands (Greece) during the Nineteenth Century. *Comparative Studies in Society and History* 36:4 (1994): 702–19; chapter 6 as: Honor, Masculinity, and Ritual Knife-fighting in Nineteenth Century Greece. *American Historical Review* 105:2 (2000): 359–82; and chapter 8 as: Peasant Ideology and Excommunication for Crime in a Colonial Context: The Ionian Islands (Greece), 1817–1864. *Journal of Social History* 24:3 (1990): 485–512.

PREFACE

Dominance in India was doubly articulated. It stood, on the one hand, for Britain's power to rule over its South Asian subjects, and on the other, for the power exercised by the indigenous elite over the subaltern among the subject population. The alien moment of colonial dominance was thus matched by an indigenous moment within the general configuration of power. (Guha 1993: 69).

All resistance is not constructive, nor are all subordinate peoples able to critique the conditions of their subordination. (Merry 1995: 14).

These two passages aptly capture the focus of this book. Guha's comments remind us that we need to be attuned to the layers of power relationships that exist in any society but that may achieve an even deeper stratigraphy in colonial situations. Merry's observation, based on her assessment of the importance that law played in shaping imperial rule, suggests that we need to exercise care in identifying acts of "resistance" because we always run the risk of imputing motives that may exist more in the mind of the modern analyst than in that of the historical actor. As I delved deeper into this study of the interaction between British representatives of the Colonial Office and the Greeks of the Ionian Islands whom they were sent to rule, I became increasingly uncomfortable with the emphasis on resistance that has become prominent in the contemporary literature on imperialism and colonialism. Conceptually, I found the antinimous pair of resistance and accommodation too constraining for a deeper understanding of the colonial experience. I increasingly came to share the concern recently voiced by Michael F. Brown (1996) and others (e.g., Fox and Starn 1997) that we need to "resist resistance," or at least to conceive of it in more complex and nuanced ways. Not all actions of the ruling groups, either foreign or domestic, are hegemonic, and not every response by the subaltern constitutes resistance.

What I want to capture in this book is the complex, variegated, and often-ambiguous *experience* of imperial rule shared by Britons and Greeks when the islands were part of the British Empire. Conceptually, I have chosen *dominion* to express the thing that they experienced. Because *dominion* emphasizes the unity of power, authority, and sovereignty, it better conveys the complexities and ambiguities of imperial rule than do *hegemony*, *accommodation*, and *resistance*.

The central aim of this book, then, is to undertake an engagement with debates on hegemony, power, and identity in contemporary historical and anthropological literature. Each chapter individually engages a different aspect of that literature.[1] Together they are intended to move the discussion away from an emphasis on a simple polarity between hegemony and resistance, and instead to focus our attention more on the shared interaction between colonizers and colonized, rulers and ruled, foreigners and locals. I want to emphasize contingency and historical agency, to examine intentionality, to explore the processes of accommodation and, when warranted, resistance, and to reconstruct the world Britons and Greeks made together on the Ionian Islands during the nineteenth century through their shared experience of dominion.

Few readers, besides those who have an interest in the Hellenic world or who are aficionados of Lawrence Durrell's novels, have probably heard of the Ionian Islands, let alone know that for much of the nineteenth century they were part of the British Empire. Moreover, it is indisputable that in the annals of the empire, the isles occupied only a marginal position and were simply a sideshow in the great game of European imperial expansion. The Ionian Islands lacked the sense of exoticism, romanticism, and adventure that the British associated with Africa, India, and the Far East. To visit Kerkira was not to traverse into the heart of darkness. But it is precisely because the islands did not fit neatly in the usual colonial categories that an analysis of the experience of dominion there can be especially fruitful.

Basic elements that shaped the colonial encounter were more ambiguous in the Greek case than elsewhere. Were the Ionians, for example, racially Europeans? Were they culturally "western"? Answers to these basic questions about their identity were not self-evident. How could the descendents of the ancient forebears of western civilization *not* be "western"? How could the cosmopolitan Greek bourgeois merchant or the crimson-cloaked Italianate Ionian aristocrat *not* be "European"? In short, on the Ionian Islands, the British confronted a complex, sophisticated, white, Christian indigenous culture, and so the process of identity formation and cultural categorization was different from elsewhere. And this further complicated the dynamics of imperial rule. Compounding the complexity of the situation was the anomalous political status of the islands. They were, in theory, a sovereign state under the protection of the British crown. Perforce, the local Greek political elite had to be accorded a greater degree of political power than in other types of direct-ruled colonies. In sum, since the Ionian Islands presented the British with a situation different from elsewhere in the empire, an analysis of how Greeks and Britons experienced dominion and hegemony, resistance, and accommodation here will enrich our historical understanding of imperialism more broadly.

Chapter 1 briefly introduces the reader to the Ionian Islands and explains the genesis and development of the British protectorate over them from 1815 to 1864. Chapters 2 and 3 are related and deal with the issue of identity. In chapter 2, I examine how the British crafted an identity for the Greeks. In so doing I engage the literature on identity and "Otherness," and on Orientalism and postcolonialism. I argue that much of that literature simplifies the process of identity formation by envisioning it as a straightforward process predicated on bipolar opposition. Instead, using the case of the British and the Ionian Greeks, I show that the process was more complex than that and that it was based on the construction of colonial stereotypes through analogies rather than through single dichotomies. In this case, the British created an identity for the Ionians either as "Mediterranean Irish" or as "European aborigines." But identity formation was a two-way street, and in chapter 3 I explore how the Greeks understood Britons and the West. The challenge with this, of course, is rooted in the sources. The voices of the ruled frequently come to us in muted whispers and oblique asides. Using the legal statutes passed by the municipal council on one of the islands, Zakinthos, I show that the Greeks understood that "Western" meant to be ordered, regimented, and segregated, but that such traits were only a façade, masking public presentation but not affecting private reality. The dialogue over identity highlights key features such as private versus public space, inner character versus outward presentation, and civic virtues versus personal interest that shaped and informed the process of colonial rule on the islands.

Chapters 4 and 5 explore two related but different aspects of the colonial experience. In chapter 4, I examine how colonial initiatives, regardless of how well intentioned, could produce very different results when transformed in local hands. In this case, using the establishment of foundling hospitals and orphanages aimed at caring for society's most vulnerable group, I show that there was a vast difference in political culture between the British and the Greek elite members and that this difference influenced the way that state institutions operated in civil society. To the Greeks, the state primarily constituted a bundle of resources that existed to be exploited for partisan advantage. The Greek elite, then, frequently did not resist "hegemonic" colonial initiatives, like the foundling hospitals, but instead embraced and exploited them in creative ways unforeseen by the dominant power.

Chapter 5 explores acts of open resistance, but does so in such a way as to exemplify the difficulty of reconstructing and understanding the "hidden transcripts" (Scott 1990) of resistance. Greek peasants spoke a language of resistance that was oblique and that was rooted in metaphors rather than political slogans. They understood power relations and expressed their protests to them through allusions to sex, honor, masculinity, and integrity. Politics and protest, hegemony and resistance between Ionians and Britons and between Greek aristocrats and peasants were filtered and *shaped* through a complex lens of culture and language that were grounded in a rich language of sexual metaphors.

Chapters 6 and 7 continue the theme of colonial initiatives and unintended consequences, but in a different realm: courts and the law. As I suggest in a variety of places in the book, the Colonial Office saw law and justice as the key pillars justifying the legitimacy of British rule over the Greeks. Consequently, the British placed great emphasis on reforming the courts and the criminal justice system.

Chapter 6 explores how the British endeavored to deal with the extremely high level of male interpersonal violence, exemplified most vividly by the ritualized knife duel so favored by Ionian plebeians. I reconstruct the knife duel, uncover the system of masculine honor on which it was based, and then examine how the British tried to abate it through legal reforms. In particular, I show how the expansion of the role of the courts eventually led Greek men to incorporate them into their disputes over honor and reputation, but in creative and unexpected ways.

Chapter 7 picks up this theme but adds a gendered dimension. One of the unintended consequences of the Colonial Office's legal reforms was to create a new civic space that was exploited initially by Greek women rather than men. In spite of being immured in a gendered cultural system, very reminiscent of the ones examined by ethnographers in contemporary Greece in which women were strictly forbidden to encroach on public space, Ionian Greek women flocked by the thousands into the sacred halls of justice and there leveled charges of slander against one another. The story of women's interaction with the criminal justice system exemplifies from a different angle the complexity of the interplay between rulers and ruled. In this we can see how an explicitly hegemonic institution, the colonial criminal courts, could actually be transformed into an empowering experience for the ruled.

Chapter 8 examines the crucial topic of religion. At the heart of how Britons and Greeks experienced dominion was religion. Both were Christian cultures, and Christianity constituted a vital element of each culture's self-identification. Religion provided the British with legitimation of their rule. As I show, they considered it their God-given mission to bring Christian enlightenment to the Greeks. On the other side of the coin, religion provided the Greeks with a rationale for resistance. Using the example of the British-sponsored policy of issuing excommunication against Greeks accused of secular crimes, I explore the complexity of the relationship between religion, culture, power, and identity, and how that struggle was at the heart of how each side experienced dominion.

Collectively, these case studies address key topics and questions in contemporary social and cultural history and historical anthropology. I have tried wherever possible to engage debates in as many relevant fields as possible (identity studies, gender, legal history, postcolonialism, etc.) and to place the Greek case in as broad a comparative context as possible. This volume thus speaks to many audiences: historians and anthropologists of Greece, students of the British Empire, and scholars from various disciplines interested in empires, the imperial experience, and contemporary trends in the study of colonialism. Adopting such a broad comparative perspective opens the work up to criticism from various regional specialists. Such is to be expected. One of the primary goals of this book is to contribute to a post postcolonialist paradigm for examining the imperial encounter and another is to further the increasingly closer ties between history and anthropology. Finally, I hope that this book suggests some of the ways that historians of modern Greece can adopt a more vigorous and explicit engagement with mainstream historiography (Gallant 1997, 1999, 2001).

ABBREVIATIONS

A&P Acts and Proceedings of Parliament

CO Colonial Office

IAK Istoriko Arheio tis Kerkiras

PRO Public Records Office. Citations to documents from the PRO employ their recommended citation style.

TIAK Topiko Istoriko Arheio tis Kefallenias

EXPERIENCING
DOMINION

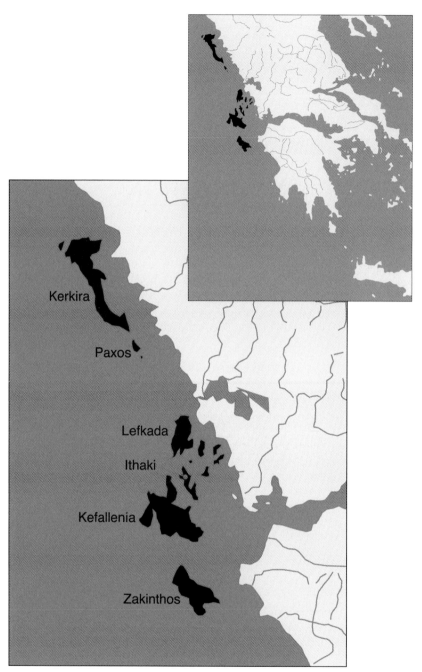

The Ionian Islands.
Courtesy of the General Libraries, the University of Texas at Austin.

CHAPTER ONE

Introduction

The Ionian Islands

The Ionian Islands

The Ionian Islands are a string of verdant isles lying off the western coast of Greece at the edge of the Ionian Sea (see facing map). There are seven major islands and numerous smaller, largely uninhabited ones. Thus, they are often referred as the *eptanisia*, or "Seven Islands." In order from north to south, they are Kerkira, Paxos, Lefkada (or Lefkas), Kefallenia, Ithaki, Zakinthos, and Kythera. With the exception of Kythera, they form a fairly coherent geographical unit. That Kythera, located thirty-five miles south of Cape Maleas at the southern tip of the Peloponnesos, was included in the group was the result of history, not geography.

The six western islands present a landscape quite different from peninsular Greece. Unlike central and southern mainland Greece or the Aegean Islands, the Ionian Islands are not characterized by an arid, barren, and seasonally desiccated landscape. Instead they are lush and verdant, though not in the way that the more alpine regions of Northern Greece are. Instead, rolling hills, upland karst basin, and small but fertile coastal plains characterize their topography, and because of their location they enjoy precipitation levels well in excess of much of peninsular Greece. For these reasons, the island of Zakinthos, for example, was often referred to as the "flower of the Levant," and the same could be said of the other islands as well.

Though geography may not be destiny, in the case of the Ionian Islands it has surely shaped their development. In the days before steamships, possession of the islands could give a state mastery of east-west maritime movement across the northern Mediterranean. For that reason from antiquity until the recent past, they were a hotly sought-after commodity by any power with imperial pretensions in the region.

The Long Imperial Past

The case studies in this book focus on specific situations and events, an analysis of which can provide us with insights into how the experience of dominion had a deep impact on both the British and the Greeks. What I want to do in this section is provide a reader with the historical background needed to contextualize the chapters that follow. The islands had been inhabited on and off since the Paleolithic period. During the Late Bronze Age (1550–1050 B.P.), some of them, but especially Kefallenia, were part of the Mycenaean cultural domain. Mycenaean civilization flourished in southern Greece and was one of the major cultures of the eastern Mediterranean during the late prehistoric period. Its presence on the Ionian Islands indicates that from an early date, the islands were connected to developments on the continent. It is also this period of its past that has most interested archaeologists, because of the so-called "Homeric Question." For those who ascribe to a literalist reading of Homer's *Odyssey*, the search for Late Bronze Age Mycenaean remains was driven by the quest to identify the hero Odysseos's Ithaca. For some it was the modern Ithaki; for others it was either Kefallenia or Lefkada. The result of their expeditions has not solved the question, but they have brought to light solid evidence that Mycenaean Greeks occupied all of them and that, even in the second millennium B.C., they were a prized stepping-stone for east-west travel in the central Mediterranean (Souyoudzoglou-Haywood 1999).

This role was even more crucial to their development during the period in which the Greek city-states flourished. Kerkira was one of the earliest places colonized by mainland Greeks as part of the process of Greek colonization of the Mediterranean during the eighth and seventh centuries B.C. During the Classical and Hellenistic periods it was the only one of the islands to achieve any degree of prominence. The others remained essentially on the fringes of the more developed world of the Greek city-states. With the rise of Rome, the islands were once again a sought-after possession for geostrategical purposes. The archaeological remains suggest that the islands were both a way station for trans-Mediterranean traffic and a playground for wealthy Roman citizens.

With the transformation of the Roman Empire into an eastern and a western half, the islands went from being geographically in the center of a multinational polity to being on the frontier of two increasingly estranged powers: Rome in the west and Byzantium, the great medieval empire of the east. One major consequence of this shift was to reduce the islands to a liminal status, uneasily existing on the edge of two competing powers, and this resulted in the islands becoming an infamous haunt for pirates and marauders. At times during the twelfth century A.D., for example, pirate chieftains like Maio Orsisni on Zakinthos and the Genoese adventurer Vetrano on Kerkira emerged as virtual rulers of the islands (Nicol 1984: 2; Miller 1903: 209). As the power of the Byzantine Empire waxed and waned, Italian city-states sought to advance their mercantile interests in the Near East by occupying the geostrategically important Ionian Islands. Venice, for example, briefly incorporated Kerkira into its empire in the aftermath of the Fourth Crusade. The rise of the Despotate of Epiros quickly led to the island being reincorporated into the Byzantine sphere of influence. But the other islands to the south passed back and forth between various Latin rulers and their families. Throughout the medieval period, the Venetians harbored desires to conquer and control the islands, and the emergence of the Osmanli Turks as a dire threat to the great Orthodox empire of the east provided them with an opportunity to do so. In 1402, their dream was thus partly achieved when they bloodlessly became masters of Kerkira (Miller 1903: 212). After the fall of Constantinople, through various stratagems and schemes, they acquired Zakinthos in 1484, Kefallenia and Ithaki in 1502, and Lefkas in 1684. The island of Kythera was already in their hands as part of the Cretan domain. When the doge lost control of Crete to the Ottoman Empire in 1669, administration of the island was transferred to the *proveditore generale del Levante* based in the Ionian Islands, and so Kythera, in spite of its distant location, became one of the Ionian Islands. From this point on, the history of the Seven Islands would be profoundly different from the rest of the Greek world.

The Islands under Venetian Rule

The Venetians ruled the islands wholly or partly from 1402 until 1797, when they were liberated by the advancing armies of Napoleon Bonaparte. Venetian rule profoundly shaped the development of society and economy on the islands, and so we cannot understand the circumstances that confronted the British when they took over the islands without first briefly discussing the development of the islands under Venetian rule (Andreades 1914).

The Venetians modeled their administration of the islands on their own system of government (Margaritis 1978). A *bailly*, or governor, was appointed by the doge in Venice, and he sat at the head of council composed of a vice *bailly*, a commander of the military garrison at Kerkira, and a captain of the fleet. The Venetians provided for Greek participation in government through the establishment of a council of 150. This body was composed of noblemen elected annually by an assembly of the heads of the aristocratic families whose names had been enrolled in the Golden Book, and the group was accorded some minor administrative and oversight functions. Ionian society was juridically divided into three groups: nobles, burghers, and manual laborers. The aristocracy, or Signori, dominated both the political and the economic systems. The Venetians kept intact the feudal system that they found on the islands, and in fact, they sought ways to strengthen it. There were twenty-four feudal baronies on the islands, though the number did fluctuate, dropping to a low of twelve in the mid-eighteenth century. The Venetians used the bequeathal of feudal estates as a way of recruiting and rewarding loyal followers. The peasants tied to the great estates had neither political nor property rights. They were considered the "movable goods" of their lord (Alvanas 1984). Each noble household possessed a gang of retainers who managed their estates. A Venetian law of 1641, which mandated that no man could vote in the noble council unless he had a house in the city, fueled the already manifest tendency of the feudatories to become absentee lords. This enabled members of their gangs to become de facto petty lords on their estates (Miller 1903: 217). There thus developed a system in which private gangs of violent men called *bravi* came to play a prominent role.

The estate system, encouraged by Venetian imperial policy, produced a particular form of agrarian regime. The agricultural landscape of the islands became dominated by a single crop, which varied from island to island. The northern isles of Kerkira and Lefkas specialized in the production of olives, while Kefallenia and Zakinthos to the south were given over to the production of currant grapes (Gallant 1985; Asdrachas 1994; Franks 1997). On Kerkira, for example, olive trees covered 44 percent of the cultivated surface area, and an additional 19 percent was under vines; on Lefkas, 51 percent was devoted to olives and 28 percent to vines. On Zakinthos, in contrast, currant vines covered 54 percent of the surface area and olives 17 percent. What the islands had in common was that the bulk of the production of both commodities was destined for export to European markets. Some of the grapes were processed into wine for domestic consumption, but most of the crop was sold as dried raisins to markets in England, Belgium, and elsewhere. The olives and olive oil served domestic needs, but in the eighteenth century the bulk of the crop was shipped to central Europe, where it was used as an industrial lubricant. Moreover, since so much of the available cultivable land was devoted to the monoproduction of cash crops, all of the islands produced insufficient food to feed their population. Consequently, long before other regions of the Balkans, the Ionian Islands were incorporated into the burgeoning Eurocentric mercantile world system as a seller of export cash crops and a buyer of basic subsistence commodities. In other respects as well, the Ionians were connected to Western Europe in ways that their Hellenic brethren on the continent were not.

The great aristocratic families took advantage of the opportunity open to them under the Venetians to gain an education at the universities of Italy. Many young Ionian noblemen studied law or medicine at the University of Padua or Pisa (Leontsinis 1994). While there, they were exposed to the ideas of the Enlightenment. The merchants and commodities factors who traveled abroad to conduct the business of the wealthy landowners also developed ties to the burgeoning Greek diaspora communities and so were also exposed to new ideas and trends. Consequently, islanders came to play a critical role in the dissemination of ideas about liberty and natural rights into the Greek world during the second half of the eighteenth century. Ionian islanders, then, contributed in crucial ways to the emergence of a Hellenic consciousness. This meant that any struggle for emancipation of the Greeks from "foreign"—either Ottoman or other—rule would include the Ionians, and indeed, islanders played vital roles in every Greek uprising, including the successful one of 1821. As we shall see in a number of instances later on, the Ionians' heartfelt connection to the larger Greek struggle shaped their interaction with the British authorities in numerous and meaningful ways. For now, what needs to be appreciated is the role that islanders played as a window to the West.

According to popular legend, when plotting his Mediterranean campaign Napoleon observed that capturing the Ionian Islands would make him a master of the Mediterranean (Stoianovich 1949: 1; Kukku 1983). After his whirlwind defeat of the Austrian forces in northern Italy, Napoleon's France obtained the islands with the Treaty of Leoben on April 18, 1797. Shortly thereafter, French forces under the leadership of General Gentili seized the islands, and the Treaty of Campo Formio, which signaled the demise of the Serenissma Republic of Venice, then formalized that occupation. The French Revolution came to the Greeks along with the Gallic army. Liberated Greeks planted trees of liberty. The aristocracy was abolished. A popular government based on the French Constitution of 1795 was installed. Factional squabbles between competing aristocratic parties jockeying for power erupted in intrigue and violence. Sectional fighting plagued the islanders for the next twenty years, as they were passed back and forth between the Great Powers. The French held the islands until 1799, when the Russians drove them out (Mackesy 1957). Their Orthodox coreligionists from the north, in turn, occupied them until the Treaty of Tilsit ceded them back to Bonaparte in 1807. The islands' strategic importance led the British to launch a military expedition against the French forces on them in 1809. There had previously been fighting between pro-British Greeks and the French, but the landing of British forces elevated the conflict to a new and higher level. French resistance on all of the islands except for Kerkira proved limited. By October 1809, Zakinthos had fallen; within a matter of three months, the others followed suit. Only the garrison on Kerkira stood firm, and did so until shortly after Napoleon's abdication in 1814. Henceforth, Britain would dominate the islands.

"A Peculiar Connexion":
"King Tom" and the Protectorate (1816–1832)

The British took control of the islands as the primary protector of their sovereignty.[1] This decision was arrived at by consensus among the Great Powers at the Paris Peace Congress of 1815. The tempestuous events that had engulfed the islands after the French takeover showed that the rambunctious Greeks could not be accorded home rule. But because of their strategic location, each of the major powers was reticent about letting any one of the others annex them completely. The solution arrived at was for the islands to be granted limited autonomy within the framework of Great Power guaranteed protection. The islands were, thus, united into a single independent state, called the United States of the Ionian Islands. Basing their argument primarily on the grounds that their forces had liberated the islands and that they still had troops there, Great Britain sought and obtained an agreement that placed the islands under the protection of the British Crown (Dietz 1994: 66). How heavy or light Britain's protective hand would be was an issue left open. All that the treaty stipulated was that a lord high commissioner would be appointed by the Crown to coordinate Anglo-Greek affairs. Among his duties were that he would convene a constituent council to draft a constitution detailing the system of self-rule, that he would oversee the British military forces, and that he would wield control over the islands' mercantile, commercial, and foreign affairs. The protecting power was to construct a system of modified self-rule, and the Greeks were to be responsible for maintaining the military forces. To implement this peculiar arrangement the Crown selected Lieutenant-General Sir Thomas Maitland.

When he accepted the post of lord high commissioner of the Ionian Islands in 1815, Maitland had already compiled an impressive record as a military officer and a colonial administrator (Dixon 1969). He had previously sat on the Board of Control for India and the Privy Council, and he had successfully served as Governor of Ceylon and Governor-General of Malta. In the latter two capacities, he had earned the reputation as a man who brought order and reform to the subjects under his command, even if it took more than a modicum of coercion to do so. His autocratic bearing and haughty demeanor earned him the nickname of "King Tom." He seemed to the British government to be the ideal person to bring order to the chaos that had reigned on the islands since 1797. Since technically the islands were a sovereign state, one of the first orders of business for Maitland was to oversee the drafting of a constitution. He made crystal clear to his Colonial Office associates that the purpose of the constitution was "to give us pretty nearly all the real power" (CO 136/300: Maitland to Bunbury, May 3, 1816 PRO). The trick was to devise a system of government that paid lip service to Ionian sovereignty while establishing British control. As to any semblance of democracy and liberty, he was equally blunt: "a free government is incompatible with a strong one" (Dixon 1969: 185), and he was bent on establishing a very strong one.

The charter eventually passed by the Constituent Assembly received royal ratification on August 26, 1817 (A&P 1818 (132), XVII). It created a complex system of government that gave the appearance of providing legislative and administrative power to the Greeks while maintaining real power in the hands of the colonial administration. There was to be a bicameral, national legislature consisting of a senate and an elected legislative assembly. The senate consisted of six members, five of whom were elected by the assembly. The lord high commissioner selected the sixth member, who also served as the senate's president, and he could veto the assembly's selections. Local electoral bodies elected the assembly from a double list of nominations. The right to vote and to hold public office was open only to a tiny percentage of the population based on wealth qualifications. Each island was accorded a local administration headed by a regent, elected by a syndicate but subject to the approval of the lord high commissioner, and a municipal council. Law and order were also key issues of the day, and the Colonial Office made sure that the institutions needed to keep the peace were firmly under its officers' control. The courts and law were revamped and new police forces established. While ostensibly operated by Greeks, key positions, like posts on the Supreme Court, were largely in British hands. Also, each island housed a garrison of British troops.

Real power both nationally and locally was clearly vested in Colonial Office appointees. Nationally, the lord high commissioner possessed enormous discretionary veto power: all laws, decrees, and most appointments had to meet with his approval. He also enjoyed special judicial powers that gave him control over a special executive police force and the ability to detain, imprison, or exile anyone without a trial. Locally, residents appointed by the lord high commissioner exercised similar powers over the regents. In short, the 1817 Charter of the United States of the Ionian Islands provided a semblance of democratic, republican rule, but in fact vested the real power in the British colonial administration.

Many islanders saw through the façade and agitated against the constitution; indeed, a deputation led by Count Ioannis Kapodistrias, member of a prominent Kerkiran family and a former official in the Russian foreign office, formally complained about it to Prime Minister Lord Liverpool in 1819. But other developments soon shifted both Greek and British attention away from the constitutional question and turned it instead to an issue that would complicate immeasurably British rule over the islands: Greek nationalism and Ionian unification.

Even before the first blows were struck in the name of Greek national liberation, Ionian islanders were deeply involved in the revolutionary struggle (Thompson and Sosnowski 1994; for an account of the war generally, see Gallant 2001: 9–31). In 1814, a secret society, the Filiki Etairia, was set up to further the cause of Greek nationalism. Ionian intellectuals, nobles, and merchants were active in the organization from its inception, and it was widely assumed that the leader of the movement was Ioannis Kapodistrias. He was not, but members of his family were. This was sufficient to fuel the rumor that he was, and the belief in the veracity of the rumor was enough to incite many of his fellow islanders to join the rebellion. In spite of the risk of excommunication, Orthodox priests on the islands preached to their flocks the gospel of rebellion. Thus, when hostilities broke out first in the Danubian Principalities on March 5, 1821, and then in the Peloponnesos twenty days later, Ionian islanders were eager participants. Within weeks of the war's commencement, over four thousand men crossed over to the continent to join the rebellion. Soon their numbers were large enough to form a special Ionian Brigade. Those who did not leave to fight gathered and sent arms, supplies, and money. These developments placed the British in an awkward situation because the official government policy was one of neutrality. Consequently, as subjects of His Majesty, the islanders were also supposed to be neutral. Imposing nonintervention would prove difficult and would irreparably impair Anglo-Ionian relations for the next forty years (Wrigley 1987a; 1987b; 1988).

War fever swept the islands. When some Moslems refugees, for example, attempted to find refuge on the southern island of Kythera, the locals slaughtered them (CO 136/1332: Adam to Hethcoate, September 9, 1821 PRO; CO 136/1332: Adam to Hethcoate, October 18, 1821 PRO; Leontsinis 1987: 283; Wrigley 1988: 113–15). On another occasion, some shipwrecked sailors from the Porte's fleet were washed up on the shores of Zakinthos. Before an angry lynch mob of Ionians could reach them, British troops intervened, only to be themselves pelted with rocks and other debris. The resident's response of executing the stone-throwers—including a child of tender years—only served to exacerbate tensions on the islands (CO 136/1085: Duffy to Hankey, October 11, 1821 PRO; Wrigley 1988: 109–12). As the Greek war of independence progressed, the British had to adopt more and stricter policies to sustain Ionian neutrality. Among the most aggressive and hated were: (1) confiscation of weapons, especially firearms; (2) confiscation and sale of property belonging to men who had left the islands to join the rebellion; (3) strict application of quarantine laws, which carried a capital sentence, against those caught clandestinely reentering the islands; (4) blockade of shipping and commerce between the islands and the mainland; (5) the British policy of selectively favoring Moslem over Greek refugees. These policies, however, only added fuel to the fire of Greek nationalism, and the Ionians either ignored or actively resisted them.

Sustaining and enforcing these draconian measures became even more difficult when British and other western European and American philhellenes started to use the islands as their base of operation. That men like Lord Byron and Edward Blaquière moved back and forth from the islands to the continent only served to raise Ionian expectations about a change in their possible involvement in the war. Those expectations and their belief that the islands would be included in a free Greek state were elevated even further as British forces began to play a more active role in the conflict, culminating with the crushing defeat of the Ottoman fleet by Anglo-French forces at Navarino and the election of Ioannis Kapodistrias as the first president of an independent Greece. Even the Kerkiran's assassination did not dampen the Ionians' belief that they would be included in the new state. Those hopes were dashed, and with their demise, Anglo-Ionian relations entered a new phase. From this point forward, a new issue separated rulers and ruled: Greek nationalism and Ionian unification.

The Reformist Imperative (1832–1848)

The ascendancy of a Whig government in Great Britain after decades of Tory rule and the establishment by the Great Powers of an independent Kingdom of Greece under the rule of Prince Otto of Bavaria marked crucial turning points in the history of the Ionian Islands. The treaty that granted independence to the mainland Greeks deliberately and explicitly omitted the Ionians, thus dashing the hopes of the vast majority of islanders. Their fate was still linked to the British Empire. The incoming Whig administration appointed a new group of colonial administrators with a very different agenda than their predecessors. As in the United Kingdom, the Whigs came to power on the islands with an ambitious, reformist agenda. Lord Nugent from 1832 to 1835 and then his successor as lord high commissioner, General Sir Howard Douglas, embarked on a series of major legal innovations and economic and social reforms (Bowen 1861: 326). It was their goal to bring enlightened civilization to the islands by providing them with liberal institutions. It was their hope that by so doing they would show the people the benefits of British rule, and that this would dampen the still seething ambition for union with Greece. Through the 1830s and 1840s, various lord high commissioners, regardless of which party governed in the metropolis, sustained the reformist imperative. Repeatedly in the chapters to follow, I return to this key moment in the history of the empire and the protectorate because it was during this period when we can see best how both sides experienced the process of colonial rule.

Nothing the British tried could diminish the swelling tide of support for national unification. Secret societies formed. Radical newspapers spread the nationalist cry—until the authorities shut them down. Priests preached the gospel of Hellenic Orthodox unity—in spite of orders from the ecumenical patriarch in Istanbul forbidding them to do so. Public ceremonies from religious processions commemorating Orthodox saints to civic festivals almost invariably ended in some form of public protest in favor of unification. As the pitch of nationalist agitation rose, so did the Colonial Office's endeavors to suppress it through force.

Douglas in particular began to use fully the dictatorial powers vested in his office by the 1817 charter. Constructing civil society through institution-building increasingly took a backseat to maintenance of the public tranquility through force and coercion. With the appointment of Lord John Russell as head of the Colonial Office, Douglas lost London's support for his hard-line response to unrest amongst the Greeks. In 1843, Lord Seaton took over as lord high commissioner with the specific charge of solving the Ionian issue. Lord George Bowen (1861: 327), a colleague, described him as a "tall and dignified man, traits that were no mean element[s] of success in governing Orientals." Seaton's strategy was twofold: first, to continue the building of civil society by incorporating more Greeks into the administration and, second, to revamp completely the 1817 charter by incorporating many liberal elements intended to place more power in Greek hands. His hope was to assuage the moderates' desire for constitutional reform, and by so doing to undercut the power of the more radical nationalists (Calligas 1994). The violence that erupted on the islands in 1848 only complicated matters.

The Ungovernable Rocks: Nationalism and the Unionist Movement (1848–1864)

1848: the year of European revolutions, the "springtime for the people." Even these distant Greek isles were not spared the contagion of nationalist revolt. Though the various secret societies at work on the islands had planned for there to be a series of coordinated uprisings on all of the islands, only Kefallenia experienced actual violence. I discuss the 1848 and 1849 riots in a number of the chapters, focusing on various aspects of them (Hannell 1987; 1988; Paximadopoulos-Stavrinou 1980; Tsouganatos 1976).

As with most of the 1848–49 revolutions on the Ionian Islands, there was no single element that united all of the participants. For some peasants, the uprising presented an opportunity for them to get back at exploitative landlords; others took up arms at the behest of their patrons and protectors. For committed revolutionaries like the notorious Papas Listes, or Bandit Priest, this was to be the start of a holy war of liberation against the infidel. In any event, the rebellion never spread far from its epicenter on the island of Kefallenia. Nonetheless, it had an impact.

"Determined not to loose the initiative, Seaton argued for one bold stroke of policy to restore Britain's position and confound the extremists. Throughout 1848 and 1849 he remained an optimist, convinced that enlightened self-interest favouring the British connection still outweighed the emotional attraction of union with Greece" (Pratt 1978: 132). And so he pushed for more liberal constitutional reforms. Once enacted, these changes shifted the balance of power from the lord high commissioner to the legislative assembly. The failure of open rebellion and the new opportunities presented by the constitutional reforms led the ardent nationalists to change their strategy.

The Radical Union Party grew in numbers and importance. The newly enshrined freedom of the press opened the way for publications like *Fileleftheris* ("The Liberal") and the even more radical *Anayennisis* ("Renaissance") to spread openly the gospel of national unification and expound the new tactic of peaceful noncooperation against the British.

Through the power now vested in the Greek-controlled legislative branch, the radical unionists endeavored to make the island ungovernable (Calligas 1994a; 1994b; Knox 1984; Stavrinos 1985; Gregory 1986). Repeatedly through the 1850s they disrupted the working of the government, voted for unrealistic budgets, and submitted petitions designed to humiliate Her Majesty's government. Administrative gridlock resulted. Not even a special mission by noted philhellene and liberal William Gladstone could salvage the situation (Souris 1989; Sandiford 1981). As the islands became more ungovernable and their strategic importance to the British diminished, a discussion began in Colonial and Foreign Office circles about ceding the islands to the Greek kingdom.

Three options were seriously discussed. Option one called for an expansion of the British military forces on the islands and the restoration of a more restrictive constitution. This course of action was rejected; the price in men and material would be too high when balanced against the strategic value of the islands. Option two envisaged the British keeping control of Kerkira while giving the other six islands to the Kingdom of Greece. But many officials familiar with the islands suggested that this plan was unworkable: the Kerkirans would rise up in open opposition, if not revolt. The only remaining option was to cede all the islands to the Kingdom of Greece. But the Colonial and Foreign Offices recognized that they needed a context in which to do so that would make it appear that they had not given in to the radical national unionists. The perfect occasion arose for such a gesture when Danish Prince William of Glücksburg was selected by the Great Powers to ascend to the Greek throne as George I in 1864 (Eldridge 1969; Temperley 1937). The protectorate had come to an end. Henceforth, the fate of the Seven Islands would be linked to that of Greece.

CHAPTER TWO

European Aborigines
and Mediterranean Irish

Identity, Cultural Stereotypes, and Colonial Rule

In June 1859, I first arrived at Corfu, and put up, with my family, at the Hotel de l'Europe, till we could find suitable apartments. . . . The living in Corfu was of course inferior to that of the countries in the West of Europe. But such things can be borne by most persons with patience, and by some, perhaps, even with indifference. The worst evil to me was the difficulty of sleeping. . . . [T]he town was alive with noisy pedestrians from about eight in the evening until three or four in the morning. . . . The loud conversations, the sharp disputes, and the irritating laughter, teazed and tormented the ear and brain struggling vainly for sleep. . . . Under these torments the hapless Briton tossing on his bed, . . . writhed with mingled anguish and despair. He had work to do by day, and if he slept at all, he must do so by night. His tormenters slept for half the day, and walked and sang during the greater part of the night. The Englishman truly felt that he had no business there. (Viscount Kirkwall 1864: 5)

Now I am once more among the merry [Ionian] Greeks, who are worth all other nations put together. I like to see [them], to hear them; I like their fun, their good humour, their Paddy ways, for they are very like Irishmen. (Sir Charles Napier 1852: 357)

These two passages capture the contrasting reactions that British officials and travelers experienced when they arrived on the islands. On the one hand, there was a feeling of *familiarity*. The Ionian Greeks resembled other peoples, in this case the Irish, with whom Englishmen had an intimate knowledge. Furthermore, the ideas of romanticism, with their reverence for the Greece of antiquity, on whose lofty foundations modern Western Europe was built, heightened this sense of local knowledge. The islanders in this scheme were constructed as Europeans. On the other hand, there was a distinct feeling of *exoticism*. Viscount Kirkwall felt that, in spite of its Italianate architecture and the European dress of some people, he was entering a land no less unfamiliar and foreboding as Bombay or Timbuktu, and a place where no Englishman belonged.

This chapter examines the ways that the British constructed the Ionian islanders and their culture. By focusing on how the dominant colonizers crafted identities for the colonized, I consciously draw on the Orientalist paradigm. Much has been written about Edward Said's work, and a lively debate has grown up around it (Said 1978; Mani and Frankenberg 1985; O'Hanlon and Washbrook 1992; Breckenridge and van der Veer 1993; Prakash 1992; 1995; Dallmayr 1996; Seidman 1996). In his pathbreaking study, he developed the idea of Orientalism as a way of explaining how the West constructed an identity of the East. There were two nuanced meanings of Orientalism (Said 1978: 4–8). One revolved around the creation of an eastern stereotype by academic eastern studies centers; the other focused more on the definition of an eastern distinctiveness by travelers and others who had direct, nonacademic, contact with the East. With extended usage the full meaning of the term *Orientalism* has become diluted. It has been reduced sometimes to a shorthand way of expressing otherness, used even when the non-western culture involved was not eastern. James Carrier has encouraged us to employ a new term, *ethno-Orientalism*, to refer to the process of exotization of cultural Others by Europeans (1992a: 198). Whatever we call the process of creating cultural differences and identities through opposition, we still need to utilize models that are more multidimensional than the simple bipolar "Us-Them dichotomy" paradigm that has been widely employed to date. When different cultures attempted to render each other intelligible, to label and to categorize one another, I would argue, they did so not by drawing simple contrasts, but through a more complex process that relied mainly on the selective application through analogy of stock stereotypes of different groups (Thomas 1994: 13–14).

The power of stereotypes lies in their capacity to provide people with a form of shorthand for comparing and categorizing other people and things, when only partial similarities are evident or incomplete information available (McDonald 1993: 220–22). I show in this chapter that the English created identities for the Ionians not by drawing contradistinctions between Greekness and Englishness, but by forging chains of analogies between the Ionians and stereotypes of other cultures (e.g., Irish, Hottentot, and Indian). There had to exist, however, some perceptible attributes or characteristics that provided the basis for the initial comparison between the Greeks and others. Once this cognitive connection had been established, then the capacity of stereotypes to construct complete identities from partial resemblances became operative. The process is relatively simple, operating with a series of "just like" comparisons: culture A and culture B manifest a similar cultural trait X; therefore, culture A, by analogy with the stereotype of culture B, must also possess traits Y and Z just like B. In regard to the Ionian islanders, the British selected cleverness and mendacity as the paramount characteristics for comparing, comprehending, and castigating Greek society. These two traits stood out for a number of reasons. First, they were perceptible and real attributes of the islanders: they did lie and consider deviousness laudable. Second, other cultures in the empire also manifested them, and so they provided the crucial analogues that facilitated the imposition of stereotypes of those groups onto the Greeks. Third, English society considered them to be defining characteristics of the difference between a civilized and a noncivilized race. We shall examine, then, how and why the British constructed the Ionian islanders as European aborigines and Mediterranean Irish through analogies and stereotypes.

Turning back to the Mediterranean world for a moment, because of their location it might seem that the more canonical Orientalism stereotype might be applicable to the Ionian Islands, but this is the case only in a limited way. The shortcomings of Orientalism with respect to the Balkans have been articulated recently by Maria Todorova, who argues instead for a "Balkanism" model (Todorova 1994; 1997). Both internal and external identity formation processes occurred in opposition to the oriental. Geographically, western Europeans saw the Balkans as not part of Europe, and certainly not part of the East. The region's Christianity set it apart from the Islamic cultures to the south and east, as did the absence of direct colonial control. Internally, many Balkan groups constructed self-identities in opposition to the Orientals (Todorova 1994: 454–55). There were distinct differences in the context in which this process occurred on the islands compared with the Balkans generally; the most important of these was the colonial experience whereby the British were on the islands as rulers, not just interested travelers or diplomats. There were additional distinctions between the Ionian case and the situation of other groups in the British Empire. The most significant of these was that the Greeks were not readily categorizable either racially or culturally as non-Europeans (Stoler 1992: 322). As has been often noted, Greece falls between East and West (Herzfeld 1987: 2–3; 1995; Kotzageorgi 1992; Peckham 1999: 167–69). Since neither an intuitively nor manifestly obvious oriental or occidental identity could be applied to the Ionians, the British constructed contrasting identities for the Greeks that reflected this ambiguity based upon a number of different stereotypes: one, as the Mediterranean Irish, that emphasized their Europeaness, and another, as European aborigines, that underscored their non-Europeaness (Peckham 1999: 165).

Before they could construct an identity for modern Greeks, they had to grapple with the long historical legacy of the past. The Ionians of the present were "debased," as evidenced by their habitual mendacity and immoral deceitfulness. Victorian romantic Hellenism required that these sad relics of a people somehow had to be disassociated from the Golden Age Greeks of antiquity. Otherwise the status of the ancients as the spiritual forefathers of modern Europe could be challenged. To denigrate the Ionians of the nineteenth century, and thus to justify their rule in the face of Greek nationalism, the British tried to deny them a place in the idealized ancient world by showing that even in antiquity Ionians were morally corrupt, cheaters, and liars. When this failed, they postulated instead a rupture with antiquity and a fall from grace. Venetian rule came to be seen as the epoch during which the entire "western" heritage of the Golden Age was lost and ironically the essentialized "eastern" or exotic characteristics of the present were developed.

The next two sections reconstruct the dominant dual identities that the British constructed of the Ionians, that as European aborigines and as the Mediterranean Irish. Two cultural characteristics stood out in these constructions: the cultural exaltation of cunning or deviousness and mendacity. I analyze these two behavioral forms and their cultural reception, endeavoring to explain how and why they came to be definitive characteristics in the process of identity formation.

"Degenerate Descendants": The Denial of History

The story of how British and other European philhellenes came to the Balkans with images of Perikles and the Parthenon dancing in their heads and found instead dirty shepherds and dark, dangerous Orientals has been told too often to require repetition here (Herzfeld 1985: 18–21; 1987: 3; Kotzageorgi 1992: 211, 214–17; St. Clair 1972: 51–65, 195–204; Tsigakou 1981: 72–75; Leontis 1995; Augustinos 1994; Peckham 1999: 168–70). The ironic twist to the tale in the Ionian Islands was that, first, the British went there as rulers, not just travelers, and so their interaction with the Greeks was qualitatively different than it was with Greeks on the continent or in Asia Minor, and, second, because they were situated in a specific place, an ancient past peculiar to that place had to be evoked as well. In discussing continental Greece, much of the travel literature collapsed historical space so that classical Athens came to stand for all of the Greek states of antiquity. Such an elision was still possible, but it was more difficult to apply the unitary vision of Hellenism to the Ionian Islands because they had been home to separate, and in some cases numerous, autonomous states in antiquity and each had its own history (Gallant 1982). In either case, the deplorable moral condition of the Ionian islanders in British eyes required an assessment of the antique past. As the heading of this section states, for the British the Ionians were but degenerate descendants of the Greeks of the Golden Age (Goodison 1822: 203).

Nineteenth-century romanticism discovered and glorified classical Greece as a Golden Age and then enshrined it as Ur-Europe. Herzfeld has pointed out "since Europe claimed ancient Greece as its
spiritual ancestor, Europe also decided what was, or was not, acceptable as Greek culture in the modern age" (1987a: 28). In constructing
those criteria that defined ancient Greece, romanticism collapsed
the cultural complexity of the ancient world into a unitary ideal of
Hellenism. In place of a messy reality in which there were over 120 autonomous Greek states scattered across an area from the Caucasus to
the Straits of Gibraltar and linked, if at all, only by a common language and religious practices, there emerged a single ideal type that
drew its inspiration primarily from an oversimplification of fifth-
century Athens. Western Europe then traced its own self-defining
characteristics—aestheticism, reason, democracy, individualism, liber-
alism, rationalism, and capitalism—back to this idealized Hellenism.
Moreover, as Herzfeld and others have suggested, westerners subsequently utilized this romantic ideal type as the basis for a cultural critique of modern Greece and its inhabitants (Herzfeld 1987a; Leontis
1995; Gourgouris 1996). For the Ionian islanders and other Greeks, antiquity became both a blessing and a curse.

The British felt a fundamental tension between their perceptions
of the idealized Greeks of antiquity and the Ionian islanders whom
they confronted on a daily basis, and it was a tension that had to be resolved. One way the British attempted to relieve this pressure was to
dissolve the unitary vision of antiquity and to focus instead on the islands separately, as being not really part of Golden Age Greece and
the Hellenic tradition it spawned. The difficulty with this strategy
was the paucity of ancient sources on the islands. Throughout antiquity,
they were peripheral to the major centers of ancient Greece and so
only occasionally did they warrant mention by classical authors (Gallant 1982). The only exception to this was Kerkira, which was featured
prominently in sections of Thoukydides's *History of the Peloponnesian
War*. If the Ionians were to be dissociated from the Hellenic ideal but
still have their character shortcomings traced back to antiquity, then it
had to be on the basis of Thoukydides's description of them. And that
is precisely what Lord George Bowen attempted to do (1862: 311–41).

Bowen was a very learned man whose knowledge of the major ancient texts was wide and deep. He claimed to have found the roots of

all of those character flaws that the British highlighted as deplorable among the Greeks—cunning, duplicitousness, violence, irreligiousness, and fractiousness—in Thoukydides's account of the civil war on Kerkira. "It [Kerkira] cannot, however, be said to occupy a peculiarly honourable place in the records of any age. The seditions of Corycra [sic] have become a by-word among readers of ancient history; and, unfortunately, both in that and the sister isles, the tendency thereto does not seem to have abated during the lapse of twenty-three centuries" (1862: 315).

What better evidence of the islanders' unchanging propensity to fractiousness than the civil war itself? In the conflict between the (good) democrats and the (bad) oligarchs, Bowen saw the primordial roots of both the contemporary conflicts between the nobility and the peasantry and between the (good) pro-British and (bad) anti-British Greeks. Examples of cunning and duplicity abounded in the civil war, from the democrats freeing slaves to fight on their side (Thoukydides 3.73) to their tricking the oligarchic leaders into coming to a meeting at which many of them were assassinated (Thoukydides 4.48). Of course, as with any civil war, violence was especially ferocious.

Based on the ancient texts, he was also able to essentialize irreligiosity as an ancient trait. "But the modern Corcyraeans seem to have as little reverence for the Holy Eastern Church as their predecessors—we cannot call them their forefathers—for the sacred groves of Zeus and Alcinous" (Bowen 1862: 341). The episode referred to (Thoukydides 3.70) is as follows. After his acquittal on the charge of treason, Peithias, the leader of the democratic pro-Athens group, accused the five wealthiest leaders of the oligarchic pro-Korinth faction of having cut vine-props from the vineyards sacred to Zeus and Alkinous. The governing council of which Peithias was the leader found them guilty. Rather than face their punishment, the accused attacked the council and slew Peithias. This event started the civil war. I recite this episode at length because, for Bowen, this story had it all; here was proof positive of cunning, double-dealing, duplicitousness, corruption, irreligiousness, and violence. In Bowen's view, then, all of the character flaws of the Ionian Greeks could be traced back to classical antiquity.

Note also how even as he was attempting to tar them with the sins of the past, Bowen's classical prejudices crept through and led him to get in a shot by diminishing the Ionians' connection to antiquity—the ancients were their "predecessors," not their "forefathers." The end result of his analysis was to render the Ionian islanders' cultural defects timeless and immutable, as he put it: "In this region . . . the same game, or nearly so, has been played over again repeatedly" (1862: 316). If this was so, if history was doomed to repeat itself because of the Ionian Greeks' essential character flaws, which had not, after all, changed in twenty-three centuries, then liberal reform was futile and an iron-fisted imperial rule wrought by the "guardianship of wise and wealthy strangers" (Ansted 1863: 15) was fully justified.[1] Moreover, his argument kept intact the romantic ideal of ancient Hellenism by dissociating the Ionians from it. They were, in his view, "bad" Greeks even then.

This strategy failed. Few of his colleagues followed Bowen's lead in tracing the flaws of the present to the ancient past. Some of the reasons for this may be: first, most colonial officers and official functionaries did not possess Bowen's familiarity with Thoukydides and the other relevant texts. Most of the lower tiers of the administration were filled by military men who had little time for the classics. Subtle arguments on the fate of Peithias and the democrats meant little to them. Instead they drew on examples and situations from other parts of the empire or from Great Britain with which they were far more familiar. Second, the unitary vision of Hellenism proved hard to challenge even among the better-educated bureaucrats of the empire. After all, everywhere around them in the form of ruined temples and city walls and theaters were indications of the islands' participation in the Golden Age.[2]

Third, the educated elite on the islands contested the arguments about their place in the past. Many Ionian islanders were as versed in the classics as the British, and they employed the ancient texts as a vehicle both for critiquing the protectorate and for linking themselves to the Golden Age. Greek politicians propounded in their speeches and public writings the idea that there was a direct connection from democratic Kerkira as described by Thoukydides and their own supposed democratic inclinations. Moreover, the classical texts provided them with a vocabulary of political protest that they turned against the British. When, for example, Ilias Zervas Iakovatos suggested that more than ever, the Greeks needed a new Thrasyboulos or Pelopidas to arise from their midst, for they had too many Demosthenes (1854: 132), it was clear both to Greeks and Britons who he was suggesting were the new tyrants to be overthrown by these two renowned tyrant-slayers from the ancient world. Classical texts, then, provided a vocabulary of resistance for the Greeks.

Fourth, the reemergence of the "historical Homer" debate recentered the islands in the mainstream of an idealized ancient Greece. During the early Victorian period it became accepted as a matter of fact that the *Iliad* and the *Odyssey* depicted an actual historical epoch (Turner 1981: 135–40). What became a matter for dispute was, among other things, the geography of the epics. This debate centered attention on the Ionian Islands. Colonel William Mure, a colonial officer whose account will be referred to repeatedly, specifically asked to be assigned to Ithaki so that he could look for the palace of Odysseos (1852). William Gladstone's interest in the islands flowed directly from his fascination with Homer (Turner 1981: 165–77).

All scholars agreed that the Ionian Islands were the site of the *Odyssey*, but controversy raged over the precise role played by each island; e.g., some considered Ithaki to be the home of the epic hero Odysseos while others favored either Kefallenia or Lefkas (on this controversy see Dörpfeld 1927). If Ithaki was the home of the epic hero Odysseos and Kerkira the land of the Phaecians, then how could the islands not but be an integral part of glorious Greece?

Konstantinos Asopios, professor of ancient history, language, and literature at the Ionian Academy, took this line of argument even further by arguing that the Ionians were the direct racial ancestors of Homer's Greeks. His proof of this was that only Ionians could read Homer by accent and quantity. Granted, not everyone accepted his view uncritically. After Asopios give a public recitation of sections of the epic poems, the acerbic British cleric the Reverend Wilson opined that clearly the learned professor "had learned to read Homer, not from his fathers, but at a German University" (Wilson 1839: 517). While somewhat extreme in his beliefs, many Ionians felt like Asopios that the Ionian islanders were the last best vestiges of the classical world.

This view of the Ionians' Homeric, and thus classical pedigree, was further propounded by classically minded philhellenes like Lord Byron and Frederick North, the fifth earl of Guilford, whose newly founded (in 1824) Ionian Academy was to be the place where the Greeks resurrected the Academy of Plato and Aristotle (Henderson 1988). What better way to emphasize the link with the Golden Age model than to create a center for its glorification: complete with mock ancient dress and adorned with the co-opted symbols of the classical period. Numerous symbols from antiquity were employed at the school. Professors, referred to by the ancient title of Ephor, were garbed in a tunic and mantle, red sandals and leggings, and bound their hair with a filet; students wore tunics and mantles, a broad-brimmed felt hat modeled on the ancient *petasos*, and sandals. Winners of academic prizes were crowned with olive wreaths. The owl of Athena, symbol of wisdom and the totemic icon of the ancient Athenian polis, became the Academy's emblem (Henderson 1988: 21–24). Together these factors fostered acceptance of the idea that the Ionian islanders were indeed descendants of the classical progenitors of Europe, but they were nonetheless decadent descendants and so the root cause of their fall from grace had to be found elsewhere in the past.

Legends of the Fall

If the classical heritage could not account for the cultural short-comings of the modern Ionians, then another locus of degeneration had to be discovered. This was to be the Venetokratia, or period of Venetian rule. Michael Herzfeld has argued that the years of the Ottoman occupation played an analogous role in shaping western attitudes toward the rest of the Greek world. The western construction of modern Greeks postulated that during the centuries of foreign rule symbolically polluting elements became imposed onto Greek culture by the Turks, the most important of which were "shiftiness, double-dealing, illiteracy, influence-peddling and rule bending, disrespect for norms and admiration for cunning individuals who twist them to their own advantage" (Herzfeld 1987a: 29). A very similar process expressed in almost identical terms took place on the Ionian Islands, except that the Venetians rather than the Ottomans were cast in the role of the corrupting snake responsible for the Greeks' fall from Hellenic Eden.

Even before the protectorate had been officially established, the Venetian period was blamed for all of the Ionian ills. Henry Holland in his account of the islands in 1815 argued that because of the capricious and corrupt character of Venetian imperial administration there

had developed on the islands a cultural ethos that encouraged violence, crime, fractiousness, and rampant immorality. The corrupt
feebleness of the Venetian government, not surprisingly in his view,
produced a duplicitous and cunning aristocracy and a debased and
cowed peasantry (Holland 1815: 23, 40–41).

Sir Thomas Maitland, the architect of the protectorate, had no
doubts that centuries of Italian rule had acted only to exaggerate the
worst tendencies of an already degenerate society (Dixon 1969: 183). The
metaphor of the fall and its attribution to the Venetians was especially
important to Sir Charles Napier. He was an ardent philhellene who
until the end of his life looked back on his days on the islands as the
happiest of his life. The dilemma for him was how to reconcile his love
for the islanders with their manifest cultural defects. As we shall see
shortly, one way he did so was to analogize the Greeks as Mediterranean
Irishmen, but he also accomplished this by systematically tracing the
roots of every character flaw he perceived to some aspect of Venetian
rule. Napier argued that the Greeks' propensity for cunning and duplicity was due solely to years of habituation in a corrupt environment
(Napier 1833: 52–53). He also assumed that the want of self-discipline
and ambition stemmed from the same source (Napier 1833: 193).

William Goodison, writing in 1822, concluded that the morality of
the Greeks was excessively bad, and he argued that they still retained
their character for cunning and duplicity, which had developed during the long years of Venetian misrule (1822: 194–95). His contemporary, Tetius T. C. Kendrick, had no doubt that it was "the introduction
of Italian vices [that] may have created a greater degeneracy in their
morals, which are generally excessively bad and call for the severest
punishment" (1822: 17). The London *Times* lent its weighty support to
the idea that the Greeks were debased by the Venetians (September 17,
1849): "We took under our aegis a people who combine Italian crime
with Greek cunning; who are strangers to the private honesty or
public virtue; who are remarkable for strong passions, dark superstition, ignorance and laziness."

Dr. John Davy was surgeon general on the islands during the
reform years of the 1830s and early 1840s. He found "that the Venetian
manner of ruling the Ionian Islands was bad, is commonly admitted;
and as Venice degenerated, probably from bad it became worse, till it
was atrocious" (1842: 13). He argued further that the Greeks had been

reduced to a virtual state of "slavery" under the "despotism of the Venetian government," whose policies led to a situation where "religion, life, honour, personal liberty, the sacred rights of property, were [reduced to] a state of humiliation" (Davy 1842: 14). The result of this was that the islanders were treated either like slaves or as children and, that as a consequence of this treatment, they were more like children than men in their conduct (1842: 13). The notion that the manners and morals of the islanders were childlike was a view espoused by most British officials.

Benjamin Martin Montgomery, writing about the islands in the early 1850s, noted, "So long as the Ionians remained under the Neapolitan rule, little or no improvement could be expected; and the ascendancy of the lion of St. Mark wrought, of course, no great change in their moral condition. The criminal guilty of ten murders was punished with ten years in the galleys; whilst the offence of having spoken once disrespectfully of one in high office, received a similar sentence; hence, a powerful incentive was given to great crimes, and the national tendency to obsequious flattery fostered" (1852: 141). Venice sent "miscreant hordes" of soldiers and officials to govern the island. Crime and banditry flourished, and justice could be easily purchased. For Montgomery, then, lying and cunning, disregard for the law and self-help justice in the form of feuds legitimized by the ethos of blood vengeance, and a flourishing patron and client system were due in large measure to the corrupt and corrupting influence of Venetian rule. Edmund Spencer echoed these sentiments when he argued that the islanders could not be blamed for the centuries in which they dwelled in darkness, cut off from the new civilization being wrought by the Anglo-Saxon race (Spencer 1852: 223).

Two other accounts written during the waning days of British rule show the power of and the persistent need for the metaphor of the fall. Very little about island society escaped the critical eye and poison pen of Lord Bowen. As we saw earlier, he was the official who most directly confronted the tension between the romanticized ancient Greece and the debased modern Greece. In spite of his lengthy arguments on this point, he was never able fully to convince himself or others of its merits. So he also looked to the more recent past in the same way his predecessors did. After reciting the usual litany of character defects, he concluded that the "centuries of bondage, culminating in the corrupt debasing tyranny of Venice, have effectively done their work [and so even now] they have not outgrown the needful discipline of paternal government" (1862: 321). But, unlike earlier writers, Bowen could not leave the argument there because to do so would have called into question the civilizing mission of the empire: why had not civil society and the Greek character been reformed after forty-five years of British rule? And why should imperial rule therefore continue? That is why we see a slightly different gloss on the argument: it was not just the quality of Venetian rule that was at fault but also the *length of time* that the Greeks lived under Italian misrule. How, after all, could the British be expected to reform in decades what it had taken the Venetians centuries to create? T. D. Ansted found himself in the same situation and adopted much the same line of reasoning as Bowen, except that he placed greater responsibility and blame on education and religion. The moral devastation produced by Venetian rule would only be eradicated when generations of young Greeks had received proper education and when the baneful influence of the clergy had been removed (1863: 49).

From the inception of the protectorate until its demise, British officials explained the moral and cultural failings of Ionian society, especially mendacity and duplicity, as the result of centuries of Venetian misrule. They postulated that it was during that reign of corruption that all of the attributes that made classical Greeks the forefathers of western civilization came to be lost. By so arguing they were able to keep intact the image of a pristine Hellenism grounded in Golden Age Greece while dissociating modern-day Ionian islanders from their own history and heritage. Paternalistically, the English used this argument to deny them responsibility for their condition: it was not the islanders' but the Venetians' fault that the former were as they were. By rendering the Ionians as passive and childlike, this explanation served as a justification for imperial rule. Just as mankind could overcome the Edenic fall from grace through faith, so too could the Greeks be restored to western civilization, which was, after all, their ancestors' legacy to the world, by the guiding hand of Britain. Spencer captures well this sentiment: "Let our friends the Ionian Greeks . . . regard England as what she really is—a protecting power, performing her part in the Divine mission intrusted [*sic*] to her for the dissemination of enlightened civilization" (1853: 224). Venetian rule corrupted them. British rule would redeem them.

The metaphor of the fall only went partway toward explaining who the Ionian Greeks were. More accurately, it accounted more for who they were not. Such a negative image could not provide the basis for any meaningful cultural understanding. If the nobles and peasants of the islands were not modern-day Perikles or Plato, then who were they? The British still needed to construct identities for these enigmatic islanders. And they did so in one of two ways—stereotyping the Greeks either as European aborigines or as the Mediterranean Irish. I turn to the former first.

European Aborigines

Recently historians and anthropologists have begun to pay more attention to the ways that the colonial encounter shaped cultural identities both in the foreign and the metropolitan communities. There is a long tradition of scholarship regarding the ways that Europeans created the images of the exotic cultures of the colonial world. Much attention has been focused lately on the role that anthropology played in this process of creating the "primitive" (Boon 1990a, 1990b; Fabian 1983; Kuper 1988; Stocking 1988). The construction and confrontation with the "Other" in the colonial world provided a conceptual framework and a vocabulary for defining otherness inside of European societies either along class lines, e.g., between the middle class and the underclass or between the bourgeoisie and the peasantry, or along ethnic lines, e.g., between the English and the Scots or the Irish (Carrier 1995: 12, 22; Marshall 1995: 384–86; N. Thomas 1989; 1991; 1994: 66; Schwartz 1996; Daunton and Halpern 1999). Drawing on colonial analogies, the Irish became "black," London's costermongers became "red Indians," and peasants became "Hottentots." Romanticism and ethnic nationalism contributed to this process of internal identity formation by focusing attention on European peasants. Nationalists saw the peasantry as the repository of the nation's primordial traits. In integral ways, the development of the discipline of folklore was inseparable from the nationalist imperative to essentialize ethnic identity and cultural characteristics (Gellner 1983: 39–52; Herzfeld 1985; Smith 1987: 174–208).

Simultaneously, there was a train of thought running from the early romantics up through Durkheim and beyond that constructed a

European peasantry and a rural society free from the dehumanizing and alienating ills of modern society (Brettell 1986: 161; Durkheim 1960 [1891]; Friedman 1989: 250–53; 1992). These noble savages were portrayed as Europe's picturesque ancestors before the blight of modernism set in. Paired with this vision was another that saw rural folk as Hobbesian primitives, as savages (Brettell 1986: 161–62; Friedman 1989: 250–53; Gorky 1987: 382–84). Rather than nostalgic reminders of some halcyon past, peasants were seen as evolutionary relics on whom the light of progressive civilization had yet to shine. Common to all of these endeavors was the delineation and stigmatization of a European aborigine. Vital to this process was a blurring of discourses between the historical cultural constructionism of alien Others in the colonies and indigenous Others in the metropolitan communities. And, moreover, stereotypes provided the analogical language that linked the two discourses.

Noble Savages and Children of Nature

A number of British authors highlighted character traits of the islanders that portrayed them paradigmatically as noble savages. They were childlike in their innocence and naiveté, and so were easily duped and led astray either toward evil or good (Kirkwall 1864: 56). Like Spanish peasants or Papua New Guineans, the Greeks were a happy and kind people, who valued hospitality and would give a stranger the shirt off their back if need be (Brettell 1986: 159; Kirkwall 1864: 69; Kotzageorgi 1992: 211–12; Memmi 1990: 145–55; Spencer 1853: 218). The want of civilization was best seen in the islanders' incapacity for rationality, their impetuousness, superstitiousness, and inability to be truthful (Ansted 1863: 17; Bowen 1862: 321; Davy 1842: 15–16, 36, 51). All of these traits shared a common thread of meaning: they created a ready analogy between human development and cultural evolution. The Greeks were conceived of as children while the British cast themselves in the role of dutiful parents; such a construction also stigmatized the Ionians as human beings lower on the evolutionary scale of civilizations as well.

Further exoticizing the Greeks were the long descriptions of picturesque costumes and customs. The lengthy discussions of young maids in flowing skirts whose heads were adorned by coin-laden silken kerchiefs or of mustachioed men with baggy trousers, embroidered silk waistcoats, and coarse wool capotes emphasized the cultural distance between the Greeks and the West. So too did the long passages that recounted the arcane and bizarre beliefs and rituals of the islanders. The British found the knife ceremony at Ionian weddings, for example, to be particularly offensive and alien. In this ritual, the bridegroom jabbed his knife into the doorjamb of his father's house. It remained there phallically protruding from the doorway until the newlyweds returned from church, at which time the bride ceremonially removed it and replaced it into her husband's sheath. They were almost as fascinated by the ritual exhumation and examination of the bones of a recently deceased person undertaken a few months after interment (Jervis 1852: 227; Kendrick 1822: 18; Napier 1833: 220; Tuckerman 1872: 195–96). Such depictions stood alongside the timeworn anthology of exotic rites among "primitive" peoples that European travelers had been compiling for centuries.

In the noble savage model, these exotic elements were given a somewhat favorable cultural interpretation, but even so this gloss still served to accentuate the Ionian islanders' alienness and to provide comparability with other colonized peoples in Asia, India, and Africa. Some British officers and commentators, then, imposed the noble savage image on the islanders, but far more prevalent was a picture of them that was much more primitive and frightening.

Just Savages

Another, far less sympathetic portrait of Europe's internal marginal groups depicted them as analogous to non-European, nonwhite "savages" (Brettell 1986: 159; see also Walvin 1982: 62 for full list of the attributes of the savage). In like vein, many British commentators on the Ionian Greeks compared them to groups with whom they had come into contact in Africa and India. So, for Kendrick, the customs of the peasantry were so devoid of all humane and generous principles and so mired in ignorance and wretchedness that they reminded him of the Hottentots (1822: viii). Fitzroy as well compared the Ionians to the Hottentots in their crude barbarism (1850: 34). Others were less culturally specific in the analogies they drew, but their point was equally clear. Martin, for example, found them wanting in the "refinements" he so enjoyed among the Asiatics (1856: 141). To General de Bossett, no direct comparison was needed: the Ionian Islands were quite simply a land of savages (cited in Kirkwall 1864: 86). Most British officials and commentators did not name the other barbarians to whom they likened the islanders. Instead we find their models embedded in the stock repertoire of elements of Greek culture and character that they chose to describe. It is in their observations that we see the construction of Ionian islanders as primitives (Kotzageorgi 1992: 212–13 for a discussion of the literature on the Greeks in general as "barbarians").

For some, the Greeks' savagery was epitomized by their lack of reason and inability to exercise self-control. These were traits best exemplified by their propensity for drunkenness, violence, and duplicity. Calumny, detraction, and slander were the stock and trade of social discourse, and the only thing quicker than a Greek man's tongue was his knife (Martin 1856: 141). Goodison, for example, found the want of civilization in the islanders' readiness "to raise the dark knife and bloody stiletto against the breast of unoffending innocence" (1822: 204). Like less civilized peoples elsewhere in the empire and the world, the Greeks' childlike inability to control their baser feelings and emotions, their giving free rein to their passions, and their impulsive resorting to violence defined them as dwellers outside the orbit of the civilized West.[3]

With near unanimity the British bemoaned the incorrigible laziness of the Greeks. According to Jervis, for example, "The Corfiot peasant loves to lounge away his time in the market-place, catering for a trifling bit of news. Indolent beyond belief, he is satisfied with the food which Providence affords him off the neighboring olive tree; which he patiently waits to see drop to the ground. For the best part of the year his hardest labour consists in smoking his pipe at the village wineshop" (1852: 265–66). Martin argued that the Ionians elevated their *dolce far niente* attitude to life to the status of a national emblem (1856: 141). All manner of social ills, e.g., drunkenness, vagabondage, gambling, and the like, and most economic problems, including every subsistence crisis, were blamed on the Greeks' natural slothfulness.[4] Often paired with laziness was the islanders' supposed lack of cleanliness and sanitation. But, since this is a subject which I discuss in some detail in the next chapter, I shall not comment further on it here.[5]

Two defining characteristics of the savage were ignorance and superstitiousness, and the British found both prevalent on the Ionian Islands. For sheer viciousness, few descriptions rival the following from Kendrick: "Rude barbarism predominates throughout all classes [of Ionian society] having with it the usual appendages of cruelty, credulity, and superstition" (1822: 90). Particularly offensive were "the peasants [of Kefallenia, who] are superstitious, cruel and barbarous in their manners" (1822: 107). Ignorance was seen by many as being an essential characteristic of all Greeks, regardless of class. Where there existed a difference of opinion, it was over the causes and remedies of it. For some, it was an indelible, almost genetic, trait and thus unchangeable; others blamed the sociopolitical and cultural environment, noting especially the baneful role played by the clergy, and so argued that improvement was possible through education and reform of the church (Davy 1842: 40, 125; Bowen 1862: 321; Ansted 1863: 56; Kirkwall 1864: 33). For all of them, however, the Greeks' ignorance was proved by their deeply rooted superstitiousness. Belief in the efficacy of the evil eye, the power of witches and curses to heal or to harm, the existence of spirits, demons, vampires, and nymphs who could enter and possess peoples' bodies, the veneration of holy relics and icons that had the power to cure, and of saints who rose from the dead to save the Ionians from danger in their hour of need, all were seen by the British as evidence of the Greeks' primitiveness, their irrationality, and consequently, their aboriginality (Bowen 1862: 340–41; Kendrick 1822: 107; CO 136/1286: Fraser to Sutherland, June 6, 1841 PRO; Davy 1842: 46, 101–2, 147; Jervis 1852: 267; Kirkwall 1864: 34). Their belief system, thus, marked the Ionians as being well down on the scale of civilizations.

Contributing to the image of the Greeks as aborigines, some British writers even depicted them as physically resembling non-Europeans. Kendrick, for example, described them as being "short, squat and muscular with features of a villainous cast" (1822: 17). Martin emphasized the Ionians' exotic appearance, choosing to accentuate their well-developed and bulging foreheads, their swarthy complexion, their dark eyes, black bushy hair, and good teeth. Their "constitution," he noted, "is often of a sanguine and choleric cast; the gestures vivacious; the gait erect and elastic, and the enunciation voluble and emphatic" (1852: 140). Even when attempting to cast the Greeks in a favorable light, the resulting descriptions still ended up emphasizing their otherness, as in the following, also from Martin: "No people are more patient under privation; hunger, thirst, heat, and cold they endure with undaunted resolution. A morsel of bread, a few olives, an onion and his capote,—thus fed and sheltered, the Ionian, supported by climate and constitution, is contented and happy" (1852: 141). The resulting portrait portrays Greeks who were part Negroid and part Indian in their physical appearance, *bête humaine* in their physical attributes, and wholly aboriginal in any case.

All the elements of Ionian culture and character discussed above were part and parcel of the set of stereotypical traits Europeans evinced to create the non-European primitive. Syed Hussein Alatas (1977), for example, has amply demonstrated that the myth of the lazy native was a vital core element in shaping European perceptions of colonized people. This leitmotif was not confined narrowly to European colonies, but instead became almost a defining attribute of most "uncivilized" groups, ranging from Black slaves in the southern United States to peasants in Latin America and southeast Asia (Colburn 1989; Scott 1989; Wyatt-Brown 1988).

Oriental Nobles

In the colonial encounter, Europeans tended to collapse the indigenous class or status hierarchy of the cultures they dominated. Natives became of a piece, and all members of a group were seen as being roughly the same (Allen 1994: 28). Obviously, this was more easily accomplished in some situations than in others. In the Royal Provinces of India, for example, the nobility could not so easily be reduced to a single ideal type identical with the peasantry. Much the same held true on the Ionian Islands. The British could not ignore the Ionian aristocracy. This was a very cosmopolitan group. As one of them, the Baron Theotoki, told D. T. Ansted, "A stranger coming amongst us [the Ionian aristocracy] would have difficulty believing that we are Greeks" (cited in Ansted 1863: vol. 2, 129). Most of the men had some form of higher education, many in Italian universities like Venice and Padua, but others held degrees from institutions in Paris, Berlin, and Moscow. Many others were very successful entrepreneurs who had traveled extensively in Europe and the East. Almost all were polyglot and culturally sophisticated. Many had visited or temporarily resided in England; some even came to call Albion's island their home. They wore western dress, held many mainstream European bourgeois views, and were as *au courant* with the latest intellectual trends as any of the colonial officers. How then did the British accommodate the nobility in their constructions of Greek identity?

Ironically, since the Ionian aristocracy was the group that was *most westernized*, in order to exoticize them and to create a greater amount of social distance, they were the group to whom the British applied the *most orientalized* stereotype. Noblemen were portrayed as being effete, vainglorious, cunning, indolent, foppish, solicitous, and cruel; they were prone to love of luxury and to pursue those vices characteristic of a debased race—gambling, infidelities, and whoring. Martin, for example, found "the Corfiot gentleman [to be] subtle and adroit, cloaking his evil qualities under the mask of courtesy" (1856: 141). Jervis had nothing but contempt for the young Ionian noblemen who "lounge about the streets, in a perfect state of moral, industrial, and professional idleness and vacancy, smoking their cigarettes, and discussing politics, of which they do not so much as understand the terms" (1852: 238). Kirkwall (1862: 179) was appalled by the moral turpitude of the aristocracy that led them to spend their nights at the casino and their days in bed—and often not their own. Bowen explicitly compared the aristocracy to other Orientals he had encountered in their love of pomp and circumstance (a monumental conceit coming from an Englishman), in their inability to discern the Colonial Offices' lofty goal of bringing lenient and enlightened rule to the islands, and in their attributing the British government's reasonableness in exerting that rule to either weakness or folly (1862: 325, 338). He argued further that like all "Orientals [the Ionian nobility is unable] to separate the idea of government from that of monarchical authority, and invariably ascribe[s to] fear or imbecility all concessions yielded to violence and clamour" (1862: 352).

The elements of the nobles' character that the British chose to emphasize belonged fully to the stock repertoire of traits that defined those alien denizens of the East. The stereotype of the Ionian nobility depicted them as non-Europeans, as Orientals, as nothing more than eastern potentates in black suits and bowler hats. Just as the peasantry had to be exoticized, so too did the nobility. Since the latter obviously could not be accounted for in the paradigm of the primitive, another mechanism had to be devised to differentiate them. The one we see employed most frequently was the construction for them of an Oriental identity. Moreover, there was an especial need for the British to portray the Ionian aristocracy as non-western.

Christine Bolt (1984: 139) has argued that one of the most important consequences of Victorian racism was its capacity to insinuate a linkage between a race's inherent cultural characteristics and its capacity for self-government. Since the peculiar political status of the Ionian Islands made them a sovereign state under British protection, and since the local nobles were the ones destined to rule it, it became imperative for the British to devise rationalizations for their exerting effective control over the islands instead of the aristocracy. Construing the nobles as Orientals was the primary one they developed because it rationalized British rule by postulating that, just like all eastern peoples, the Ionian nobility was unfit and incapable of achieving self-rule, and so, even though technically the Greeks should rule themselves, until they became enlightened and westernized the British would have to do it for them. We shall see in the next chapter how the local aristocracy endeavored to show that they were in fact becoming western by launching a "civilizing mission" of their own based on their understanding of what constituted western civilization.

The Mediterranean Irish[6]

Just as one culture employs selected stereotypes to exoticize another with the intent of creating social space between the two, so too does it need to render the other group's culture intelligible, to familiarize the unfamiliar. In this case, the British tried to understand who the Ionian Greeks were by culturally constructing them as the Irish of the Mediterranean. Just as there were two mirror images of the Irish—one as Paddy, the devil-may-care, Hibernian hedonist, and the other as the Black Irishman, brooding, dark and dangerous—so too did the British construct dual "Irish" identities for the Greeks (Waters 1996: 2). Identity formation is an ongoing process, and so we cannot see the Irish-Ionian comparisons as having a single starting and end point.

What occurred was that when the English came into close contact with the Greeks and began to perceive some similarities between them and the Irish, as the English had constructed them, they imposed on the Ionians the stereotypes of the Irish and this set up a series of self-fulfilling expectations. In other words, once the Greeks had been Hibernianized, an entire repertoire of cultural traits became apparent because those characteristics were evident among the Irish. One could ask why the Irish were used as an analogue in this way. Some possible explanations come to mind.

First, as with any imaginary construction, there has to be some basis for it in reality, and so there were some superficial similarities between the Greeks and the Irish. Second, both societies were in a subordinate position vis-à-vis the English and were part of the colonial order, but unlike most of the other colonized cultures these two stood out because they were Christian and white. Third, they were both among, if not the most, ungovernable dependencies in the British Empire during the nineteenth century. For these reasons, when the British endeavored to understand Ionian culture, they effortlessly turned to a near-to-hand analogue that they pretended to know well: the Irish.

Paddies of the South

One stock stereotype of the Irish devised by the English was as Paddy. This image bears a marked similarity to the "noble savage/child of nature" discussed earlier. It depicts the Irish as being hospitable, good-natured, quick in perception, much given over to singing and dancing, curious, and garrulous. More negatively they were seen as puerile, emotionally unstable, and possessive of a general inability to exert any self-control, which in turn led to a propensity for drunkenness, high passions, and violence (Chapman 1982: 137; Curtis 1968: 50–51, 53, 59; 1971: 18; Lebow 1976: 39, 61, 64; Gibbons 1996: 25). In his assessment of them, Matthew Arnold (cited in Curtis 1968: 43) concisely observed that "the unfortunate Irishman is a prisoner to his emotions." It was this vision of the Irish that Charles Napier had in mind in the passage quoted at the beginning of this chapter.

Napier was one of the leading contributors to the Ionians-as-Irish argument. He was in a good position to do so as well, having spent the

better part of his childhood on his father's estate at Celbridge, County
Kildare. As a young man he took part in the military campaign to suppress Emmet's Rising, and in 1835 he rejected an offer of command of
the military in Ireland. Napier returned there in 1839 instead to develop a program of agrarian education for the poor. Throughout his
life, Sir Charles was involved in the debates about policing in Ireland,
and it is not coincidental that his experiences there informed his attitudes toward policing in the Ionian Islands and later in India; one
model that he advocated for Ireland and that he implemented in India
was developed first on Kefallenia. On a number of occasions in his
first book about the islands (*The Colonies*, first published in 1833) he remarked in passing about the similarities he detected between the two
cultures (e.g., 1833: 126). It was, however, in the biography written
about him by his brother William (*The Life and Opinions of Sir Charles
James Napier*) that he articulated most explicitly the resemblances he
saw between the Ionians and the Irish. Napier made particular note of
the characteristics previously mentioned: happy, merry, playful, song-
ful, easily contented, loyal, and trusting (1857: 357–59). Other observers
also saw more than a bit of the Paddy in the Greeks. Ansted, for example, found them to be "acute, shrewd, and good natured . . . and as
quick in repartee as the Irish" (1863: 56). To many English observers,
there were marked similarities between the Ionian islanders and the
Paddy image of the Irish.

Black Irish, Black Greeks

There was a more prevalent stereotype of the Irish that accentuated a
darker and more dangerous side to the Hibernian character (Taylor
1996: 215), and this image of the "Black Irish" was equally applied to
the Greeks.

Lord John Russell (cited in Lebow 1976: 16, 64), a key figure in
this tale because he was active in both Irish and Ionian affairs, characterized the Irish as follows: "The Irish . . . hate our order, our
civilisation, our enterprising industry, our sustained courage, our decorous liberty, our pure religion. This wild, reckless, indolent, uncertain
and superstitious race has no sympathy with the English character,"
but instead are "cunning but ignorant, cowardly but brazenly rash, religious and superstitious, indolent, complacent and addicted to both

violence and alcohol." These passages capture many of the major elements of the Black Irish stereotype. All of the characteristic traits of the non-European savage were applied to the Ionian islanders as well. I want to focus our attention here on just a few of these "natural" elements and to suggest some reasons why the British drew closer comparisons between the Ionian Greeks and the Irish than they did between the Irish and any other culture in the empire.

A critical element in compelling a comparison between the Greeks and the Irish was that they were both Christian cultures and this distinguished them from the vast majority of cultures in the British Empire. It seems to me that it was precisely because of the common Christian link between colonizers and colonized that religion and the differences between Protestantism, on the one hand, and Orthodoxy and Catholicism, on the other, became so crucial. Since the Glorious Revolution of 1688 and the consequent development of the Penal Laws, Catholicism had been enshrined as the core social organizational principle of Irish society. The Act of Union in 1800 did little to displace religion from its place of primacy. Throughout the period of direct English control over Ireland the tension between Catholicism and Protestantism remained high, and the religious divide was never far from the center of any cultural construction of the Irish.

Much the same can be said about the perceived role of Orthodoxy in Ionian society. The English readily drew analogies between the two faiths, and in each case, saw religion as a crucially important social institution, and the one that was largely responsible for social backwardness. The images of the church and the clergy in each case were mutually reinforcing. The English assumed, for example, that village priests in Ireland and the Ionian Islands wielded enormous influence over their parishioners. Lebow cites numerous instances where the English popular press portrayed Catholic priests in the villages as ignorant intriguers who misled the even more ignorant peasants (1976: 6). The following passage from Kendrick captures a sentiment widely held among the colonial officers on the islands: "The [village] priests . . . have infused opinions and sentiments of the most dangerous tendency into the minds of the lower class, who are incapable of discriminating with judgement" (1822: ix).

Very similar views regarding the role of the clergy in fomenting violence were propounded. J. C. Colquhoun, for example, railed against

those "dark ministers of dark faith" who stood at the altar and incited their congregations to venture forth and destroy the property of
Protestants and even to kill them. From the priests came the call:
"Blood is the Order—Blood is the Cry—Blood is the Doom" (1836:
64). In like vein did Dr. Hennen depict the influence of the Orthodox
clergy on Greek society: "The clergy are taken from the scum of the
population, and are, with few exceptions, illiterate, superstitious, and
immoral, and . . . few, if any, acts of private atrocity or rebellion have
occurred in the islands, which have not been planned and in part executed by the priests; [furthermore] even the gangs of robbers or pirates have their regular chaplain" (cited in Martin 1856: 141).[7] Others as
well repeated the conclusion that the Orthodox Church in the village
was a moral and practical source of corruption (in chapter 7 we shall
examine how the Colonial Office tried to deal with this problem). The
English envisioned religion as being central to the identity of both the
Irish and the Ionian Greeks. And I would suggest further that their
assumption about the role of Orthodoxy among the Greeks was
shaped by their perception about the centrality of Catholicism to the
Irish.

Another set of comparisons was based on the image of the Irish,
and by analogy the Greeks, as being prone to passionate outbursts,
drunkenness, and violence. The following observations from James
Johnson can stand as exemplary of a very widely held view of the Irish
that saw them as "the most savage, most desperate, and most uncivilized people on the face of the earth." Johnson found the evidence for
this assertion in "the [numerous] murders of this country [that] would
disgrace the most gloomy wilds of the most savage tribes that ever
roamed in Asia, Africa, or America" (cited in Lebow 1976: 46).[8] I selected this passage over the numerous other possibilities because it
demonstrates the linkage that existed between the cultural construction of the Irish and the discourse of colonial rule. The European
aborigine model, discussed earlier, directly tied into this discussion because it allowed the stereotype of the savage Greek to be given an
"Irish" interpretation, i.e., all of the traits that made Greeks like colonial barbarians could also be used to render them Irish since the Irish
themselves were like aboriginal savages, but, like the Greeks and
unlike the others, they were white. Thus, when the British realized, as
they did very early on in the life of the protectorate, that interpersonal

violence was extremely common between Greek men, they immediately drew the parallel with the Irish and assumed that, just like
among the Irish, violence was integrally related to drunkenness and
Greek men's inherent inability to control their passions. The conclusion they therefore reached was that Greek culture was puerile, just
like the Irish.

Another example whereby the British interpreted Greek culture
through the lens of Irish society refers to the perceived propensity and
social estimation of cunning and duplicity. I discuss later in this chapter why these two elements played so important a role, but for now I
want to focus on the way they connected even more closely Irish and
Ionian cultures. Compare the following passages regarding the prevalence of perjury in Ireland and the Ionian Islands. The first is taken
from a letter from Prime Minister Sir Robert Peel to his Home Secretary James Graham (Dec. 3, 1845): "There seems a general impression
in Ireland that nothing will effect this [perjury] but a pecuniary
motive, that the people are so radically corrupt and sanguinary that
there is a sympathy for the Murderer—and that selfishness and the
fear of pecuniary [loss] must supply the motives to give evidence
against an Assassin which the natural and intuitive feelings of
mankind supply in more favored Countries" (cited in Lebow 1976: 49).
Peel's sentiments echo those expressed at around the same time by
Lord High Commissioner Nugent in a missive sent to the colonial
secretary, Viscount Stanley (cited in Davy 1842: 322–23):

> Perjury is an evil so widely spread, that it ought in the new
> [law] code to be especially considered. In Santa Maura [Lef-
> kas], the purchase and loan of false oaths are spoken of as a
> notorious fact; and I believe that the same may be asserted of
> various other islands. The ordinary means conceded to judges
> being manifestly inadequate to its suppression, I fear that it
> cannot well be reached unless through the medium of special
> tribunals, endowed with extraordinary powers. The terror in-
> spired by salutary severity, added to the infusion of moral
> principle, by means of education, would, undoubtedly, in a
> generation or two, produce the desired effects. As to immedi-
> ate eradication, by human means alone, I hold it to be impos-
> sible, yet think much might be done if sufficient power were

granted not to punish with severity, but to facilitate conviction. If it be thought that such powers could not, compatibly with constitutional principles, be entrusted to a tribunal, I cannot imagine how this dreadful evil is to be reached, and must continue to wonder why sworn testimony is allowed such tremendous weight, when it is known to be without the slightest foundation in truth. I have been assured by judges that they frequently decide contrary to their conviction, and the fiscal advocate of Santa Maura has assured me that he has seen the lawyers paying witnesses for false testimony, in the vicinity of the tribunals. How can improvement be hoped for, while every man, however, respectable in character and station, is liable to be the victim of false swearing, and whose only chance for defence and redress, is by having recourse to the same revolting crime? What must be the situation of a conscientious man so circumstanced?

Napier noted that on Kefallenia it was as easy to purchase a false witness as it was to buy a flask of wine and that there were well-known shops where such professional liars were to be found (1833: 139). Just as with the Irish, then, the Greeks were believed to be inveterate liars. Consequently, in both cases special measures needed to be taken in order to establish effective criminal justice systems. *Graecae mendax* was the same as *Hiberniae mendax*, and this led directly to the view that the policies of social control implemented in Ireland would work in Greece.

There were two very clear additional examples where the English cultural construction of the Ionians as the Mediterranean Irish had a direct impact on how colonial officials understood and reacted to critically important developments on the islands. The first focuses on Greek nationalism and the unification (Enosis) movement, and the second on class conflict and rural violence. We saw in chapter 1 that Greek nationalism and the movement for the unification of the islands with the Kingdom of Greece became increasingly important issues from 1832 onward and that from the late 1830s the protest movements that they spawned dominated the political scene and generated such widespread unrest that the islands eventually became ungovernable. In the way that the colonial officers understood the Enosis movement we can see the power of the Irish stereotype. They considered Enosis to be exactly like the Irish Repeal movement, and they predicated their response to the Greek case on this comparison.

From the turn of the century until the Great Famine of 1845, no issue dominated Anglo-Irish relations like the movement to repeal the 1800 Act of Union and to establish Irish home rule. There were some superficial similarities between the developments in Ireland and the situation on the Ionian Islands, and these resemblances combined with the already tacit understanding that Ionians were culturally just like the Irish simply drove home the point. Like the Repealers, the Ionian radicals sought to separate from the empire and were not averse to using violent means to achieve their goal. Also, in both cases nationalism provided the central ideological core of what were becoming in both cases mass movements. Moreover, both Greek and Irish nationalisms developed in opposition to English imperialism. Based on these resemblances, the British superimposed their interpretation of the Repeal movement onto the Greek Enosis movement. For example, they considered the role of the Orthodox Church in the movement to be comparable to the part played by the church in the Catholic League party in Ireland; we shall examine elsewhere how this view led the Colonial Office to misunderstand considerably the social position of the church in Greek society. Leaders of the Enosis movement were directly compared to prominent Repealers; ardent Greek nationalists like Nikolaos Tipaldo Giakommatos, Nikolaos Fokas Repoublika, Vasilis Pigantore, and Elias Zervos were seen as demagogues and rabble-rousers like Daniel O'Connell, Robert O'Brien, John Mitchell, and Charles Gavan Duffy (Bowen 1862: 328). Bowen found the two movements to be very similar, noting that "the great mass of the peasantry in the southern islands have been deluded by the artful representations of their demagogues, and by the atrocious calumnies of the press, into expectations of deriving moral and physical blessings of every kind from union with Greece; just as we lately saw the lower classes of Ireland duped into looking for all imaginable felicity from a repeal of the union with England" (1862: 346). A positive feedback loop was in operation: the Greeks were like the Irish in character and temperament, the Enosis movement must therefore have been the same as the Repeal movement, and this provided further evidence that the Greeks were just like the Irish.

One more example of this process in operation will drive home the point. In both Ireland and the Ionian Islands, violence of a type that the British categorized as "rural outrage" was common. Greek and Irish peasants committed arson, maimed animals, maliciously destroyed property, and killed other men at alarming rates. On Kerkira, for example, in the years 1830, 1844, and 1856, arrest warrants were issued for 121 cases of arson, seventy-three animal thefts, eighty-two episodes of animal maiming, and 137 cases of destruction of property (usually this referred to the cutting down of vines and the mutilation of olive trees). When colonial officers attempted to understand Greek rural violence, instead of turning to episodes from the British countryside, like the Captain Swing outbursts of 1831–32 or the Scottish anti-clearance outrages of the 1840s and 1850s (Archer 1985; 1989; 1991; Dunbabin 1974: 263–64; Hobsbawm and Rude 1975; Mingay 1989), they chose instead to analogize it to a very specific type of Irish rural violence: Whiteboyism. Whiteboyism refers to the rural violence that rocked Ireland from 1800 to the Great Famine. A number of different movements (e.g., the Shanavests and Caravests, the Captain Rockites, the White Feet, and the Terry Alts) were subsumed under this label. These were secret societies consisting of tenants, small farmers, and laborers who banded together to protest rural conditions in Ireland through acts of violence—assassinations, animal maiming, arson, and the like (Beames 1987; 1983; Broeker 1970; Clark and Donnelly 1983; Donnelly 1983; Palmer 1988). Given the superficial resemblances between the Irish and Ionian situations and their predilection to see things Irish among the Greeks, it is not too surprising that the British saw the two situations as almost identical. The 1819 tax revolt on Lefkada, the 1832 electoral riot on Kefallenia, the 1835 peasant march on Argostoli, and the 1848 and 1849 riots on Kefallenia, for example, were compared not with the Newport rising of 1839 (Jones 1985) or the Welsh Rebecca Riots during the late 1830s and early 1840s (Jones 1989) but instead with the Young Ireland uprising of 1848 (Knox 1984: 506). To the colonial officers, rural Greek violence resembled Irish, but not English or Scottish or Welsh, rural violence.

There were similarities in the structure of rural economic and social relations between Ireland and the Ionian Islands that fostered a comparison, the most important of these being the dominance of a sharecropping system and a consequent division of social classes into landowners, usually aristocrats, and dependant tenants. But I suggest that equally important was the more widespread notion that the Irish and the Ionians were culturally analogous. As with the Enosis movement, the Irish analogy obfuscated more than it clarified. In the case of rural violence it led the Colonial Office to see Ionian outrages as being more organized, more political, and more class-oriented than they actually were. For example, while most Whiteboy attacks were perpetrated by poor farmers against estate owners and factors (Beames 1983: 71–89, 200–226), a preliminary analysis of the Greek data suggests that most of the acts of arson, animal maiming, and animal theft were aimed at other peasants and not at landlords or their agents. Likewise, most rural homicides on the islands resulted from vendettas or knife fights between peasant men contesting honor and status through ritualized displays of aggressive masculinity rather than the more common assassination of landlords by disgruntled tenants that characterized the Whiteboy movements: though to be sure, these did occur on the islands.[9] At numerous points throughout the remainder of this book we shall see where the construction of the Greeks as the Mediterranean Irish led to profound cultural misunderstandings between the Ionians and their English masters.

One last area where the discourses of Irish and Greek identities intersected relates to their physical and racial composition. I have noted already that one element setting these two cultures apart from others in the empire was their whiteness. Like the common Christian link that established similitude between the Ionians, the Irish, and the English, whiteness also demonstrated a degree of similarity between them. Some commentators described the Greeks as possessing aboriginal physical features that resembled Black Africans and subcontinental Indians. I argue that this process was directly related as well to the construction of the Irish as being Black. L. Perry Curtis, Jr., has collected and analyzed hundreds of published caricatures of the Irish during the nineteenth century; he found that one of the dominant trends from midcentury onward was the simianization of the Irish (1971: 29–58; see also Lebow 1976: 39–40). Irishmen were depicted with exaggerated Negroid facial features and apelike bodies. English writers as well portrayed them this way: "I am haunted by the human chimpanzees I saw [in Ireland] . . . I don't believe they are our fault. . . . But to see white chimpanzees is dreadful; if they were black, one would not feel it so much." (Charles Kingsley in a letter to his wife, quoted in Curtis 1968: 84; see also Ignatiev 1995). Black Irish in the discourse of colonial rule had begot Black Greeks.

Clashing Characteristics

To this point we have examined how the British crafted various identities for the Ionian Greeks, and how they situated these cultural constructions into the broader discourse of categorizing colonized peoples within the British Empire. In whichever of the dominant models we examined, cunning or duplicitous behavior and disingenuousness appeared as central elements in defining cultural differences. In this section I pose and provide some possible answers to the question of why these two elements were the ones that established the links between the Greeks and other colonial stereotypes that then enabled the British to castigate Ionian culture as being uncivilized and un-European. First, following Brettell's lead (1986: 162), we have to appreciate that there was a "reality out there" and that Greeks and Englishmen did look upon cleverness and lying in very different ways and that their cultures estimated these behaviors in completely opposite manners. Understanding why this was so can enable us to comprehend better the reasons these clashing characteristics assumed the crucial position in the process of identity formation.

The Cultivation of Cleverness

An Ionian nobleman told the following anecdote at a banquet hosted by Lord High Commissioner Sir John Young (Kirkwall 1864: 12–13). The diametrically opposed reactions of the Greeks and the British present at this commensal gathering provide us with an entry point for examining the clash of cultural characteristics

A young Kefallenian count found himself down on his luck in Rome. He had insufficient funds to pay for his passage on the steamer from Ancona to Kerkira, let alone the cash needed to purchase a carriage fare from Rome to Ancona. So he hit upon the following ruse. Under Roman law, in order to ensure that a carriage man arrived at the agreed-upon time, he would give a deposit to the client. The money would be returned when the fare was picked up. Frantically, the count raced around Rome booking passage with as many carriage men as he safely could—collecting from each, of course, a deposit. He told all but one of them to pick him up at his hotel at 9 A.M.; that one he told to be there at 7 A.M. The scene at the hotel was chaotic as over twenty carriages arrived to pick up the count. Some carriage men ran to the police, others took off in pursuit of the swindler. The two-hour head start proved too much. The clever count eluded capture, and not only was he able to pay for the ferry, but he made a profit as well.

The assembled Greeks, all of whom were pro-British in political orientation, roared with approving laughter at this exemplary tale of cleverness, or in Greek *poniria*. The British found little to laugh at. Barely able to contain himself, Viscount Kirkwall furiously wrote of the episode: "The toleration of such conduct as above described is a sad stain upon any society. . . . If the Greeks are in earnest in their desire to cultivate the friendship of the English, they must turn over a new leaf in their manner of treating such delinquencies. These are not simply to be laughed at as good jokes. They must be denounced as a national abomination and disgrace, unworthy of any country calling itself Christian and anxious to obtain all the moral as well as material advantages of civilization" (1864: 14). Civilized men, then, did not deceive one another, nor did they find humor in the deceptions perpetrated on others. Candor and civilization went hand-in-hand.

Another example highlights further the cultural dissonance over cleverness. Some Ionian islanders "it is said, point to the [British-funded Ionian Bank] as a thing pregnant with evil,—'a horse of Troy' (this is their word of alarm), hiding speciously mischief incalculable, utter ruin. The British government, they say, by means of this bank, mediates a transfer of the landed property of the islands to British subjects, by the cunning process of taking advantage of the distress and necessities of Ionian proprietors, making pecuniary advances to them on mortgage, and then (after some changes made in the law relative to real property) taking possession of the property by foreclosing! Never, perhaps, was a *mala mens* in a party more preposterously exhibited, or in a manner more insulting to common sense of the people whose fears they wish to excite" (Davy 1842: 74–75). This story is replete with significance, but I want to emphasize here only the way in which Ionians automatically assumed that there had to be some deeper meaning, some clever ruse being enacted by the Colonial Office's establishment of the bank. If this institution and its practices were not part of some elaborate scheme to steal their land, then why would the British lend them money at reasonable rates but secured by land? Obviously after the proprietors became ensnared by English debts, the Colonial Office would use the power of government to change the laws and foreclose. The Greeks held a culturally inscribed expectation of deception and a reflex assumption that their foes would manipulate the levers of legislative power to partisan advantage.

Cleverness and cunning, the ability to gain materially or socially by deceiving one's opponents, were for the Greeks characteristics denoting moral superiority, whereas to the British they were an abomination and disgrace. Ionians considered the use of deception, depending on the context in which the act took place, to be most honorable. Honor, for the British, by definition precluded such behavior. Clearly here we have a clash of behavioral and attitudinal norms.

First, we need to comprehend why cleverness was for the Greeks a socially acceptable, indeed laudable, character trait, and second why the British found it so disagreeable and repugnant so as to be one of the prime manifestations of the islanders' want of civilization. There is a considerable body of anthropological literature on Greek cleverness, and it is to those works that we must turn first.

Ethnographers working in rural Greece have found that cleverness was considered to be an essential quality that a man, as the head of a household, had to possess (e.g., Campbell 1964: 282–83; du Boulay 1974: 197; Friedl 1962: 80; Herzfeld 1985: 198); recent research among immigrant urbanites suggests that the pattern was not restricted to the village (Hirschon 1989: 176). In Greek culture it was accepted, indeed expected, that men would employ trickery and deception as means of advancing or defending the interests of their households. Honor, in the form of the esteem in which his peers held a man, was directly related to his ability to display cleverness and to outwit his opponents. Charles Stewart captures well the view that cunning behavior was both normative and that to boast about it was required when he states that "guile is such an expected component of local action [on the island of Naxos] that one learns to suspect appearances strongly, even when going along with them, and assume that there is a hidden, unexpected motivation. Someone easily taken in is *koroiaudo* [a shorn goat]. The premium on trickery has created a situation where virtually no plan, even if it may be realized by perfectly straightforward means, is aesthetically pleasing unless there is a hidden trick to it" (1991: 63). The use of trickery and duplicity to obtain material gain for one's household was thus mandatory, but such actions alone did not constitute cultural capital until the deed was revealed in settings like the local *kafenion* or other male gatherings. It was not just the revelation of the deceitful act alone that gave it meaning, but also the way that the narrative of the deed was presented (Herzfeld 1987: 24–26). We can thus comprehend the reason why the story of the clever count evoked such strong emotions among the Greeks (it was an exemplary act recounted in a well-told tale) and the British (because it so offended their notion of what constituted civilized behavior and because the Greeks so obviously reveled in the story's message). Viscount Kirkwall and his comrades might have felt more than a little discomfort when they realized that by not getting the humor in the story they exposed their susceptibility to Greek *poniria*.

As early as the middle of the nineteenth century one explanation for Greek cunning blamed it on the long years of tyrannical Ottoman rule (Finlay 1971 [1871], vol. 1: 14). The ability of clever Greeks to outwit their Turkish overlords was a stock theme of Greek popular shadow theater from the nineteenth century onward (Danforth 1976; Myrsiades 1992; Couroucli 1993). Even though the Ionian Islands escaped the grip of the Porte, they were still under foreign rule for centuries and so this explanation could also account for them. This underdog culture model finds comparative support in studies of other cultures as well. James C. Scott has argued that trickery and deceit were weapons of the weak wielded against superiors (1990: 88–89). In his detailed study of a village in Malaysia, he documents how such stratagems operated (1985). Bertram Wyatt-Brown, in an assessment of male slave psychology in the Old South, argues that cunning was an integral component of the Sambo persona which slaves sometimes adopted in confrontations with their masters (1988: 1241–43; he also cites numerous examples that suggest that cunning and trickery were behaviors adopted by slaves in many different cultural settings; see also Greenberg 1996: 12, 99). The underdog culture explanation only partially accounts for the high estimation in which members of subordinate groups regard cleverness. It is evident that Greek men, for example, employed trickery and duplicity not just in dealings with their superiors but with their equals as well. I suspect that the moral ethos that elevated the self-interest of the household over other forms of cultural organizations played a vitally important role. A view of the world as a zero-sum game, like Foster's ideology of the limited good (1965) or Banfield's amoral familism (1958: 10), established a social climate in which behaviors like duplicitousness that advanced the fortunes of one's own were deemed acceptable and praiseworthy. When combined, these two explanations help us to understand why the Greeks considered cleverness good. Before discussing why the British found it so bad, I want to analyze the closely related phenomenon of Greek mendacity.

Truth and Disingenuousness: It's the Context That Counts

British colonial officers, diplomats, and travelers unanimously considered that one of the hallmark features of Mediterranean peoples was their utter lack of candor and their penchant for lying. Charles Newton, for example, observed that "people in England wonder how it is that, after a long residence in the East, Europeans become suspicious, jealous and generally cantankerous; but they forget that an Englishman in the Levant passes his life surrounded by [liars]. The very air we breathe . . . is impregnated with lies" (1865: vol. 2, 75). And nowhere was the atmosphere more full of falsehoods than in the Ionian Islands. "Nothing sets in a clearer point of view the dereliction of every thing virtuous and honourable amongst [the Ionian Greeks], then the total disregard to truth, in which they are brought up; they seem to take as much pains to discourage ingenuousness and candour, as a people of more elevated principle would, to detect and punish prevarication and falsehood: the probability is, that a young Greek will deceive you, even in matters of the greatest indifference; although he gains no immediate advantage by this sacrifice of candour, yet he considers that, by holding you in ignorance, he is ready to profit by his craft at some future emergency" (Kendrick 1822: 195–96). Others agreed (Ansted 1863: 450; Davy 1842: 8, 322–23; Kirkwall 1864: 252). Charles Tuckerman, United States consul to Athens in the 1870s, believed that all Greeks naturally embellished facts with the same flair and ornateness as their ancient ancestors adorned their architecture

(1872: 332). Lying was thus an oriental trait. Not only did Greeks lie, but they also did so even when they stood to gain no utilitarian advantage. But one form of lying above all others was seen as being particularly destructive and offensive: perjury.

Throughout the duration of the protectorate, the ubiquitousness of perjury was seen as the paramount obstacle to the installation and effective operation of a modern criminal justice system. During his tenure as resident on Kefallenia during the 1820s, Sir Charles Napier continually bemoaned that he was unable to obtain untainted, or sometimes even any, testimony in criminal proceedings regardless of the nature of the crime (Napier 1833: 125; CO 136/303: Napier to Kennedy, March 16, 1824 PRO). He even spoke once about there being shops where litigants could buy false witnesses for so much a head, and he was being only slightly facetious. The long passage quoted earlier from Lord Nugent shows that little had changed in the 1830s. I discuss in chapter 8 many of the stratagems employed by the Colonial Office to try and elicit unperjured testimony from the Greeks in the 1830s and 1840s, and in particular how they tried to use the church and the practice of excommunication to accomplish this task. In spite of all these efforts, the British believed that the Greeks continued their disingenuous ways: they lied to each other; they lied to officials; they lied in court. And the British were probably right.

Anthropologists working in Greece are as unanimous as the British Colonial officers in seeing lying as an integral element in village discourse. Juliet du Boulay, during her ethnographic fieldwork in an Evvian mountain village, found that "lying . . . is . . . a talent indispensable to village life, and one which is almost universally possessed" (1974: 172–73). Mendacity was a social skill taught to Greek children from childhood onward. Villagers spoke of getting together to "tell each other lies" (Friedl 1962: 80–81) as a euphemism for having a conversation. One woman summed it up concisely when she told du Boulay, "You cannot live without lies" (du Boulay 1974: 191).

Lying was expected and, in the assessment of Sarakatsani shepherds at least, any man who did not lie when the context called for it was not only a fool but also not a real man, i.e., one lacking in honor (Campbell 1964: 283; see also Herzfeld 1990: 306). This passage also suggests the explanation for why manipulation of the truth is essential in Greek life, and du Boulay perceptively articulates it: "Because the truth of the honour of his family is to the villager a reality much more important than the factual truth of what has actually happened, the lesser truth of the pragmatic event is manipulated to clear the way for the greater truth of family honour to appear" (1976: 405). Just as with cleverness, prevarication was seen as a socially essential strategy needed to defend the household's reputation, to advance its material interests, and to attack its rivals and exact vengeance on its foes when necessary. Lying when one's vested interests required it was not just expected, it was a duty (Campbell 1964: 283; du Boulay 1974: 77–78, 172–73, 192–99; 1976: 399–405; Herzfeld 1990: 319; Hirschon 1989: 179; Peristianny 1976: 23; Stewart 1991: 112). Consequently, no guilt was attached to lying, and Greeks had no difficulty in reconciling mendacity with the moral precepts of Orthodoxy. As one woman storyteller related in her gloss of a folktale in which lying, duplicity, and cunning were all prominent: "God wants people to cover things up, He wants there to be no fuss . . . God wants concealment [of the truth]" (du Boulay 1974: 82–83).

It is not surprising then that the epistemological status of the truth changed little when Greeks went to court. For a start, many Greeks did not see litigation as a means of determining right or wrong, or as a way of attaining the truth. Instead, prosecution was employed as a device to restore one's own reputation while sullying that of another when it was not possible to do so in informal village discourse (du Boulay 1974: 197). Two aspects distinguished the court of law from the court of public opinion: the first was that the former necessitated the intrusion of the state into households' affairs (meaning that information meant for insiders would have to be revealed to outsiders), and the second was that oaths would have to be sworn to vouchsafe the information revealed as the truth. Without oaths, there could be no perjury.

Oath-swearing, however, occupied a very problematic place in Greek society. Herzfeld found, for example, that among Cretan shepherds, when one man demanded that another swear an oath as to the veracity of a charge or accusation (usually for animal theft) that one levied against the other, this in itself constituted a challenge to the accused's *filotimo* (a term often glossed as "honor"). In investigating this process further, he discovered that there were rituals involved, that the oaths were sworn between men in private (only accuser and accused stood together as witnesses), and that they were sworn in churches (Herzfeld 1990). The differences with oath-swearing in a courtroom are fairly evident: one was public, the other was private; one was conducted in secular space, the other in sacred. So, even though all oaths are by definition sacred (Rouland 1994: 267–68), for Cretan shepherds at least, the binding transcendental power of an oath stemmed equally from the words themselves and from the sacredness of the place in which they were uttered. As one sheep thief told him: "In a law-court, to get some-one else off [a charge], they say, [perjury] is not important. . . . In a church you shouldn't do it. In a church, you're afraid" (Herzfeld 1990: 318). Lying in court, then, was merely a logical extension of the prac-tice of concealing and manipulating information in the village square or in the local wineshop.

The ethnographic evidence from the recent past amply supports the conclusions regarding Greek disingenuousness drawn by Napier, Nugent, and their colleagues during the nineteenth century. The rea-sons why lying was acceptable in Ionian society are the same as the ones propounded earlier to explain the cultural veneration of cunning. There is a plethora of comparative material that demonstrates that lying is a very prominent weapon of the weak against their supe-riors (Bailey 1991: 66; Barnes 1994: 81, 83–86; N. Brown 1989: 104–5; Gilsenan 1976: 196; Kloos 1983: 135; Scott 1990: 3, 89, 131). Once again, when this underdog mentality was combined with an ethos that encouraged or even required members of a household to enshrine its interests over all others, they produced a cultural setting in which pre-varication was perceived as a morally good action. In sum, when it came to telling the truth or performing some deceitful act, it was the context that counted above all else.

Why did cunning and disingenuousness so offend the English and lead them to elevate these two behaviors to the status of the most prominent manifestations of the Ionians' lack of civilization and to essentialize them as the most important primordial Greek character flaws? At one level what we are dealing with is a collision of variant ethical systems, in which there were diametrically opposed views over the types of behaviors each system deemed estimable. Take veracity, for example. Mendacity was considered by Greek men to be both ad-mirable and honorable, but in both the English aristocratic code of honor and the ascendant bourgeois moral code, it was deemed to be the most dishonorable of traits.[10] Charles Kingsley (cited in Gay 1985: 412) made the point with his characteristic forcefulness: "The virtue you admire most? TRUTH. The vice to which you are most lenient? ALL EXCEPT LYING." And no form of lying was more offensive to Victorian sensibilities than perjury, because it both violated the virtue of the truth and it was blasphemous (Baker 1990: 87–88; Barnes 1994: 79; Green 1985: 360–63; Hill 1850–1851: 102; Harwood 1843: 196). Popular ethics and nineteenth-century Christian morality combined to make perjury a truly offensive act.

The same gulf existed between the English and Greeks in regard to probity and honesty. Ionian islanders found honor in duplicity, cunning, and cleverness if the context warranted them; the English bourgeois moral code of Christian commerce enshrined honesty as the highest virtue regardless of context. What truth was to Kingsley, honesty was to Robert Owen (Perkin 1969: 279). For Max Weber, honesty constituted one of the defining elements of the "Protestant ethic" (Weber 1975: 161).

The exalted position occupied by honesty and veracity in the new Victorian hierarchy of virtues also explains why they were two of the paramount categories used for defining cultural difference in the empire. Herbert Spencer, writing at the end of the nineteenth century, carefully described the relationship between these two behaviors and modernity. For him, the progress of civilization was directly related to the cultural propensity to tell the truth. Wild tribesmen (African savages, Amerindians, and Filipinos, for example) capriciously lied all of the time; semicivilized peoples (ancient Greeks and Romans, eastern Europeans, and Orientals) lied some of the time; modern Englishmen intentionally lied none of the time (1891: 401–2). He was not naive enough to believe that Englishmen never lied, but what separated them from the lower orders of races was that they never did so except when moral necessity required it (1891: 403). Equally important, I would argue, was his idea that veracity was connected to liberty and freedom. Free men in a free society did not lie (he cites the case of the English, who habitually lied before the Glorious Revolution). His point had to do with liberty and equality, but others could easily turn it around: those who lie are *not worthy* of political liberty. Liars were, therefore, incapable of self-rule.

The idea of truth being related to moral enlightenment was also evident. During the nineteenth century there was a debate concerning the role of oath-taking in the justice system. Religious opponents argued that it violated the biblical proscription against taking oaths; other abolitionists maintained that, in an enlightened Christian society, oaths were redundant because men would not need God to play the sheriff—to paraphrase Jeremy Bentham (cited in Baker 1990: 88)—in order to tell the truth. They would do so as a matter of course (Empson 1834: 447–50; Forsythe 1860: 196). Finally, there developed during the early Victorian period a notion that lying and cunning were quintessentially childlike traits (Gay 1985: 421).[11] This strongly reinforced the idea that veracity and mendacity were connected to evolutionary stages of human races on the road of progress. For the British, then, nothing demonstrated the Ionian islanders' complete want of civilization, their cultural inferiority, and their lack of moral enlightenment than their predilection for mendacity and deviousness.

Stereotypes and Rule

In this chapter I have investigated how the British constructed identities for the Ionian islanders. Colonial governance necessitated that the dominant group render the cultural system of the subordinate group intelligible not only as a mandatory prerequisite for ruling them but also as a means of legitimizing their position of power. These were of even more importance on the Ionian Islands because of their "peculiar connexion" to the empire—by right they were to have been self-governing—and because the Greeks occupied an ambiguous position in the panoply of colonial cultural categories—Ionians were neither manifestly Occidental nor Oriental, European or non-European. They had to be created as one or other, or a hybrid of both. The British did not arrive on the islands without any preexisting notions of who these people were: they had the classical tradition to guide them. But their confrontation with modern Greeks challenged the image of romantic Hellenism, and so the Ionians had to be distanced from their own history. We saw how Bowen and others did this, first by denying them continuity with their ancient Hellenic past and second by situating that rupture during the long centuries of Venetian rule. This left open the question that if these were not the Greeks of old, then who were they? Through the application of analogies of colonial stereotypes the British created a series of identities for the Greeks. One set acted to exoticize them and to render them as comparable to aborigines. The other sought to familiarize them by turning the Greeks into the Mediterranean Irish. We also saw how common to both images and integral to the cultural critique of the Ionians were deviousness and mendacity. These behavioral traits provided the links between the various stereotypes. The British used these variant identities as the bases for their policies and for justification of them. Whether it was as Oriental poobahs in bourgeois garb, Balkan Hottentots, or swarthy Paddies, one overarching conclusion flowed from any one of these identities: the Greeks were a baser, uncivilized race that was unworthy and incapable of self-rule. Therefore, they had to be governed by whatever means necessary to guide them on the path toward enlightenment. Once the illuminating influence of English rule had sufficient time to work its magic, then and only then would the Greeks be able to join the ranks of the civilized peoples of Europe. But identity formation was a two-way process, and while the English were busily crafting identities for the Greeks, the Greeks were also undertaking a cultural critique of the English and the West. In the next chapter, we examine how the Ionians went about creating a "western civilization" on their islands.

Figure 1. "View of San Marco," by Edward Dodwell. Printed by permission of the British Library, no. 649.b.1.

CHAPTER THREE

Creating
"Western Civilization"
on a Greek Island

Edward Dodwell's painting *View of San Marco* imaginatively captures the cacophony of sounds, the kaleidoscope of sights, and the variety of smells that struck the visitor to the Piazza San Marco on the water-front of the capital city of Zakinthos (see facing page). Dominating the center of the scene he depicts an aged countrywoman attempting to control her unruly flock of milk goats; a young boy, her grandson perhaps, offers her a milk jug. Actively engaged in conversation are groups of merchants, recognizable by their characteristic attire that combined western and eastern styles of dress, and aristocrats, fashion-ably attired in top hats and long coats and holding elaborately adorned canes. Sitting nearby is an idle carter, waiting for the next merchant ship to arrive. Peasants in the traditional costume of baggy trousers, kneesocks, overflowing linen shirt, and soft cloth cap mingle about the square seeking an audience with their landlords or work from an over-seer. The ever-present priest stands side by side with a monk and an aristocrat, watching as a street vendor tries to sell meat to the man-servant from some great house. Idling on the seawall, a group of young men smoke and play cards. Through this turbulent scene hur-ries the customs agent, recognizable by his cocked hat and ledger book. Off to one side, segregated from this Greek social gathering, stand the red-coated troops from the British garrison, seemingly oblivious to the slice of life surging all around them. Also separated off to the side stand some younger women, gossiping in the doorway of a house from which they dare not stray or risk being castigated as a "Magdalene"—an adulteress or a prostitute, for reasons we shall see in chapter 7. Scattered through the scene are the ubiquitous dogs so reviled by British travelers and residents. Providing a backdrop to this social tableau are the large colonnaded buildings whose first floors housed the businesses, shops, and taverns of the city's square. The upper stories above them, meanwhile, served as the townhouses for the island's wealthy and, in their style, attest to the long years of Venetian rule over the island.

What strikes us viewing this scene, and what appalled British visitors to the island, was the seeming disorder of Ionian society. Not disorder as in unrest—though there was plenty of that—but rather as a lack of coherence or regimentation. There was seemingly a chaotic mixture of elements that created the sense of things out of place. Side by side stood countrymen and urban denizens, aristocrats and street vendors. Functions and activities seemed to occur willy-nilly: buying and selling, gambling and gossiping, work and play seemed to take place without any semblance of order or structure. The intermixing of class is evident as workers, vendors, soldiers, merchants, and aristocrats vied for space in the busy square. Goats and dogs added a variety of sounds, smells, and refuse to the crowded piazza. Rich and poor, young and old, colonizer and colonized, men and beasts, all commingled in the center of the island's capital. Numerous British sources commented scathingly about Ionian civic culture and public spaces, finding in this lack of order proof of the Greeks' exoticism and inferiority.

We saw in the last chapter how representatives of the British Colonial Office and other members of British society constructed certain cultural stereotypes of the Ionian islanders as a means of categorizing and exoticizing them. The British consistently and predictably enacted policies predicated upon expected patterns of behavior based on those stereotypes. The emphasis in that discussion was on an identity projected onto the islanders by outsiders. I focused there on how the western "Us" created an objectified and recognizable "Them" in order to go about the business of imposing rules and order. But identity-formation processes are multifaceted and complex. At the same time that the British were pigeonholing the Greek islanders as European aborigines and the Mediterranean Irish, the Ionians were actively designing a collective representation of themselves as "civilized westerners," an identity shaped by their imaginary construction of British, "western culture." Two discourses were operating simultaneously but interconnectedly.

In this chapter, I examine the other side of the process of identity formation. The problem that confronts us, however, is how to make the "subaltern speak" (Spivak 1988; Sivaramakrishnan 1995). How can we discover the ways that Greeks understood the British? How did they interpret what constituted "western" civilization? Unlike the British, learned Greeks for the most part did not leave the types of writings used in the last chapter to describe British culture. To be sure, there were sharp social critics like Andreas Laskaratos and Antonis Matesis, whose works will be referred to elsewhere, but they turned their critical eyes on Greek, not British, society. In political pamphlets and memorials to the press, Ionian intellectuals railed about the British occupation of the islands as unjust and tyrannical, but they did not critique British culture. In a later chapter we shall see that Greeks of all political persuasions agreed that the central divide between themselves and the British was religion, with each side claiming the right to define itself as *the* Christian culture. But that was a different discourse. Finally, there was no equivalent to the western traveler who felt the compulsion to put pen to paper and to describe his or her experience among the alien, other culture. In the absence of such sources, how can we explicate the ways that the subordinate culture viewed the dominant one?

There is a source that can provide some insights into how the Greeks viewed the West, and that source is municipal laws and statutes. What I argue here is that during a particular moment of transition in colonial rule, a group of pro-British Greeks attempted to mold Greek civil society to resemble that which they considered western through the mechanism of law. As we saw in chapter 1, the advent of the liberal administration of Sir Howard Douglas witnessed an even more explicit attempt than had occurred under his predecessor, Lord Nugent, to reform Greek society through the implementation of liberal policies and institutions, like the foundling homes to be discussed in chapter 4. If anything, Douglas wanted to increase the administrative capacity of the local, Greek-controlled institutions, especially the municipal councils (CO 136/70: Douglas to Glennig, Nov. 30, 1835 PRO). Under the Ionian charter, revised by Douglas, the regent, an elected official with responsibility for the entire island, and the municipal council, a body of wealthy men selected from a double list, had the power to legislate and regulate local society. They did not, however, have full autonomy. As mandated by the 1817 charter, all new laws and statutes were subject to review by the British resident on the island and to veto by the lord high commissioner.

Over a sixteen-month period immediately after the accession of the Douglas government in 1835 and continuing for the first sixteen months of his reign, the regent and the municipal council of Zakinthos passed 136 pieces of legislation aimed at the reordering and the redefinition of Zakinthiote civic society and public space.[1] Together this body of law provided the core of the civilizing process, as defined by Norbert Elias (1978), through which Greeks would become westernized; indeed this episode goes beyond Elias's idea of a slow, evolving process and instead resembles more Arthur Mitzman's (Mitzman 1987) notion of a civilizing mission. Moreover, since the laws had to meet with British approval, at least partly I would argue, the statues were intended to impress colonial officials and so we can draw inferences from the laws about what some Greeks believed the British thought to constitute civilization. The Greeks believed that for the British, being civilized denoted a sense of decorum and superficial appearance manifested in public. Indeed, they took their cue from such utterances as this from Douglas: the social defects of the Ionians, the lord high commissioner wrote, were rooted in their wanton disregard for "cleanliness, classification, [and] discipline" (CO 136/75: Douglas to Gleneig, Jun. 6, 1835 PRO). Douglas's emphasis on the connection between sanitation and civilization flowed out of the discourse on this issue that was occurring in England during the mid-1830s (Hennock 2000).

Western civilization for the Greeks, however, was not a state of being but a mode of public presentation; it was not about beliefs, character, and morality, but about decorum, appearance, and conduct. To pro-western Greeks, being civilized meant a society that possessed ordered public spaces—in the sense in which Mary Douglas employs the term—regimented people, and segregated public spheres. Civilization was not about who you are but how you appear (Douglas 1973; 1975).

A detailed examination of the municipal statutes, then, can provide insights into how Greeks constructed the "West." The statutes can be divided into a number of categories. Some of the laws were utilitarian and make perfect practical sense, like those relating to weights and measures employed in the public market. Most of them, however, had more of a symbolic than a utilitarian function. Indeed, as I show below, many of them were unenforceable and the city fathers knew that they were unenforceable. Thus, the intent of the legislators was not necessarily to change the way their fellow Greeks behaved, but to show the Colonial Office that they too believed in the civilizing mission of the empire and that they were prepared to act to bring the West to the East. I begin with a discussion of the largest group of laws, those pertaining to the ordering of public space.

Ordering Public Space

Anthropologists working on contemporary Greece have noted the significance accorded to the distinction between public and private space. Most frequently highlighted has been the very marked gendered aspect of space. Another aspect that has received less attention has been that Greeks place great emphasis on differentiating the outside from the inside, the street from the home (Herzfeld 1991). Hospitality, for which the Greeks are justly famous, represents a symbolic bridging of public and private (du Boulay 1991; Herzfeld 1987). There is then a cultural construction whereby it is chaos, dirt, and disorder that separates the domestic from the public, the inside from the outside. Ordering public space, then, engages some deep-seated ideas about society as a whole. It is in this context that we should assess the civic statutes aimed at reordering public space in Zakinthos.

A bevy of statutes regulated the marketplace. Some of them aimed at regulating shopping hours. Statute #90 (1836), for example, stated that all shops and market stalls had to cease all business at 11 P.M. between September 15 and March 15. The only exceptions to this law were wineshops, cafes, and other drinking establishments, which were to close at 10 P.M. (statute #37). This latter was further revised by law #89 so that drinking emporia would close at 11 P.M., like other shops, during the winter and 12 P.M. during the summer months. The markets and shops were to close on "Easter Sunday and Monday, the Pentecost, the festival of Agios Apostolos, the feast of the Virgin, Christmas Day, the Epiphany, the feast of the Apostles, Agios Dionysios, and on all of the other festivals of the great saints and martyrs" (statute #37).

In addition to time, market space was also to be regulated. Merchants selling wares and goods from a market stall were required to register their location with the market police, to do business only from their registered stall, and to restrict the size of their stall to the limits set by the police (statute #101). Statute #86 set the precise spatial boundaries within which stalls could be built. The police would summarily destroy any stalls set up outside of this zone, and the owner would be ineligible for any compensation. Vendors operating out of a shop did not escape the heavy hand of the city fathers. In addition to regulating the hours of operation, statutes #102 and 104 mandated that each shop owner hang a wooden plank sign on which was inscribed his name, trade or craft, and license number. The laws also stipulated the size and color paint to be used on the sign, and where the sign was to hang. The market, then, was to be neat, orderly, and uniform.

As part of this process of segregating and ordering market space, the city fathers passed laws controlling the meat trade (#5). Meat could only be sold at registered stalls located either in the central public market or at a designated area on the outskirts of town at Ammos beach. All butchers required a license, and their stalls were subject to periodic inspections. No young, old, or ill animals could be killed. All slaughtering and deposition of waste materials had to be done at designated areas located outside of the city limits. In total, no less than nine separate statutes were passed controlling the meat trade.

Marketplace perfidy did not escape the city fathers' attention. All weights and measures had to be tested by the market police and marked with an official seal. Anyone tampering with weights or caught selling fake seals was severely punished. If a customer requested it, a butcher or fishmonger had to reweigh items for sale in front of two witnesses. Fishmongers caught mixing seaweed or sand with items for sale were heavily fined. Financial penalties and even jail time awaited those merchants caught watering down wine, mixing fillers in their bread, or adulterating olive oil (statutes #5, 39, 130, and 132). Finally, all prices had to be posted in writing at the start of the business day and could be altered only after obtaining written permission from the police (#110).

Of course regulating the purity of products, the location of abattoirs, and the like are all perfectly good examples of sound, sensible sanitary measures. Similar legislation was passed in cities and towns around the world. But, as with the municipal statutes enacted on Zakinthos, there was another motivation behind them as well. As Nicholas Thomas (1990; 1994: 105–42) has argued, British sanitation policy in Fiji, while motivated by benign intent, also aimed at reshaping Fijian society. Timothy Mitchell has remarked about British policy in Egypt that sought to bring order to the chaos of the Orient: "The [British] colonial process would try and re-order Egypt to appear as a world enframed. Egypt was to be ordered up as something object-like" (Mitchell 1991: 33). As he goes on to show, the process of enframing, as he calls it, was about ordering both people and place. Reforming space, therefore, also had a deep symbolic meaning. By attempting to alter some of those aspects of city life that the British found most offensive, the pro-empire Greeks added explicitly "occidentalizing" reform. In short, what the city fathers wanted was a marketplace and a cityscape that looked more like Covent Garden than an "oriental bazaar." They did not, however, stop there. Molding civil society meant more than just the public markets, and so they endeavored to westernize domestic space as well.

Another set of statutes dealt with the ways people were to deal with dirt and human waste from their homes. "It is forbidden to throw from one's house into the public street night soil, shit, and garbage. Such materials should not be allowed to collect outside the door, but should be kept inside until they can be properly disposed of" (statute #4). So reads the first of many laws designed to regulate the disposition of dirt and waste. Another, passed immediately after the first, gave people eight days during which to clean out their courtyards (#27). On the ninth day, the police would begin household inspections. The other statutes defined where Greeks could properly deposit wastes—at three dumps outside of the town limits and on the beaches, but only at sites specifically demarcated for that purpose and only if the person had purchased a permit (#99)—and when they could remove refuse—only between the hours of 10 P.M. and 2 A.M. (#48). The police were given wide discretionary powers to enter a house if they smelled "foul rather than sweet" water emanating from within or if they suspected that the house's chimney was not properly cleaned (#11 and #27).

Here again, these appear at first glance to be reasonable measures aimed at maintaining public health and sanitation. And they were. But something deeper was going on as well. Anthropologists have noted that Greeks draw a sharp distinction between the inside of the family dwelling and the outside, and that it is a divide rooted in ideas about purity and pollution (du Boulay 1974; Dubisch 1986b; Herzfeld 1986; Pavlides and Hesser 1986). According to Jill Dubisch, "The opposite of the house, which is the realm of cleanliness and order, is the 'street,' a place of both dirt and immorality. Here, order and control are, to some extent at least, absent. In the village, the street is the place where trash is thrown, where humans and animals defecate, where strangers pass by. The street and the fields that lie beyond symbolize the 'wild,' the outside, the realm of competitiveness and danger" (1986b: 200). Women scrupulously sweep dirt and refuse from their courtyards and deposit them into the street. Dirt and pollution symbolically separate the inside and outside, the safe from the dangers, the home from the street. The 'natural' order of things, then, is for the public space to be unclean and for the domestic realm to be clean.

Moreover, the symbolic boundary between domestic and public space touched key elements of both masculine and feminine identity. For police and other nonkinsmen to enter into a man's home represented a threat to his reputation (see below, page 113). Greek men were willing to die to keep state officials out of their houses. The statutes aimed at cleansing domestic space were unenforceable, and the city fathers knew it. No sustained effort was ever made to enforce these intrusive laws. I have been able to find only two cases in which someone was prosecuted for violation of the sanitation codes, and in both instances the charges were as lesser and included offenses. In one case, a man was cited for improperly disposing of night soil; he was also charged with insult and public insubordination. He dumped the effuse on a constable passing by his balcony (TIAK, *Ektelstikon Astinomia Katagrafis Anaforon Epitheoriseon Stathmon Peripolon*, Fak. 23, 1859–1860: #1137, Aug. 30, 1860). In the other, a man was charged with emptying buckets of waste in front of the British garrison, as a violation of statute #99 (TIAK, *Ektelstikon Astinomia Katagrafis Anaforon Epitheoriseon Stathmon Peripolon*, Fak. 23, 1859–1860: #574, Apr. 24, 1860).

If the laws were known to be unenforceable, then why pass them? The answer is that it was the symbolism behind the action that had meaning for the Greeks. The pro-British Zakinthians were answering the oft-repeated characterization of Greeks as dirty, and thus uncivilized (Giffard 1837: 104; Davy 1842: 13, 199, 203; Jervis 1852: 267). What they conveyed instead was that it was not an essential characteristic of Greeks, but instead a result of history. By passing the laws they wanted to show that they appreciated the link between cleanliness and civilization, and that they would do their best to reform their own people. But they wanted to use law not only to order things out of place, but people as well.

All of the major settlements on the islands were both ports and bases for garrisons. Prostitution was therefore, not surprisingly, a flourishing trade in them. One of the statutes passed in 1835 set out how prostitution would be regulated. The measures adopted on Zakinthos became the standard procedure for the other islands as well. Like elsewhere in Europe, the Greeks turned to the system employed in France (Harsin 1985: 3–55; Corbin 1990: 9; for Italy, see : 14–16), which combined toleration of prostitution with control over it. I cite in full statute #25, enacted on June 17, 1836:

1. All public women (*koinai yinaikai*) are forbidden from loitering on the streets, avenues and alleys of the city. They may only work out of special residences (i.e., brothels) located in areas not frequented by respectable people.

2. All public women must register with the police in a special book upon entering the town in which shall be entered their name, patronymic, age, home village, when they entered the city and the place of residence.

3. It is strictly forbidden for girls under the age of 18 to lead the life of a public woman.

4. It is strictly forbidden for public women to receive into their residences any girl who has not reached 18 years of age.

5. Anyone renting a house to public women must inform the police within 24 hours of doing so, and they must pay a surety for the keeping of the public tranquility.

6. Amongst the public women it is forbidden for them to have children with them, either boys or girls, over the age of 8, not excepting their own children. If they wish to practice their trade, they must board children elsewhere.

7. All public women must be examined in their houses once a month by a Doctor appointed by the Chief of Police.

They must pay him two dollars for each visit. If they do not have it, then he may charge them as he sees fit.

8. The Doctor shall examine all public women, their servants, and anyone else living with them. If he finds upon examination that a public woman is suffering from venereal disease, then he shall take her to the Police Station where she shall be detained in the Public Gaol at her own expense until such time as she is cured.

9. If any public woman knows that she is suffering from venereal disease and yet continues to ply her trade, she shall be guilty of a misdemeanor and fined not more than $5 and be confined at her own expense for a maximum of 20 days in the House of Correction.

10. If any public woman is found plying her trade in any but the designated residences, she shall be guilty of a misdemeanor and fined not more than $5 and be confined at her own expense for a maximum of 20 days in the House of Correction. Habitual offenders shall be exiled from the town at their own expense.

The aim of the prostitution law is clear: segregation of the women away from polite society, regulation of the type of women who could ply the trade, and protection from venereal disease for male clients. An examination of police records and the register of prostitutes kept by the police on Kerkira suggest that the only section of the law that the authorities took seriously was the one relating to spatial segregation. Based on the information recorded in the police register (CO 136/784: Jul. 7, 1848 PRO), for example, many women entered brothels well before the age of eighteen. Others continued to ply their craft in spite of contracting venereal diseases on numerous occasions. The "sanitation" component of the law was taken seriously only when British troops were involved (TIAK 23/793, 1241: 1858). Conversely, the police aggressively patrolled the spatial boundaries of prostitution. Bambi Katavria, for example, was given two days in the house of correction for soliciting in a restricted area (TIAK 1734/14: 1838). On another occasion, to protest the police's rough handling of a couple of girls, all of the whores working for Dionisoula Spathi invaded the financial district and proceeded to proposition men entering and exiting the

Ionian Bank. A squad of constables soon arrived and carted them to jail (TIAK 23/1122: 1858). Regulating prostitution, like so many other of the measures we have examined so far, related to control over the presentation of public space. People, women of a certain type in this case, had to be kept in their proper place. Another law relating to women demonstrates this even more obviously.

The purpose of statute #14, enacted on May 10, 1836, looks relatively unambiguous. Its first clause states the hours at which public bathing is permissible at certain beaches. So, at the busy beach by the harbor, swimming was allowed only between the hours of midnight and five A.M. At the more remote beach near the quay of Agios Konstantinos, one could take a dip anytime of the day except between six and nine P.M. These provisions clearly had safety in mind. It is the final clause of the statute, however, that intrigues: bathing by men is forbidden anytime that *women are present.* Why did the city fathers believe that swimming segregated by sex was a mark of civilization? This certainly was not the custom in England, where not only did men and women swim together, but it was extremely common for men to bathe nude well into the nineteenth century (Lenek and Bosker 1998: 83–84). Some qualms about bathing in the buff began to be heard during the 1830s, but few raised a voice in favor of segregated swimming. That discussion would begin later in the century. The only place where segregated bathing was in force was Prussia, and perhaps that was the model of the West that the Greeks turned to (Lencek and Bosker 1998: 92). In any event, it was not from the British that they got the idea that segregated bathing by sex was civilized. I suggest instead that they took their cue from the widely voiced idea about segregation and order, about the propriety of things being in their proper place. As with the other areas we have discussed so far, to be western meant to be organized and categorized. An examination of some other aspects of social life which the municipal authorities endeavored to regulate suggests that even the most utilitarian statutes discussed so far had symbolic significance as well.

The artist Edward Lear, a longtime resident of the Ionian Islands, recorded in his diary the following exchange: "The evening before, a man, after growling at all 'Greeks' with the contemptuous annoyance of an Anglo-Saxon, spoke as bitterly as he could of a nice young Englishman—an officer—married to a really nice Greek girl: 'He was ceasing to be English entirely, & becoming Greek altogether.' 'But how?' said I. And after obliging my man to confess that Captain ———— was as good-tempered, as attentive to his duties, as fond of exercises, as regular at church, etc. etc., as before he married, he began to get cross, & at last grumbled out, 'Well then! I'll tell you what he does! He breakfasts *à la fourchette* at 11 or 12—and if you can say a man is an Englishman who does that, the devil's in it'" (Lear 1988, 190: diary entry for Feb. 8, 1863).

To the anonymous, crusty "John Bull," being an Englishman was not about religion, culture, or beliefs, it was about when you ate. The evidence that the unnamed captain was no longer a true Englishman was not a change in what he believed or which church he attended. The proof that he had "gone native" was that he ate when Greeks ate. Identity, then, was bound up with eating habits. Lear's friend was not alone in feeling this way. Other Englishmen riled against Greek eating habits as well (Jervis 1852: 254; Ansted 1863: vol. 2, 130–31). In both British and Greek culture, dining was about more than merely eating; male sociability was a key element of it. One difference in male commensality, however, further separated Greeks and Britons: Greek men entertained each other at public eating and drinking emporia rather than at home. The British made constant reference to the fact they were never invited into Greek homes to dine (Ansted 1863: 154–56). To be civilized then meant eating at specific times of the day. It could also mean altering where men chose to eat together.

Zakinthos's city fathers accordingly endeavored to make Greeks eat like Britons by redefining when men could eat in public. I suspect as well that they hoped to force more men to dine the British way: at home. But they could not simply shut down the taverns, wineshops, and cafes where men chose to gather. Instead they sought to regulate the hours during which such places could operate, and by so doing mold men's behavior. Law #85, passed June 22, 1835, mandated that all cafes must close for business at eleven P.M. in winter and midnight during summer; taverns and wineshops were to cease operation at ten P.M. in winter and eleven P.M. in summer. The regulation stipulated that winter commenced on September 15 and ended on March 15; the remainder of the year was considered summer. Law #89 closed a slight loophole: it mandated that any establishment that manufactured alcoholic beverages would be covered by the same rules as cafes. Another law (#37) required that all such establishments be closed on Sundays and on days of major religious festivals, likes Easter, Christmas, Epiphany, and the like. In all, taverns and wineshops had to close on over thirty-five days for religious observance.

These laws flew in the face of popular custom. On the Ionian Islands, then as now, the eating regime included a large, late lunch followed by a siesta and then a meal taken late in the evening. Men did not even begin to gather in public at night until nine or ten, or even later. The taverns and wineshops of the towns and the villages reached their peaks of activity sometime during the early morning hours. Strict enforcement of the new regulations would have necessitated a complete transformation in the ways Greek men socialized. I would submit, thus, that the city fathers harbored no expectations that the laws would be effective. Indeed, an examination of the relevant police and court records in the years after passage of the statutes suggests that the police rarely enforced them. Indeed, in the few cases that I found in which they did, violation of the opening-hours rules was an infraction tacked on to more serious charges like operating without a license or allowing gambling to take place on the premises. In other words, these laws were largely unenforceable and merely gave to the police additional discretionary powers. The purpose of the laws, therefore, was not substantive but symbolic. Instead of altering the behavior of Greek men, the statutes were intended to convey to the British the image of a public culture that was civilized, that conformed to western models of comportment.

There were other regulations that had an even more explicit aim of shaping the appearance of civil society to conform to an idealized image of the West. Both had at their heart notions about superficial appearance, hierarchy, regimentation, and segregation. The first of these, law #103 from 1835, dealt literally with the color of public space. The law read: "It is forbidden to have on the outside of a house colored lamps except as follows: it is permitted to display lamps with only one color, either all white, red, or dark green. All white is recommended." In this case, as with some of the others, I have not found any evidence that the law was enforced. And once more, it seems to me that there was never any intent to enforce it. The measure was surely not utilitarian; what possible practical difference could it make what color lights people chose to display on the front of their abode? Instead, this measure was purely symbolic in intent. Its purpose was connected to the oft-repeated diatribe that "Orientals" were fond of garish colors and outlandish color combinations. In a variety of situations, Greeks could not help but be made aware of the negative view that the British espoused about the, in their view, garish appearance of lower-class Greeks. The city fathers of Zakinthos, taking their cue from such utterances, sought to make the appearance of their town more sober and somber. To be civilized, as they saw it, was to be monochromatic.

No other public event portrayed Greek culture at its most stereotypically "oriental" than the wild festivities of Carnival. The celebration of Carnival on the Ionian Islands was even more important than in other regions of the Orthodox world because of the long period of Venetian domination (Davy 1842: 135). Carnival was the quintessential celebration of disorder; during its festivities, the world is turned upside down. Class order and gender were inverted as men and women, regardless of class, donned masks that hid their real appearance and indulged in nightly bouts of dancing and drinking. Some men dressed as women and women as men. Gaggles of young men strolled the avenues and alleys of the cities and towns, serenading and dancing throughout the night.

As elsewhere where Carnival has special importance, there was a palpable sense of danger to the festivities. Men drank and gambled. They traded insults and fought duels with knives. Moreover, because everyone wore masks, there was a level of anonymity absent from normal times. As Gilmore (1987: 105) has noted, because during Carnival "shame takes a holiday," people feel a freedom to behave in ways differently than if their identity was known. The anonymity provided by the masks emboldened members of the lower classes to insult and provoke their status superiors in ways that would be unthinkable otherwise. Masked men would sing songs that mocked members of the aristocracy, that vilified the British, and that insulted anyone in power. The British saw in the ribald and raucous Greek celebration of Carnival vestiges of a pagan past and believed that it demonstrated the Greeks' lack of civilization (Ansted 1863: vol. 2, 135–36). Once more taking their cue from the British, the city fathers endeavored to tame the Dionysian festivity and to impose order on it.

Law #58, passed in January 1835, mandated the following. First, over the last three weeks of *apokreas* (Carnival) the wearing of masks and costumes on the public roads and streets was prohibited. Women could not wear masks at all during the entire period of the celebrations unless they were going directly to the theater. Clearly, this prevented all but the wealthy ladies of the islands from wearing masks. Men could wear masks and costumes during the first two weeks of the festival under the following conditions. No one could wear a costume that was improper, offensive, or in any way likely to disturb the "public order." Men could only be out in public wearing a mask in their village or town of residence; anyone caught on the roads or paths outside of a residential area would be arrested. "By 6 P.M. all revelers must be off the streets and at home" (clause b3).

The law, then, put temporal and geographical limits on the celebrations. Women were debarred from participating; men were restricted to their home area and had to be off the streets by a certain time. Other clauses restricted what men could do. A common element in the Greek celebration of Carnival is for celebrants to strike one another over the head with an object. In contemporary Greece, a plastic bat is so employed. In the nineteenth century, a wooden stick wrapped in sheepskin was used. Supposedly this refers back to the ancient festival of Dionysios and was intended to bring fertility. This custom was abolished, and more significantly, in the same clause of the law that did so, the police were accorded the power to arrest anyone whose behavior was "likely to give the slightest annoyance" (clause b2). The law gave the police enormous discretionary powers to detain anyone whose actions they felt might threaten the public peace. I suspect that heading the list of actions likely to cause annoyance was the singing of ribald, insulting songs. In any event, the police had the power to curtail the disorderliness at the heart of Carnival.

With the passage of this legislation, the pro-British city fathers of Zakinthos aimed to impose order and regimentation on Carnival. Women were to be segregated from the celebrations and the excesses of men curtailed. For most of festival's duration, men were forbidden to wear masks, and this removed the anonymity that enabled the ritual to serve as a forum for social commentary and symbolic reversal. With the new law, Carnival, the archetypal celebration of disorder with its garish costumes and outrageous behavior, was to be transformed from a Bacchanalian celebration to a bourgeois, British-style fancy dress ball. Like some of the other social-order pieces of legislation, this one was never enforced with any rigor or regularity. Moreover, I would contend that it was never intended to be enforced. Its aim was symbolic, not practical.

Of Men and Beasts

"Whether shut up by themselves in outhouses or yards, or roaming wild about the town all night the howling and barking [of the dogs] were incessant. The civil police with their guns, myself and servant with pistols—everything was tried. But the evil . . . was never entirely remedied. . . . But in what language can I speak of those terrible tortures [dogs] which . . . drove me very nearly frantic?" (Kirkwall 1864: 93) One element of Greek street life that appalled the British was the intermingling of people and animals. They saw dogs, as the passage cited above suggests, as the primary urban nuisance, and indeed they were not alone during the nineteenth century in holding that view. But the notion that the Greeks perceived about the place of animals in public space had much less to do with public health than it did with public presentation. Here again, what they perceived was that to be "western" meant segregation and order. So, the laws they passed regarding the keeping of animals in the city were designed to regulate when humans and animals, and not just dogs, could occupy public space.

On May 10, 1836, the Zakinthos Municipal Council passed statute #13. Henceforth it was forbidden for anyone to let their dog run loose within the city limits during the summer and autumn months. Dogs had to wear an iron-ringed collar bearing some mark of identification. Any dog found on the public thoroughfares unattended would be killed. Dealing with pesky hounds soon came to occupy a great deal of the police's time; so much so that local directors of police often petitioned the lord high commissioner for permission to establish a special animal patrol (e.g., IAK 1558/1; CO136/61: Jul. 4, 1837 PRO).

Even more legislative attention was paid to the problem of pasturing sheep and goats and feeding pigs within the city limits. Two statutes, #33 and 36 (both promulgated in 1835), and one amendment (#135, June 1836) dealt with the two areas of concern: where animals could be kept in the city and the control over access to public pastures in and around the town. Law #36 begins, "It is forbidden to move, keep, or pasture sheep, goats, cattle or any other such animal in places other than those listed below." There follows a lengthy, detailed list of public lands on which animals could be kept—for a price. Shepherds and anyone else wishing to obtain access to public land had to register with the police, pay a per capita fee for each animal, and purchase a license. People could keep animals on their own property, but each animal had to be staked. The owner was responsible for any damage his animals did to property. Any animal found wandering in the streets or feeding unsupervised on public lands would be slaughtered and the meat confiscated by the state, to be used to feed prisoners in the house of corrections.

No animals were to be driven through the city streets between the hours of 7 A.M. and 11 P.M. Law #135 amended this last point. "Since there is a need for fresh milk in the city, each day 200 milch-goats will be allowed to enter the city for the purpose of giving milk; at the end of each day, they must be brought to the designated [public] pastures. No more than twenty shepherds may obtain legal permits from the police for the purpose of bringing goats into the city. The permits must be carried and displayed at all times" (statute #136, clauses 3 and 4). This last clause carved out an exception to the ban on animals in the city.

The laws about dogs and other beasts clearly had a utilitarian intent. And they were enforced, sporadically and selectively. Loose canines were killed, unattended sheep and goats were confiscated and slaughtered, much to the delight of the state's prisoners who were fed the roasted meat of the latter (IAK 1558/1). Frequently, however, constables met resistance when they tried to enforce these laws (CO 136/0765/5: E. Drakatis, (Local Director of Police) to Baron d'Everton, Resident. Argostoli; Aug. 19, 1848 PRO). There was, I argue, a symbolic dimension as well. The ordering of civic space mandated a separation of men and beasts. Dogs running through the streets and howling through the night, as the British colonial and military officers repeatedly made clear, were hallmarks of barbarism. The goats so prominently placed by Dodwell in the painting described at the beginning of this chapter were symptomatic of broader social disarray. And so to present themselves as a western culture, the Zakinthian Municipal Council members tried to tether the goats, silence the dogs, and pen the pigs: all to no avail.

Occidentalism, or Imagining the West

Colored lights and carnival masks, loose dogs and loose women, drinking hours and segregated swimming, what did all of these have in common? Why did the city fathers of Zakinthos feel the need to embark on a concerted, coordinated effort to legislate so many different areas of public life? The timing is crucial for explaining it. By the mid-1830s, any hope that the Ionian islanders had of unification with the Kingdom of Greece had been dashed. Their quasi-autonomous status as a protectorate within the British Empire was to be continued indefinitely. The new Whig administration of Sir Howard Douglas swept onto the islands with promises of institutional reform and greater home rule. This was to be the moment when the "wise strangers" were to bring enlightenment to the uncivilized Greeks (Ansted 1863: 449).

Many members of the Ionian elite saw an opportunity to obtain local power for themselves, and they seized it. Some even believed that cooperation with the British was the right thing to do, and that westernization was the way to cultural advancement. Whether out of cynical or altruistic motives, or a combination of both, pro-British Ionians on the Zakinthos Municipal Council in 1835 believed that the moment was ripe for reform. They embarked on a civilizing mission to reshape Ionian society in the image of the West. Douglas's words, "cleanliness, classification, [and] discipline," aptly capture how Greeks conceptualized the West. Occidentalism meant order, segregation, control, and blandness. The western world was, in Greek eyes, monochromatic. But it was also a superficial world. The city fathers sought, therefore, to modify public space—clean streets, orderly markets—and to segregate and control both people and animals within the civic domain. Being western was all about public presentation, not internal character. While the British created the Greeks as either European aborigines or Mediterranean Irish, the Greeks saw the British as obsessed with order, regimentation, and restraint. Moreover, they believed that the British obsession with enforcing these in public and *in private* indicated that their presumptive rulers from the north lacked facility in the art of cunning concealment. As the next chapter demonstrates, this perspective shaped how Greeks viewed the British attempts at public policy and how they experienced colonial rule.

CHAPTER FOUR

Indirect Rule and Indigenous Politics

The Case of the Foundling Home on Kefallenia

Maria Kourkoumelis silently slipped out of her village of Valsamata on the night of July 7, 1833, and made her way down to the nearby hamlet of Frangata. Huddled in her arms was a blanketed bundle. Carefully, she entered the village square and deposited her swaddled newborn son on a pile of rocks. In spite of her cautiousness, she did not go unobserved. A shepherd returning with his flocks spied the fleeing maiden and went to investigate. He found the infant and raised the alarm. The baby was taken to the home of the Widow Lombardos, a well-known midwife and healer. A boy was sent by the village mayor to fetch Constable Petrakis from the police outpost at Fort Agios Giorgios. The next morning, the constable proceeded to the girl's parents' house and over the lamentations of her mother arrested the girl for infant abandonment. The policeman, the maiden, and the infant set off on the long trip to the capital city of Argostoli. There, the girl was tried before the magistrate's court, found guilty, and sentenced to three months in prison. The infant was brought to the police station, where the chief of police enrolled it on the growing list of babies brought under the care of the state. The girl served her time and then fled the island. What became of her thereafter is unknown. Her child was given into the care of a wet nurse, and according to the police register, the boy died of chronic diarrhea seven months later (TIAK 1787; unbound, unnumbered coroner's logbook).

This episode might seem trivial. After all, tens of thousands of infants were abandoned annually across Europe. What makes this case, and the hundreds of others like it that occurred on the Ionian Islands during the period of British rule, intriguing is that it allows us a glimpse into a number of different realms of cultural conflict between rulers and ruled. Not since the heyday of the Byzantine Empire had there existed in the Greek world a charitable institution intended to care for society's abandoned children. And even then, the orphanage was an urban institution (Constantelos 1991; Kalligas 1990). But the episode narrated above provides us with an entry point to examine three important issues related to how Greeks and Britons experienced dominion on the Ionian Islands. The issue here relates to the Colonial Office's endeavor to utilize public institutions as a means of furthering its civilizing mission. How the Greeks responded to and integrated these novel institutions into their social and political systems highlight some important cultural differences between the two groups.

Greeks held a fundamentally different view of the "state." To them the state consisted of a bundle of resources to be exploited for personal and partisan purposes. As I argue below, institutions like the foundling home quickly became integrated into the dominant patronage network that fixed power relations within the Greek community. To the colonial officers this action simply reinforced their views about the innate character of the Greeks as corrupt, venal, and duplicitous. To the Greeks, the British policy acted to reinforce their views about the British as naive, gullible, and over-trusting. I am not, of course, arguing that civic life in England was free from corruption. There are simply too many well-known criminal episodes for that. But I would submit that in the confrontation with another culture, each side brings to bear idealized images of their own. In this case, each side's behavior validated the cultural stereotypes that they had of each other.

This chapter falls logically into three parts. The first briefly discusses how the Colonial Office envisioned the role of civic institutions as a key element of the civilizing mission. The discussion can be brief because it echoes many of the points made earlier. The second examines how the foundling hospital operated compared to similar institutions elsewhere in Europe. The third focuses on how the system became part of local patronage systems. The dilemma, of course, is how can we discern that it was patronage rather than other, more "rational" considerations that shaped the institution's operation. In the end we shall see how complex and variegated the interaction was between colonizer and colonized, between British and Greek culture, and how crucial identity was to how Greeks and Britons experienced dominion.

Civilizing through Institutions of Modernity

The British Colonial Office saw its role as an essentially paternalistic one; in the words of Lord John Russell, it was their aim to "advance the inhabitants toward some qualification for institutions more liberal than those which were granted them by god" (CO 136/1121: Russell to Douglas, December 12, 1839, Diplomatic and Consular Reports PRO; see also Ansted 1863: 15). This is a splendid summation of the view that the empire had a civilizing mission. Such an outlook pervaded Colonial Office thinking. Similarly, former public coroner Dr. John Davy (1842: 16–17) firmly believed that British rule "administered under a strong, and just, and enlightened controlling power, ought to have the best effect in developing the good qualities of the public mind and in checking the bad—and in the formation of good principles and the habits, the foundation of character." As we saw in chapters 2 and 3, identity was bound up with this issue of national character.

The need to modify the Greek character was deemed of paramount importance and so here, as elsewhere in the British Empire, indirect rule was to be implemented. Thus, the local elite had to be molded into leaders worthy of these new liberal institutions, and in his "State of the Islands" report in 1824, Sir Frederick Adam indicated which institutions he wanted to develop: schools, hospitals, prisons, insane asylums, and foundling homes aimed at caring for society's most vulnerable members: abandoned children (CO 136/22: Adam to Douglas, January 18, 1825 PRO). His successor as lord high commissioner, General Sir Howard Douglas, came to power as part of the first Whig government in decades, and he aimed from the moment he arrived on the islands to institute a major program of liberal reforms.

He intended, in particular, to use the foundling homes and similar types of institutions as a way to construct an ideology of civic charity with the intention of gaining legitimacy for British rule. From its inception, the foundling home was linked to the Colonial Office's political agenda, and in addition, because of the practice of indirect rule, the institution quickly became embedded in the political struggles of the local Greek elite.

The Foundling Hospital: Its Structure and Operation

The Colonial Office established the systems for the care of foundlings with an eye to local conditions. At Kerkira and Zakinthos, for example, foundling hospitals, complete with a *tour* or a *ronde*, were constructed (Kirkwall 1865: 201); this is a device inserted into the wall of an orphanage to enable someone to leave a child anonymously. At Argostoli, there was only a basket with a bell suspended above it so that the person could alert an attendant inside the building that a child had been left in the basket (TIAK, Committee on Charitable Foundations 1856: chapter 1, clause 2–3). On the other islands, women from the countryside came to these hospitals and were hired as wet nurses for the abandoned infants. On Kefallenia, however, there was no such physical structure until 1856; instead, abandoned children were taken under the care of the state, in the form of the police department, and sent out to wet nurses and foster parents in the countryside. The decision regarding the disposition of the child rested solely in the hands of the chief of police; for the years of interest to us, he was Konstantinos Valsamakis. The children only became wards of the state if the identity of the parents was unknown or if the parents and their kin were able to demonstrate that they were so indigent as to be unable to care for the child.

A civic statute from Zakinthos provides a good picture of how the system worked initially (*Civic Publications 1863:* civic statute #30, originally passed in September 1829, revised in August 1856). The report of the Kefallenian Committee on Charitable Foundations (TIAK Committee on Charitable Foundations 1856), which outlined how the new orphanage and the foundling register were to be operated, contains scattered references to the way the system had operated previously, and these passages indicate that it was the same as on Zakinthos. I have chosen to discuss here the Zakinthos statute because it is much more detailed than the occasional comments in the Kefallenian committee's report.

When a child was found abandoned, either at the hospital or at some other public location, it was immediately taken into care. If the police had any inkling as to the identity of the parents, then it was their duty to seek out the parents. If those individuals petitioned the court and obtained a certificate of indigence, then the burden of caring for the child was shifted to the next closest agnatic kinsman. If poverty barred that person from providing assistance, then the next closest male kinsman was held responsible; and so on until the kinship domain was exhausted. If this happened, or if the identity of the natal parents was unknown, then the infant was automatically enrolled on the foundling register and the state assumed responsibility for it. From the moment that a child came under the state's care, the chief of police wielded enormous discretionary power over its future.

Some comparisons with the situation elsewhere in Europe can help us to discern the similarities and the differences with the foundling home on Kefallenia and on the causes of infant abandonment. The first level of comparisons drawn in the literature refers to the overall rate of abandonment as measured against the total number of births. Rachel Fuchs found that in Paris the average rates during the years between 1816 and 1853 were approximately 16 percent and for the entire Department of the Seine roughly 12 percent (Fuchs 1987: 72–73). Child abandonment was on the rise elsewhere in Europe as well. David L. Ransel, for example, determined that anywhere from 20 to 30 percent, and occasionally higher percentages, of the children born in St. Petersburg and Moscow were abandoned; though he is quick to point out that these figures are probably inflated because a sizeable but unknown number of children were brought to the cities from the countryside while the ratio was calculated on the basis of the total number of births recorded in the city alone (Ransel 1978: 192–93; Shorter 1980: 103). Recent work in urban Italy produced rates of a similar magnitude (Corsini 1976, 1984; da Molin 1983). The figures are appreciably lower in rural areas, however. Regionally in France, for example, Yves Blayo (1980: 278–79) found that the rates of abandonment varied from less than 2 percent in the southeast to almost 4 percent in the northeast; from this he concluded that "foundlings were rare in the rural population." Jean Meyer (1980: 254–55) cites data drawn from specific localities in France which again suggest figures of between 1 and 3 percent as the rate of abandonment. W. R. Lee's work on Bavaria (1980: 136–37) and John Knodel's on a set of fourteen German villages (1988: 192–97) also produce rates of a comparable magnitude.

Two main causes are proposed to explain the increase in the number of foundlings. The first places particular emphasis on illegitimacy. In Paris in 1830, for example, 45 percent of all illegitimate children were abandoned (Fuchs 1987: 57), and across the entire century, Fuchs found a very strong correlation between the illegitimacy rate and the rate of abandonment (1984: 73). This observation receives confirmation from Adrian Wilson's detailed study of the data in the London Foundling Hospital records for the eighteenth century (1989: 134–41) and Joan Sherwood's of the Inclusa in Madrid (1988: 5–7, 98–99).

The second most commonly cited reason for the rise in the numbers of abandoned babies is poverty among the urban lower class and among peasants coming to grips with the changes wrought by proto-industrialization (Fuchs 1984: 10–11; 1987: 73; Lehning 1982: 647; Delasselle 1978: 70–79; Ransel 1978: 196–201; Sussman 1980: 250–52; Fitch 1986: 133; Sherwood 1988: 95–98). Of course, illegitimacy and poverty are themselves causally connected through the impact that the latter exerted on the timing of first pregnancies and the incidence of marriage (Litchfield and Gordon 1980; Levine 1987: 122; Gullickson 1986: 178–92; Sherwood 1988: 68; Fuchs and Page Moch 1990: 1014–17). Still other factors could intervene (Fuchs and Page Moch 1990: 1010), but on the whole, most would argue for some combination of illegitimacy and poverty being most important.

Both explanations share a common element: the problem is the existence of a child, either because of the social impact or the economic damage it will bring. Thus, regardless of gender, the child must be forsaken. Consequently, there should not be a discernible pattern of gender distinction in the overall distribution of foundlings. In France, Fuchs (1984: 65) found that "the sex of the baby was *not* a significant factor in whether or not a mother chose to abandon her baby. From 1830 to 1869 roughly half of all babies abandoned were male." The same held true in Spain as well (Sherwood 1988: 138–39). Contrary to his expectations based on expressed cultural norms, Ransel (1988: 132–34) found that in Russia, as time passed boys were abandoned in equal numbers to girls. Unlike the others, however, he emphasizes changes in cultural attitudes toward girls and points to the influence of ideas imported from the West as the cause (Ransel 1988: 143–46). But this simply shifts attention to the question as to what was altering the pattern in the West, and, as we have seen, most scholars point to poverty as the root explanation. Women, then, compelled either by fear of the stigma of bearing an illegitimate child or by grim poverty, abandoned their children regardless of sex to the care of the state.

The incentives that induced women to become wet nurses seem clear enough: taking on an infant brought in much-needed cash to an otherwise cash-poor domestic economy (Lehning 1982: 648–49; Sussman 1980: 252–53; 1982: 141–42; Fitch 1986: 143; Ransel 1988: 198–201). In Marlhes, France, Lehning found that payment for taking in foundlings could amount to 24 percent of the family's requisite income (Lehning 1982: 650). We can agree that "wet nursing, therefore, was a significant [and] continuous part of the domestic economy" and that "it was a means of earning cash income for [the] family" (Lehning 1982: 650, 655). Essentially then, we are dealing with a market system based on wage labor.

Ransel (1988: 221) takes the analogy with the market to great lengths and continually speaks of foundlings as "perishable commodities in the system of exchange . . . circulat[ing] in much the same manner as capital." Nancy Fitch echoes similar sentiments in her study of Allier, France (Fitch 1986: 133). In like vein, Fuchs (1984: 191) concluded that "public welfare for the abandoned children epitomized the interaction between the state and the rural family. Placement of the Parisian abandoned babies with wet nurses or foster parents in the countryside fulfilled the needs of the families who accepted them and of the state and department that were obligated to feed them and preserve their lives." Foundlings provided a key mechanism for the circulation of cash between town and country, and thus, the logic dictating the operation of the institution was based on the market forces of supply and demand.

Yet significantly—and contrary to the expectation set up by this market model—every study of foundling institutions (e.g., Ransel 1988: 222–55; Fuchs 1984: 169–77; Sussman 1982: 136–37; Fitch 1986: 133, 141) found that certain villages and regions received more babies than others, indicating that there was selectivity and directionality in the distribution of foundlings. Most historians have sought structural factors to account for this patterning. Thus one possible solution argues that certain villages specialized in taking on foundlings and thus over time became traditionally known for the practice (Ransel 1988: 201). Consequently, they were continually sent them.

Another, related structural explanation centers on the economic geography of poverty (Lehning 1982: 254; Sussman 1977: 48; 1980: 253–55; 1982: 51–52; Fuchs 1984: 176–77; Ransel 1978: 206–7; 1988: 230–32). The argument here states that poorer villages sought and obtained foundlings. Fitch offers a more multidimensional explanation for the differential distribution of foundlings and orphans in Allier (1986). She looks to structural factors, in particular the increasing need for male labor power in response to changes in the agricultural system. She found as well that there was a political dimension, as evidenced by men running for office promising to bestow or withhold foundlings from households depending on how they voted (Fitch 1986: 154). But the role that politics and patronage may have played is never explored in depth; instead she falls back on the market model as the primary explanation, arguing that "children were trafficked at various rates and to particular places according to conditions affecting their supply and demand" (Fitch 1986: 133).

How we account for the spatial distribution of foundlings, however, is critical for our understanding of the rationale behind the operation of the institution and for an appreciation of the role it played in local society. The explanations outlined above place primary emphasis on the impersonal force of a supply-and-demand-driven market in conjunction with tradition, i.e., a repeated pattern of behavior, and poverty in order to explain the operation of the foundling homes of Europe during the nineteenth century. While essentially correct, none of the above explanations accounts satisfactorily for the spatial distribution of foundlings on the Ionian Islands. The market model describes in the abstract the effect of the system but does not provide a means to analyze it. The specialization hypothesis is tautologous, leaving unanswered the question as to why certain villages and certain women came to specialize in the care of foundlings in the first instance. Poverty does not explain why only a few of the numerous poor villages came to be selected, nor does it account for the selection of only certain poor families in each village.

Based on the literature then, we can draw the following conclusions about foundling homes and what a study of them tells us about nineteenth-century European society: (a) urban areas had higher rates of child abandonment than rural areas; (b) illegitimacy and poverty account for the rising rates of abandonment; (c) gender played no role in determining whether or not a child was abandoned; (d) women used wet nursing as a form of wage labor; and (e) the underlying logic driving the way the institution functioned and the role that it played in society can be explained best by reference to structural causes in general and the operation of market forces in particular. I want next to test these observations against data drawn from the foundling home on the Greek island of Kefallenia. The results of this exercise demonstrate that the orthodox model provides only an incomplete explanation of the operation and social functions served by foundling homes on the Ionian Islands.

The Kefallenian Foundling Home in Comparative Perspective

With respect to the foundling home on Kefallenia, we are fortunate in having at our disposal the detailed register kept by the police. Recorded on the register for each case are the name and residence of the wet nurse, the name of the infant, the age at which it was registered, the disposition of the infant (alive or dead), the date of death and the death certificate number, and the amount paid to the wet nurse. From the data contained in this document we can construct a demographic profile of the foundling population and then compare it to the nonfoundling population on the islands and foundlings from other parts of Europe. Unfortunately, the data are such that we cannot delve more deeply into the origins of the mothers and the overall context of the act of abandonment, as, for example, Fuchs and Sussman have done for France (Fuchs 1987; Fuchs and Knepper 1989; Sussman 1977, 1980, 1982).

Between January 1830 and December 1834, the police department enrolled 151 infants. For comparative purposes I include figures drawn from government records for the years 1858 to 1862 (Kirkwall 1865: 303). The number of children abandoned annually was fairly constant; but until data on the intervening years has been compiled it would be unwise to infer anything substantive. The summary figures are as follows: on average, the state enrolled approximately thirty foundlings per year from 1830 to 1834 and thirty-two per year during the late 1850s. Utilizing data from the annual reports of the Colonial Office, the decennial censuses, and the birth registers over the period 1830–1863, it appears that foundlings constituted on average just slightly less than 2 percent of the total number of children born and registered each year. Not unexpectedly the rate of abandonment on Kefallenia was significantly lower than in urban areas but on par with the rates recorded in other rural parts of Europe.

Concerning infant mortality rates, the same stark picture appears on Kefallenia as elsewhere in Europe: foundlings died at an alarming rate when compared to their home-bred brethren. In some places— Moscow, St. Petersburg, and Madrid, for example—over 75 percent of infants died during their first year in the foundling home. The mortality rate on Kefallenia of 30 percent is more in line with the rates recorded in Paris and Marlhes. A comparison of the mortality rate between the general infant population on Kefallenia and babies in the care of the state indicates that foundlings were about twice as likely to die during their first three years of life. Foundlings died at a rate of 251.4 per 1,000 as compared to a rate of 132.8 for infants raised by their natal parents. Here as well, the rate is similar to those recorded elsewhere (Knodel 1988: 35–101; Anderson 1988: 56–57).

There is one area where the Kefallenian data do not fit the European pattern, and that is the gender ratio among the foundling population. On the island, fifty-six males as opposed to ninety-five females were given into the care of the state. This ratio deviates significantly from the expected male-female distribution. There is, moreover, a less than 1 percent probability that this discrepancy could have occurred by chance. Obviously, mothers were selectively and preferentially abandoning females over males. This pattern differs from other parts of Europe and requires comment.

We saw previously that poverty or the stigma of illegitimacy have been proposed to explain the rise in infant abandonment. Illegitimate births obviously occurred on Kefallenia, but I have no hard figures on the relative numbers of them yet. The Greek elite certainly believed that an increase in illegitimacy, and thus immorality, was occurring (Holland 1815: 25). The following from John Campbell's ethnography of the Sarakatsani of Epiros captures the essence of a vitally held conviction during the nineteenth century about how illegitimate births should be handled (1964: 187): "Ideally, a girl who has a premarital love affair should be killed. However, there have been cases where either the father or brother had not had the courage to do it, or was persuaded by the girl that she was raped rather than seduced. But where the fate of the mother may hang in the balance, that of the illegitimate child is never in doubt. It cannot be allowed to live in the community, a testimony to the dishonour of the girl's family. It is placed on a mule-path where it may perhaps be found by others and delivered to an orphanage before it dies. No trace of pity is felt for the infant, for it is a thing without honour and therefore scarcely to be considered human at all." The incidence of "honor homicide" for illegitimacy on the Ionian Islands during the nineteenth century attests to the currency of this view (Gallant 1990: 511–12, note 84). Given this attitude, *both* male and female babies should have been killed. The gender imbalance on Kefallenia indicates that they were not and that an alternative explanation is therefore required.

I do not want to discount completely illegitimacy from the Greek case, but I suspect that peasant impoverishment lay behind the incidence of abandonment and that the nature of the kinship system lay behind the selectivity. Poverty in this case was different from that associated with industrialization and the rise of an urban proletariat or that found in countrysides coming increasingly under the sway of "cottage industries." Instead, impoverization here was associated with rapid population growth in the context of the near absence of rural crafts or industries and an agrarian system based on huge plantations worked by dependent peasant sharecroppers. The Ionian Islands were not immune to the broader developments occurring elsewhere. As the attraction of distant markets for the currants and olive oil produced on the plantations grew stronger, the terms of tenancy changed and were hardened, rendering the domestic economy of many peasants more precarious (Gallant 1986). In the face of rising numbers, peasant households had precious few options: migrate—either seasonally or permanently—try to obtain new leaseholds, or selectively control numbers.

The incidence of child abandonment reflects Greek households' attempts to control artificially their numbers, and the gender imbalance indicates that they preferred to keep and rear boys. I would suggest two reasons for this preference. First, because of the nature of the agricultural system, boys would have had greater value as laborers (Hammel, Johansson, and Ginsberg 1983). Second, agnatic kinship formed the basis of Ionian Greek society (Couroucli 1985: 47–86), as it did elsewhere in Greece (Herzfeld 1985: 52–67) and in other parts of Europe (Segalen 1986: 48–56; Fox 1967: 114–21), and this placed much greater emphasis on the household to produce male heirs for the lineage or patrigroup. Thus there might be more scope for illegimate boys than girls to be retained. Boys were needed as heirs, desired as the propagators of the lineage, and required as contributors to the well-being and security of the group. The impetus behind child abandonment on Kefallenia was due more to poverty than illegitimacy, but it would appear that the level of poverty was not so severe that some selectivity could not be exerted: thus, boys were kept and girls were abandoned when necessary (Davy 1842: 119–20). In cases of illegitimacy, if the case of the famous nineteenth-century poet Dionysios Solomos is typical, then bastard boys could be kept and reared in the paternal household without there being any stigma attached; although in this case, his father did eventually marry the woman involved (Politis 1973, 112–13). This was an aristocratic family, and the child was conceived in a relationship between a younger son and a domestic servant. Whether or not a bastard was welcome in peasant households is still an open question. In any event, the available evidence suggests that given the choice, Greek families chose to abandon female babies preferentially over males.

Turning to the motivation of women to become wet nurses, it was the same as in the rest of Europe: wages. The rates paid to wet nurses on Kefallenia fall well within the range documented elsewhere in Europe, and this supports the contention that taking in abandoned infants was an important form of female wage labor. According to the wages recorded in the foundling register, payment varied from £4, 6¾ pence in 1830 to £10, 13 shillings, and 1 pence in 1833 per infant per year. Wages during the other years are much closer to the 1830 figure. Women were paid a lump sum as initial annual payment when they received the child. To put these numbers into perspective: an assistant school teacher earned £13, 7 shillings, and 4 pence per annum; a constable of the first class earned £11 per year; and a runner for the customs department earned £12, 15 shillings, and 4 pence (Napier 1833: 498–501). An artisan, such as a carpenter or a smith, on average, made around £8 to £10 per year. A woman could contribute approximately one-quarter to one-third (or more) of the wages needed by a family to survive, a figure in line with Lehning's figure from France (Lehning 1982: 650).

One further aspect stands out from the Greek data: the distribution of babies sent out to wet nurses is markedly skewed. Two places, Argostoli, the capital, and Dilinata, a modest-sized village, received 80 percent of the babies; eleven other villages equally divided the remaining 20 percent. Explaining why this was the case will help us to understand how the political factors powerfully shaped the operation of the foundling-care system. Why so many children would be cared for in the capital city is obvious. Why so many abandoned babies were sent to the village of Dilinata is less so. If we examine the villages to which infants were sent taking into account the size of the female population, the village's distance from the city, and the village's aggregate wealth based on the tax rolls, it appears that Dilinata received over twice as many foundlings as it should have for a village of its size, at its distance from Argostoli, and for one of its aggregate wealth.

Furthermore, even if any of these factors could be demonstrated to have played a role, they would still be insufficient as explanations. First, they leave unexplained why only certain women in these villages either sought or were selected to receive babies. Second, someone on the basis of specified criteria had to determine the depth of poverty to which a village had to plummet before it could receive foundlings, suggesting that personal and political factors need to be encompassed. Clearly, a solution to the problem must be sought elsewhere.

As a first step toward elucidating these factors we can divide foundlings at Argostoli and at Dilinata into two separate populations and then compare them in order to determine whether and in what ways they differ. Two important observations can be made. First, babies died at a significantly earlier age at Dilinata; nine and one-half months as compared to fourteen months at Argostoli. Second, the distribution of babies between groups of kinswomen is much more clustered at Dilinata than at Argostoli. On average, each kin cluster received just over one infant at Argostoli as opposed to almost two at Dilinata. By "kin cluster" I refer to groupings of kinswomen that I have been able to reconstitute from birth certificates, marriage certificates, wills, court testimony, and other archival sources. These figures are for the minimum numbers involved. Moreover, it appears that a few families at Dilinata got disproportionate numbers of babies. In fact, women belonging to four families, the Andonati, the Kappati, the Pifani, and the Masahavi, received between them twenty-nine babies, or 35 percent of the foundlings sent to Dilinata. These four kin groups received on average over seven babies per group while the remainder of the kin groups in the village obtained just over one, the latter being a figure almost identical to the one from Argostoli.

Examples drawn from two kin groups make the point. The wives of the Andonatos brothers, Ioanna, Konstantina, and Spirina, each received two babies in 1831; only Spirina's second foundling, Nikolaos, survived the year, but even he was dead by the spring of 1834. Yiorgina Pifanis was sent a baby boy named Bernado in the summer of 1832; he died in January of 1834. Within weeks she received another boy, Hristodoulos; he died in June of that year; Maria took his place. She survived until December. All told, Yiorgina had earned over £31 over a period of three years by taking in foundlings. Moreover, so far, no birth certificates have been found for her during these years; if this absence is real, then she was sent babies to wet nurse when she herself was not lactating. Undoubtedly something is amiss.

A detailed examination of the data contained in the foundling-home register identified two clear patterns. First, a single village, Dilinata, received a disproportionately large number of foundlings. And second, in that village certain families obtained far more babies than anyone else. It seems clear, then, that the foundling-care system introduced by the British was operated by the Greeks in ways far from the "rational" and disinterested manner that a "modern" bureaucracy should. We need to aim our analytical focus at the level of individual decision makers and policy shapers in order to answer these questions. In this case, the identity of the key decision maker is known: Konstantinos Valsamakis; moreover, the identities of the other individuals connected to the foundling home are known: certain women of Dilinata. What remains to be clarified is the nature of the relationship between him and those women of Dilinata to whom he sent the infants. The key to understanding the linkage suggested here lay in the following tale of violence and intrigue.

Patronage and Orphans, or Putting the State to Partisan Use

Evil deeds were in the air on the night of February 22, 1833 (a full account of the episode related below can be found in CO 136/67: "Report on the Recent Riots," October 13, 1833 PRO and CO 136/77:

Memorandum from Ioannis Metaxas, July 17, 1833 PRO). Earlier that day Count Dimitrios Delladechima had been voted to the post of regent, which was, as mentioned earlier, the highest governmental position open to Greeks. The election had been hotly contested between Delladechima and his arch-foes, Konstantinos Aninos Korafa and Nikolaos Metaksas Ioannatos. Because so many kinsmen and clients of Delladechima and his patrigroup were already in power, he was able to obtain a majority vote. His enemies cried foul. A riot had almost ensued as henchmen and dependents of the losing faction expressed their outrage publicly in the main city square. By nightfall, a fragile peace had settled on the city as townsmen and peasants alike went back to enjoying the final days of Carnival, which as we saw in chapter 3 was a celebration of great importance on the islands. But through the night, plots were being hatched.

Pavlos Valsamakis was sitting at the shop of Dando Kosimatos enjoying a well-deserved glass of wine. Pavlos was a leading member of the Delladechima faction and a member of a very powerful patrigroup in its own right. His uncle, Konstantinos, was the current chief of police, and his father, Dionysios, was the secretary to the outgoing regent. All of them were clients to the count. Drinking with Pavlos were other members of the Delladechima power network, all young men occupying key positions in the police force, the judiciary, or the civil government.

Their evening libation was interrupted when Ioannis Metaksas breathlessly approached and told them of the events he had just witnessed. It seems that while walking along the harbor front, Ioannis had seen a group of *bravi* belonging to their rivals gathering at a nearby house. Silently he followed them. Hiding in a darkened doorway, he watched as all their foes crowded into the house. Crouching beneath an open window he heard Ioannis Kapsoliveri tell everyone to arrive in town early the next day and to be prepared for a fight; a *bravo* shouted out "tomorrow they [the Delladechima group] will see the bare-footed ones [i.e., peasants]" (CO 136/72: Deposition No. 5, November 5, 1833 PRO). Metaksas immediately understood the importance of this statement: under the cover of Carnival, their opponents were preparing to use force to prevent Count Delladechima's investiture as regent.

The news upset Pavlos and his associates. They had expected trouble, but more in the form of some taunting or maybe a knife fight or two. They were completely unprepared for the massed attack of peasants and *bravi* attached to the foe that seemed to be in the offing. Moreover, they had only one night in which to devise and organize a response to their enemy's machinations. Each set off to prepare for the coming conflict. Metaksas went first to find Spiridon Gentili, Pavlos Valsamakis's brother-in-law, and then to Ioannis Aninos, the former chief constable. The Gentili family held large amounts of land around the villages of Minies, Valsamata, Davgata, Omala, and Mavrata, and so most of the peasants there were sharecroppers tied to them. Aninos and his family were the major owners of land around Dilinata, rivaled only by the Delladechima family.

And so Pavlos hastened to Dilinata. There he roused Ioannis Makris, a constable first class, and his brother Agostino, a functionary in the civil court. They combined with numerous other men from Dilinata to provide the bulk of the violent henchmen for the Delladechima faction, and Pavlos Valsamakis was their leader. Prominent amongst this group were the Pifanis brothers, Mihalis and Ioannis, the four Kappatos brothers, the three Andonatos brothers, and the Mashavis brothers. Once the men of the village were armed and ready, Pavlos led them back to Argostoli.

The count himself had also been busy. First, he went to the resident, Colonel Cogers, and asked that the British garrison be put on full alert and that some of its members be given to him as a bodyguard. Cogers refused. Because "the people of the Ionian Islands were susceptible of a lively sensibility," he assumed that Delladechima was exaggerating the problem (TIAK, bound volume labelled No. 121. Letter from Cogers to the Commission of Inquiry, June 6, 1833). Next, the count called on his client Konstantinos Valsamakis. Valsamakis mustered the full force of constables and waited for his nephew to arrive with the men from Dilinata.

As the fog lifted on the morning of February 23, an eerie silence reigned over the town. Gradually groups of men started to gather at the square in front of the hall of justice, until by the time of the ceremony it was packed with people. Finally, Count Delladechima arrived surrounded by the police and his *bravi*. Members of the opposition refused to let them through to the building. Delladechima tried to speak but was booed down. Then some started to throw lemons at him; because the word for this fruit was also local slang for testicles, the symbolism of this gesture was evident to all. Fighting erupted. Men began to attack each other with clubs and knives. Then gunfire rang out from the ranks of the police and the *bravi*. Some men at the head of the crowd fell. The fighting became more intense, and it took a charge by the police to extricate Count Delladechima from the grip of the mob. The fighting continued through the streets of Argostoli. Belatedly, the British 95th Regiment arrived and after successive volleys was finally able to disperse the crowd, but the fighting did not end. Instead it extended to other parts of the city and out into the countryside. It continued for about a day. With the declaration of martial law and the arrival of reinforcements from Zakinthos, the fighting finally stopped.

Count Dimitrios Delladechima was installed as regent. Middling members from both sides were arrested, but no one was tried. The Colonial Office appointed a committee of inquiry, which conducted a full investigation and concluded that the opponents of the count as well as his own men were to blame, though they felt it imprudent to prosecute anyone. And they extolled the police for their evenhandedness and "ambitious pursuit of the truth" during the investigation (CO 136/67: "Report on the Recent Riots" October 13, 1833, p. 3 PRO).

Information contained in this narrative holds the key to answering the questions posed earlier about the foundling home by demonstrating to us the linkage between foundlings, charity, patronage, and political violence. The critical clue is the connection between men from the village of Dilinata and the power network of Count Delladechima. Approximately one-fifth of all the wet nurses who received infants between 1830 and 1834 had husbands or kinsmen who were in some way connected to it, and, if we turn to Dilinata, this figure rises to 61 percent. Moreover, the four groups of women who received 35 percent of the foundlings sent there were the spouses or sisters of the most important members of the Delladechima *bravi* gang. I stress that these are the minimum number of cases; for many of the wet nurses, I have no additional information at this time. I suspect, though, that further work in the archives will raise all of these figures substantially.

In the hands of Konstantinos Valsamakis, the foundling home became a tool of patronage employed by him on behalf of his patron, Count Dimitrios Delladechima. The final proof that Valsamakis deliberately and preferentially sent foundlings to kinswomen of men who were *bravi* in his patron's employ is that after his disgraceful dismissal from office in April 1834 and his replacement by the Greek-Englishman Captain Constantine Reade, not one of the twenty-five babies abandoned to the care of the state was sent to Dilinata (CO 136/77: Memorial from Valsamakis to Douglas, September 17, 1833, p. 27 PRO). It seems absolutely clear, then, that Valsamakis used the foundlings as tokens of payment, as a means of diverting cash from the coffers of the state into the hands of his loyal followers.

It is not my intention to imply that Valsamakis purposely sent infants out to die, or that the women of Dilinata deliberately extinguished their young lives. On the contrary, a glance at the mortality rates adduced earlier indicates that abandoned infants on Kefallenia had a better chance of surviving than those elsewhere in Europe. What I would contend is that *whenever possible Valsamakis sent foundlings to the wives and sisters of men to whom he was connected through patronage and who provided valuable services to him and his patron*. This had a profound impact on the operation of the institution, shaping the way it functioned at the most basic level. The way in which Greeks viewed public institutions reflected their beliefs about cunning, *poniria*, and the role of the state in society. I refer the reader back to the episodes recounted in chapter 2 about the conniving count and the reception of the Ionian bank. In the case of the bank, Greeks could not imagine any civic institution being established that *did not* have the aim of attaining some partisan advantage. What we see in the case of the foundling hospital, and I would suggest in the case of any other of the institutions established by the British, is that to the Greeks the state represented a bundle of resources, and that they would be fools, in their terms, not to take advantage. To them, exploiting state resources to partisan or self-interested advantage was not corruption, as the British maintained, but common sense. Indeed, the shriller the colonial officers' outrage about their actions, the more it convinced the Greeks of the British naiveté about the ways of the world.

Imperial Paternalism Meets Partisan Patronage

The liberal civilizing mission of the British on the Ionian Islands called for the establishment of civic institutions like foundling hospitals. To the British colonial officers, such institutions epitomized their goal of spreading "enlightened" public policy. Public charity and humanitarian concerns would thus be served. Such institutions would also, they hoped, demonstrate to Greek society the essential benignity of colonial rule and so dampen the opposition to it. To the Ionian elite, the newly established institutions provided a vehicle for the exercise of formal and informal power. Whenever Konstantinos Valsamakis used the constitutional power vested in his office to operate the foundling home, he demonstrated the government's responsiveness to a very real social need. Infants abandoned because of increasing poverty were given a chance to survive. Moreover, it was not just any government but the one composed of himself and his allies that was perceived to be acting in this way. Yet, at the same time, the institution also afforded him with another weapon that he could employ in the continual struggles with other factions for control of the state. When he selectively diverted foundlings to the kinswomen of men already linked to him, he reinforced patronage relations throughout the hierarchically ordered power network of which they all were a part. The *bravi* accepted the foundlings and received the cash that came with them, but they also incurred an obligation: to serve their patron when necessary, as in the violent and riotous episode of 1833. The bond of patronage was perpetuated in this manner both upward, between Valsamakis and Delladechima, and downward, between Valsamakis, middle-range power brokers, like his nephew Pavlos, and the peasant men of violence in the villages. Each member of these categories was able to perceive and to revalidate their place in the social order.

An examination of the foundling home in its full social and political context demonstrates that it served a number of functions simultaneously: at one level it helped to shape the ideology of public charity; at another, it served to legitimize the right to power of a single indigenous political faction; and at yet another it served as a weapon in partisan politics and as a key cog in an elaborate system of patronage. The Greek men in charge saw civic institutions, like the foundling home, as a well of resources that they could draw on in their partisan struggles for power and prestige. They did not "resist" the imposition of a "hegemonic" initiative, like the hospital; instead they exploited the opportunities opened up by British policies. The way that they did so confirmed in British minds key aspects of the stereotype of Greek culture, which we discussed earlier—that the Greeks were corrupt, immoral, and unfit for anything but strong, paternalistic government. The British response confirmed in Greek minds the stereotype they held of their Anglo-Saxons rulers—that they were naive, easily duped, and childlike. In the next few chapters we shall see how colonial policies repeatedly interacted with local society in varied and unexpected ways, and we can glimpse the process of dominion in this collective experience.

CHAPTER FIVE

Turning the Horns

Cultural Metaphors, Material Conditions, and the Peasant Language of Resistance

The silence of a cold wintry morning in January 1867 was broken by the sound of church bells ringing. On this morning, tenants working land in the northern section of the island of Kerkira were being summoned to the village of Agro.[1] The bailiffs employed by the local landlords and the constables ordered to protect them were to arrive in the village that day to collect the rent due on the 1866–67 olive harvest. Most peasants in the area around Agro were sharecroppers cultivating the land of absentee landlords and bound to these plantation owners both by contracts and forms of quasi-feudal obligations.[2] The annual collection of the rents was always a tense affair because under Ionian law and custom, if a sharecropper failed to pay his rent, he was subject to summary seizure and detention in prison until someone settled the debt. And from this law, there was no right of appeal (Typaldos 1846). This particular year was even more tension-filled than most. Kerkira, like the other Ionian Islands, had been ceded to the Kingdom of Greece by the British in 1864, and the terms of unification had only recently been agreed upon in the Assimilation Act of January 13, 1866. The peasants had voted overwhelmingly for socialist deputies in the elections of 1864, and had given them the specific mandate to address the "land issue" and, in particular, the question of feudalism. Article Two of the Assimilation Act, however, forbade the much-hated practice of bodily seizure for default of rent payment. The discussion surrounding the act spurred on as well widespread rumors of sweeping land reform and redistribution—talk which was greatly worrying to the Ionian aristocracy (Hitiris 1981).

Emboldened by the prospect of imminent changes in the land tenure laws and hard-pressed by two successive bad harvests, peasants all across the island were refusing to pay their rents. Indeed, violence had been threatened several times when bailiffs and their hired gangs of *bravi* had attempted to force payment of rents or to seize persons and property. Initially, the national government in Athens had resisted ordering the police to assist in the collection of private rent or compelling the arrest of peasants delinquent in their payments. They knew that the British had enforced this law and that it was one reason why so many tenants despised British rule. But bowing to the pressures exerted by some influential Ionian aristocrats, the *demearch*, or governor, eventually ordered the various police forces to assist the bailiffs. The ringing of the bells at Agro, therefore, had special significance on this cold January morning.

In keeping with usual practice, each of the major landholders or their representatives set up tables in the village square. Behind the tables, the bailiffs sat stony-faced, surrounded by a bevy of constables. Reluctantly, peasants began to gather. Some carried baskets filled with olives (the main crop in the area); others stood empty-handed, waiting to see what would happen. Into this scene strode an unidentified man. Hefted on his shoulder was a basket containing his rent payment. The crowd parted to let him through. With a single motion he hoisted the basket from his shoulder and slung it onto the table. Peals of laughter erupted from the assembled crowd when the contents of the basket were revealed, for it contained not olives but rams' horns. No further rents were collected that day as the humiliated bailiffs and their erstwhile guardians fled.

Two questions arise immediately. First, why did the bailiffs and constables feel humiliated? And, second, why did they flee? The answers to the two queries are related. Obviously, the rams' horns signified something deeply meaningful to both groups. The bailiffs and the constables were drawn primarily from the ranks of the peasantry and so shared the same cultural system of meaning. This would explain why both sides read the horns in the same way, as a sign of humiliation. We still need to explain why the horns brought on humiliation. As to why the bailiffs and constables fled, the answer may stem from the mutual interpretation of the gesture as a prelude to more direct violence. The horns signified dishonor; dishonor brought on humiliation; humiliation foreshadowed violence: why? An understanding of this chain of cultural logic, I suggest, helps us to comprehend how peasant cultures generally interpret, acquiesce, or challenge power relations.

The sexual connotation of the rams' horns, linking the refusal to pay the rent with the "cuckolding" of the landlords, seems clear enough. In numerous peasant societies across the Mediterranean and elsewhere, anthropologists and social historians have repeatedly found the horns of ovicaprids employed as a powerful emblem of sexual impotence or power (Blok 1984: 51–70; Campbell 1964: 26; Gilmore 1987: 108; Morris 1979: 118–26; Orso 1979: 163–65; Thompson 1991: 483, 489, 516–17). To give a man "the horn" was to signify the sexual conquest of his wife and thereby expose the impotence of the husband and the power of the adulterer. As Anton Blok has put it: "Successful claims on a woman entail domination of other men, both from the point of view of the husband who jealously guards his wife, and of the adulterer, who shows himself to be *more powerful* than the husband" (1984: 431; my italics). All those present in the village square at Agro—peasants, bailiffs, and constables alike—interpreted the scene being played out before their eyes in the same way and acted on that interpretation in culturally prescribed ways. The rent was symbolically transformed into a woman and, like a woman, she was poised between two men: her husband (the landlords) and her lover (the tenants). The throwing down of the horns symbolized the cuckolding of the landlords, or in this case, their representatives. In a reversal of roles, the rent/wife was now in the hands of the lover/tenants, and there she would remain. And so the husband/landlords had been proclaimed impotent and were worthy only of the derisive laughter, which mocked their public shame (Gilmore 1987: 108).

If the use of a sexual metaphor to portray popular feelings in this manner was an isolated episode, then it might be no more than a colorful anecdote about "peasant life." But it was not an isolated episode. Indeed, throughout the nineteenth century Ionian Greek peasants utilized a very rich vocabulary of sexual metaphors to express both their acquiescence and resistance to a condition of indebtedness and dependency. Furthermore, the mode of resistance and the language through which they expressed resistance was directly linked to the nature of the dependency between peasants and landlords in the nineteenth-century Ionian Islands. It also helps us to better understand the complex, three-sided relationship between the officers of the British government, the Ionian aristocracy, and the Greek peasantry. We saw in the previous chapter how the very different understanding that the British and the Ionian aristocracy had over the nature of the state and its role in civil society resulted in numerous imperial initiatives producing consequences unintended by their authors. In this chapter we shall see that because the local peasants expressed themselves in a metaphorical idiom rooted in a sexual vocabulary, the subaltern language of resistance remained masked from the sight of their rulers. On the one hand, the seemingly illogical language of the peasantry reinforced the British stereotypes of the Greeks, as discussed in chapter 2, and it in turn led also to errors and missteps that produced even greater levels of violent resistance to imperial rule.

Horns, Symbols, and Metaphors of Resistance

This chapter aims as well to build bridges between different areas of research in social history and anthropology. The first involves the considerable literature on peasant unrest, or in Charles Tilly's phrase, "modes of contention" (1986). Much of this work focuses on the actions of peasants in nation-building contexts, or in colonial situations where they play a direct role in liberation movements, or in situations where peasants are reacting to perceived threats to their traditional way of life (Feingold 1984; Frader 1991; Hobsbawm 1965; Hobsbawm and Rude 1975; Kartodirdjo 1973; Panikkar 1989; Roderick 1975; Roeder 1984: 150–68; Sturtevant 1976; Tutino 1986). Often neglected in these works is an examination of an internally generated conceptual framework which shapes both unrest and, equally important, acquiescence. Ranajit Guha, in his pathbreaking essay "Prose of Counter-Insurgency," illuminated how colonial officials constructed codes of counterinsurgency that subsequently shaped how they reported, understood, and explained local, indigenous revolts. Almost invariably these accounts portrayed peasants as responding spontaneously and violently, almost viscerally, to changes in their material life caused by the actions of others—landlords, moneylenders, merchants, etc. Such an attitude robs the peasant of agency. As Guha put it: "Either way insurgency is regarded as the peasant's consciousness and Cause is made to stand in as a phantom surrogate for Reason, the logic of consciousness" (Guha 1983: 2–3). A more recent, complementary schema has developed which focuses on "everyday" forms of resistance and this development has shifted our attention away from the most overt and widespread types of resistance to more mundane ones. What is still lacking are works which demonstrate the connection between the prosaic, low-level forms of resistance, so eloquently analyzed by James Scott and others, and open, more violent and widespread revolt (Scott 1985; 1989: 3–33; 1990; 1992: 55–84. See also the essays in Colburn [1989]).

One area, I suggest, where we might expect to catch a glimpse of the connection between the three approaches described above would be in the realm of language and discourse, and consequently it is to the recent research in linguistic analysis by social historians that I turn as my second area of interest. Drawing on an increasingly closer affinity with cultural anthropology, some social historians have stressed the need to recapture the lost voices from the past and then to pay greater attention to the ways language both symbolizes and constructs consciousness. One of the characteristics of this literature to date is its focus on the industrial working class (Jones 1983; Joyce 1987; Kaplan and Koepp 1986; Sewell 1980).[3] Rural peoples have often been left mutely standing on the sidelines. Shaping this view is the idea that peasants are politically blank slates, capable of responding to injustices with blind fury but incapable of formulating ideologies and languages of protest. This last—ideologies and languages of protest—would only emerge in conjunction with the appearance of formal parties (Kroger 1992). In formulating this view, some historians have followed contemporary witnesses, often colonial officials, in seeing the peasantry as "mystified" by the sea changes swirling around them. This point especially connects to Guha's argument. Because colonial officials could not penetrate the language and metaphors of the subaltern insurgents, they found only nonsense in the indigenous discourse. The verdict rendered, by colonial officials and historians alike, is that so long as peasantries did not express their discontent in the "disenchanted" language of modern politics (to borrow Max Weber's evocative phrase), they lack political consciousness (1958: 105; Holmes 1989).

Using recent works which combine anthropology and history, a careful examination of the language of protest and the cultural metaphors which gave that language power demonstrates that, far from being blank slates, Greek peasants, and by extension peasants elsewhere, actively formulated ideologies of protest. The approach adopted here builds on the following proposition made by Steven Feierman: "The opposition [voiced by some anthropologists] between political language and symbols on one side and political action or the distribution of power on the other, carried a strong and misleading message about social reality: that political action could somehow be treated in a pure form separate from its cultural expression, that political discourse was not itself action, and that language and symbols could exist outside of the daily flow of political practice" (1990: 9). This chapter attempts to sketch the connections between language and symbols and power and action by showing how Greek peasants expressed themselves and their feelings toward dependency in particular by drawing on a rich metaphorical, erotic language, and by demonstrating that there was a direct connection between the nature of dependency and the expressionary mode of resistance. In short, though their language may have drawn its power from an "enchanted" (to borrow from Weber again) culture, the consciousness of those expressing dissent was indeed political—but politics as power, not simply as governance.

Furthermore, there is a wealth of comparative material that suggests that the use of erotic language in the manner described above was widespread. Numerous ethnographic studies demonstrate that, in their struggles for power and social status between themselves, peasant men in a number of different Mediterranean cultures wielded erotic words with great aplomb: "cuckold," "masturbator," and "impotent lover" were all charges leveled at opponents so as to threaten their honor (Gilmore 1987: 107–23; Herzfeld 1985: 136–62; Brandes 1980). David Gilmore's work on manhood in contemporary Andalusia, for example, shows vividly the centrality of erotic words and symbols in the discourse determining status in the community, going so far as to refer to "murder by language" (1987: 117). Spanish men's actions fit into a much broader behavioral pattern. E. P. Thompson, in his study of English "rough music," found that the use of erotic language in general and the imagery of the cuckold in particular represented key elements in the symbolic language of ritual humiliation (1990: 483). David Garrioch found that eighteenth-century denizens of Paris regularly and frequently traded ritual insults, and especially the charge of cuckold, as means of shaming rivals in public (1987: 107, 115–17). Likewise, among inner-city black youths in the United States, sexual verbal wordplay, for example "playing the dozens," is a vital element in the struggle for reputation and status (Abrahams 1972: 215–40; Anderson 1978: 3, 18, 2; Kochman 1972: 241–56). Clearly, recurrently and in a number of different cultural settings, erotic language acts as a nonlethal mechanism for establishing status hierarchies in a community, as a means of maintaining communal standards of behavior, and as a way to foster intragroup social coherence. This is not to argue that the explanation of why erotic language is employed in each case is the same. Indeed, it is the task of the historian or anthropologist to elucidate the specific configuration of ideological, cultural, and structural factors that give erotic language its power. It is the burden of this chapter to do just this in the case of Ionian Greek society in the nineteenth century.

The broader implication of this argument is that social historians and historical anthropologists must pay much closer attention to the language of rural groups, not just in regard to the use of erotic language but in a multiplicity of other ways as well. In particular, they must determine the relationship between material conditions and the metaphorical and symbolic means by which groups render intelligible those conditions (Bourdieu 1991).

My argument in the remainder of the chapter will take the following form. First, I discuss two more major episodes in which erotic language was used to express discontent or was employed as a prelude to violence. After that, I analyze certain ideational and structural variables that hold the key to explaining the roots of the power of erotic language. I begin with the notion of household both as metaphor and as a social construct. Greek peasants rendered their world intelligible through the lens of this metaphor of household. Next, a prime example of this is presented in a discussion of patronage. An examination of both the form and the content of patronage leads us first to the realm of ideas and symbols (drawn from the metaphor of household) and then to the material world of production and exchange. I show here how economic and legal changes were transforming the material conditions of production and distribution and that these developments initiated what Marshall Sahlins would call a "structure of the conjuncture" (Sahlins 1985: xiv–xv). I would suggest that, more than simply giving voice to their discontent, the sexual metaphors and erotic language acted as *enabling factors* permitting an escalation of violence against the landlords by "demystifying" class relations. I then end by examining the episodes presented earlier and show how and why the peasantry drew on the same metaphor of household to express discontent as they did to acquiesce to the patronal system of power relations. The use of erotic language becomes explicable when we see it as part of the same symbolic system employed to express class and power distinctions.

Erotic Voices and Violent Acts

Two additional historical episodes will establish firmly that Greek peasants during the nineteenth century did employ erotic language rooted in sexual metaphors when expressing defiance to their lords and masters (Gilmore 1984: 31–44). I begin with an episode from the island of Lefkada in the year 1819 (Gallant 1990).

In this year, the British Colonial Office decided that as a means of facilitating commerce and communication it would dredge a canal through the shallow salt flats which separate the island from the mainland. In order to raise the revenue for the work, they determined to impose new taxes on the islanders. Various schemes were suggested for this purpose, but all of them had in common the need for a detailed census of peasant holdings. Some colonial officers appreciated from the start that prying into the larders of Greek husbandmen might cause difficulties: Frederick Adam, the lord high commissioner of the islands, suspected that "the mode of its [the taxes] collection might be harassing, by obliging the officers of government *to make a sort of inquisition* into the properties of even the poorest of the peasants" (CO 136/12: Adam to Maitland, November 20, 1819 PRO; A & P, June 1820, 1–6).

Trouble there was indeed. When the municipal officials and their posse of constables attempted to enter the first village on their list, armed peasants confronted them. The same occurred the following day when the resident of the island arrived with a body of Greek constables and British troops. In an attempt to achieve a peaceful solution to the problem, the peasants were given the opportunity to express their grievances in a petition to be drawn up by two local aristocrats of British choosing. This was dutifully done. We have, consequently, one version—an aristocratic version—of what it was about the new taxes that was pushing the peasants to the verge of open riot. In spite of this petition, fighting broke out and lasted for three days before the peasants were finally routed. Numerous arrests were made, but sufficient evidence could be gathered against only four men. At the trial of these four, many of the peasant participants were called upon by the authorities to testify, and their words have been preserved both in missives sent by colonial officers and in courtroom testimonies, providing us with another—a peasant—version of the reasons behind the rebellion (CO 136/1270: Maitland to Barthurst, October 21, 1819, contains Maitland's cover letter and the trial transcript. PRO).

The difference between the two accounts is significant. In the aristocratic petition, the peasants complained that the new taxes would drive them deeper into poverty, would prevent them from obtaining work as seasonal wage laborers on the mainland of Greece, and would therefore lead to greater indebtedness: very clear, very "rational," very pragmatic complaints. In the peasants' own version, however, that is recorded in the courtroom testimonies, they expressed in most graphic terms and with near unanimity their belief that the real *causae belli* was the Colonial Office's intended tax on *sexual intercourse*. When Vasilios Palmos from the village of Poros, for example, was asked by the tribunal why he took up arms, he responded bluntly, "Because the priest [*papas*] in the village told me the British were going to tax fucking [*mingomenos*]" (CO 136/1270: transcript 7 PRO). Other witnesses, such as Spiridon Asprogerakas and Nikolaos Fotinos, expressed the same view but in more circumspect terms, referring to "the thing that men do" [*to andriko*]. The British officials found these statements laughable and ludicrous. There were, of course, no plans to tax sex; exit visas needed to leave the island, doors, windows, salt, wheat, sheep, and goats were being discussed as possible items to be taxed.

My next example comes from the troubled year 1849. In August of that year the island of Kefallenia was rocked by a peasant rebellion which threatened to bathe the entire island in blood (Gallant 1990; Hannell 1987; Paximadopoulos-Stavrinou 1980; Tsouganatos 1976). The violence began in the southeastern tip of the island, and in spite of the ringleaders' hopes, it was confined to that area. At the epicenter of the violence was the village of Skala.

Two episodes from this drama interest us especially. The first transpired at the house of Count Nikolaos Metaksas Tzannatos Kapsoliveris. Count Metaksas was one of the largest landowners in the region and consequently had under his control numerous sharecroppers cultivating currant grapes for export to western European markets (de Bono 1985: 171). More will be said briefly about the land tenure system and the problem of debt, but for the moment, we need merely to appreciate that Metaksas was widely hated by the local peasants, who considered him to be a particularly offensive and oppressive landlord. In August of 1849, a gang of about forty-five peasants surrounded his house seeking revenge and rough justice. According to one of the participants, the peasants talked of "cuckolding" Metaksas and of turning him into a cuckold.[4] They demanded that he surrender to them and suffer his just desserts. The count refused. From the darkened windows of his villa, he responded to their demands with gunfire. The insurgents then set fire to his house and let loose volley after volley of gunshot. No one from the surrounding villages lifted a finger to assist the trapped count and his two servants. Indeed, according to one witness, they "looked on with fiendish exultation."[5] From the doorway of his burning house, Metaksas shouted:

> "What have I done to you, my children, that you should kill me?"
> The resounding response was the cry: "Cuckold, take these currants [i.e., the bullets] into the bargaining for this year!"

Cut down by a hail of bullets, Metaksas's lifeless body fell back and burned in the raging inferno that had been his home.

The second episode occurred the following day in the nearby village of Valtes. While attempting to flee from marauding insurgents, Konstantinos Metaksas, another of the powerful landlords and cousin to the man who was burned alive, was captured by Panayis Siliverdis and Haralambos Drakatos, two peasants from Skala. Rather than simply killing him, they decided, in their words, "to cuckold him good." While one held Metaksas to the ground, the other proceeded to shoot him through both ankles. They then set off in search of other landlords to "cuckold" (A & P, *Dispatches from Sir H.G. Ward to Earl Grey regarding the recent disturbances on the island of Cephalonia* (London: House of Parliament, 1850), November 11, 1849, enclosure 9, 67–71).

More episodes like these in which Greek peasants chose explicitly erotic language to express their grievances could be recounted, but the above, drawn from three different years and three different islands, suffice to make the point.

We could explain away this seemingly "irrational" language of protest by saying that it is interesting but rather peripheral to the "real," that is to say, the material basis for violent protest. But by doing so we would perpetuate the gross condescension toward peasant consciousness already noted. Alternatively, we could focus our attention exclusively on the words themselves, thickly describing or deeply probing the semiotic/symbolic discourse of peasant culture. But by so doing we would perpetuate the mistake of divorcing the ideal from the practical, and of privileging the former as a causal explanation for the latter. Words and their attendant meanings gain power and obtain resonance through cultural interpretation based on understandings or metaphors rooted both in the material world and the mental universe. We thus need to examine each of these realms, and an ideal place to begin the examination is in the core institution of peasant societies: the household.

Household as Metaphor

I turn first to the metaphor of household. A spate of recent works has emphasized the importance of the household as the primary building block of society. The household is key not simply for the role it plays in the material world, but in the cultural world as well. As a metaphor for the structure of society, the household informs a broad range of cultural beliefs. For this reason, I consider "household" to be an encompassing metaphor because it was the primary organizing principle both ideally and practically.

That the household was the key cultural and practical unit of organization in Greek peasant society during the nineteenth century is clear from the historical sources (Gallant 2001: 80–104; Sant Cassia

1992: 1–47), and the picture drawn from them resembles the one de-rived from the sizeable corpus of ethnographic and anthropological studies of rural Greece in the recent past. The centrality of the *spiti* (household) in Greek society is now almost axiomatic given the fre-quency with which it has been emphasized in the literature (du Boulay 1974; Campbell 1964; Friedl 1962; Dubisch 1986; Loizos and Paptaxi-archis 1990). Whether it be as an economic unit or a social entity or a symbol of society, nineteenth-century Ionian culture emphasized the centrality of the household (Gallant 1990: 511–12). The implications of this for our purpose are significant. First, it would suggest that the household was considered the primary unit of production and repro-duction, and thus its material viability would have been constantly in the forefront of individuals' decision making. Second, we should expect that the household as metaphor would play a major role in shaping the ways people viewed, discussed, and interpreted their world. That this second point was true for interclass relations is obvi-ous from the language used to express the well-entrenched system of clientage on the islands.

The Material Basis of Class Relations

The majority of peasants on the Ionian Islands were sharecroppers, working as contractually bound tenants on the estates of wealthy pro-prietors. As was the case in numerous cultures around the world, landlords and tenants were bound to one another by a set of social bonds referred to as patronage. The anthropological and social histori-cal literature on this topic is vast. Suffice it to say here that clientage on the Ionian Islands conformed closely to the system found all around the Mediterranean and beyond (Holmes 1989: 97–98). On the Ionian Islands, as elsewhere, while the legal, economic bond between land-lord and tenant was the contract, the social ties between them were expressed in the paternalistic idiom of clientage.

The following scene captures both the material and ideal under-pinnings of patronage and dependency. Sir Charles Napier relates the following vignette; it is a composite of real events that had been brought to his attention. He wrote it in an attempt to show how iniq-uitous the system of landlord-tenant relations had become.

Scene: A Room with a hole in the floor, down which the fruit is thrown into the *seraglia* (the drying room for currants); the door is open from the chamber into the apartment where the Seragliante (the landlord/proprietor) sits; the servant waiting with a steelyard.

Enter GERASIMO [a peasant tenant of the lord].

Servant: Well, Gerasimo, you have a heavy weight of fruit there.

Gerasimo: Yes sir, virgin fruit, not touched by rain. (His sons, who have helped him, are sent out by the servant.)

Servant: How much have you?

[Seragliante sits behind the door looking through the chinks, unseen.]

Gerasimo: A thousand pounds!

Servant: What, a thousand pounds there?—impossible!

Gerasimo: Yes sir, there are just a thousand, without the bags.

Servant: Well, come, let's see. [Weighs them, and finds that there are about a thousand.] Oh! You rascal! [Pressing the yard with his elbow, as he shoves the weights closer to the point of suspension.] Look, knave, look! Six hundred marked on the yard!

Gerasimo: Ah, sir, you know that I can't read; but there are 1,000 pounds, as I hope for mercy on myself and my children.

Servant: I lie then, do I? What is it to me how much your currants weigh: I act for my master. However, I won't be called a villain by you. There are 600; so it's of no use to argue. [Empties the currants into the hole, and gives Gerasimo a receipt for 600 pounds.]

Gerasimo: I can't take that; there are 1,000; and I must have a receipt for the whole.

Servant: You are a scoundrel, and may settle with the master yourself. Here, my lord, here Gerasimo disputes the weight.

[Enter Seragliante, with great dignity from behind the door where he has been watching. . . .]

Seragliante: Well, Gerasimo, what is the matter?

Gerasimo: My Lord, I brought 1,000 pounds and your servant says there are but 600.

Servant: Yes, my Lord; 600 exactly! but he can't read, and he says I cheated him.

Seragliante: What, scoundrel! Accuse my servant of cheating! A person whom I have known all my life, and who is the honestest man in Argostoli! Take your fruit away; you are a villain.

Gerasimo: It's down in the *seraglia,* and there are 1,000 pounds, my Lord.

Seragliante: I am sorry that it is down; however, there is your receipt for 600, so go away, and let me have no more insolence. Hearkye, my friend, you owe me ten dollars, advanced this year, to get your fruit in; if you are not content with your receipt, pay me the money this minute, and you may take your 600 pounds back; my servant, and I, are witnesses that it weighed so much; there is interest on the ten dollars due to me, so if you like to pay me, do so, or go to jail; and if any *seragliante* (landlord) takes your fruit, I shall consider it a personal insult, and so I shall tell him. [I.e., if you try to find another lord, I shall thwart you.]

[Here Gerasimo is silent, takes his receipt, and is going away after kissing the hand of the Lord.]

Servant: My Lord, as he is a good man, and to show your generosity, and that I bear him no malice for his abuse of me, let me give him credit for fifty more.

Seragliante: Well, do so; it's lucky for you Gerasimo, to have so good a master; some landlords would have had you before the [court] tribunals for defamation [see chapter 7], and a month's imprisonment would have taught you better manners to your superiors; Go Away!

[Exit Gerasimo.] (Napier 1829: 204–5).

The economic grip of the landlord over the peasant is all too clear. Not only were rents calculated in cash values, but the figure was stipulated at the time that the annually negotiated contract was signed; thus, the burden of risk was placed squarely on the tenant's shoulders. This practice was repeatedly noted and decried by colonial officers. The following from Andrew Stewart, the resident on Kefallenia, to Arthur Stanley, the resident on Lefkas, is typical: "The fixation of prices was entirely in the hands of the landlords and the merchants, they being in fact the only capitalists, and that power I have reason to believe was not always exercised with great moderation" (CO 136/66: Stewart to Stanley, September 6, 1833, PRO). The actual amount of produce required to meet the rent payment could vary greatly from year to year depending on fluctuations in the international fruit market, as well as from the very high levels of climatically controlled interannual variability of crop yields. Moreover, as the above scene shows, peasants were dependent upon their landlords for the marketing of their portion of the crop, and the system was open to obvious and flagrant abuse.

I want, however, to focus attention on the symbolic aspects of the above scene. Note the deference required of the tenant. The physical submission he needed to show and the obsequious manner of his tone all acted to diminish his social persona. Note as well how each of the actors adopted a paternalistic discourse modeled on the language of the household, with one playing the role of providing father and the other of obedient son. Other sources suggest that these respective roles were to be acted out in any social setting. Repeatedly we see that when peasants met their landlord, they were to kiss his hand, fall to one knee, or manifest some other overt sign of deference. Common, customary greetings for a landlord were "Savior" and "Providence upon Earth" (Ward to Grey, September 7, 1849, Dispatches). Ward bases his observations on patronage on the court testimony of Gerasimos Zapantis. When the parties spoke, they invariably employed a language of paternalism connected to the metaphor of household. For example, the local expression employed to convey the essence of a patron-client bond was "to eat his bread." Anastasios Lambinato Bomboti, a peasant implicated in the violence on Kefallenia in 1849, repeatedly refused to implicate his patron, Count Gerasimos Sdrin, stating, "I will never inform against him. I cannot. I have eaten his bread." (Testimony by Anastasios Lambinato Bomboti at his trial on October 11, 1849; A & P, Dispatches from Sir H. G. Ward to Earl Grey regarding the recent disturbances on the island of Cephalonia (London: House of Parliament, 1850), October 19, 1849, enclosure 7, 29–35). The importance of bread in the peasant diet has been repeatedly noted, as has its symbolic significance (Counihan 1984). Moreover, bread is often employed as a metaphor for the household, and its use in proverbs often connotes symbolic inclusion into the household. In northern Greece, for example, the ritual incantation to mark the commencement of a wedding feast is "Come, let us eat bread" (Campbell 1964: 117). The use of the idiom of commensal sharing of bread clearly demonstrates the metaphorical connection between patronage and household. Gift giving on Easter, New Year's, and the landlord's name day from the peasant to the lord further solidified symbolically the asymmetry of the relationship. In short, the landlord was to the tenant as the father was to the son, and all aspects of their ties to one another were also to be modeled on the household. Put another way, peasants rendered interclass relations intelligible through the metaphor of the *spiti*, or household.

The picture of landlord-tenant relations painted so far is a static one. But conditions on the Ionian Islands at this time were far from static; on the contrary, numerous and fundamental changes were in the works. Economically, the British protectorate encouraged and facilitated the closer incorporation of the islands into the international commodities market (Gallant 1986: 515–32; Hannell 1989; Paximadopoulos-Stavrinou 1980: 18–32; Pizanias 1988: 65; Pratt 1978: 116–19). Demand for the Ionian currant grape rose in the markets of Liverpool and Antwerp. German manufacturers eagerly sought olive oil from Kerkira and Lefkas as a lubricant for their increasingly mechanized workshops. Prices rose, but fluctuated dramatically. Nonetheless, landlords attempted to exploit these new opportunities by increasing output, shifting the burden of market risks onto the primary producer, and by altering the traditional terms of tenant contracts. They increased rents, decreased the amount of land given to the peasants for their own private vegetable gardens, and tightened their monopoly on the means of exchange by enacting tight quarantine laws (making their violation a capital crime) and by channeling all exports through specific ports.

Simultaneously, other developments occurred which reduced the ability of the peasantry to resist the changes. The first was population growth. In spite of the increasing immiseration on the islands, population grew at a sustained, high rate (Paximadopoulos-Stavrinou 1977: 20–163). The primary result was even more intense competition for leaseholds. Thus, tenants were compelled to accept the more exacting conditions laid down in the renegotiated contracts. The situation on the islands is reminiscent of developments on Sicily at this time as described by Anton Blok, and as on that troubled island, Greek landlords frequently employed men of violence as a means of controlling their labor force (Blok 1975). Backing up the landlords' efforts to extract more from the peasants were endemic debt and summary seizure for defaulture. Landlords employed the instrument of debt to bind their tenants ever more closely to themselves and to gain control over the total product from their estates. With interest rates varying from 25 percent to 300 percent per annum, it's easy to see how even one bad crop or one downturn in the commodities market would ensnare peasants in a web of debt from which they could never escape. The use of debt in this way was prevalent also on Sicily (Blok 1975: 55). But on the Ionian Islands, bolstering even more powerfully the entire edifice of control was the archaic, but now frequently employed, legal mechanism of seizure for default. Failure to pay one's rent or meet a scheduled debt payment could result in the public arrest of the debtor and his confinement, or even that of his entire household, until the debt was settled (CO 136/1258–1269, Penal Code of the Ionian Islands, section 12–18 PRO; emended in 1841, CO 136/76 PRO, CO 136/154 PRO). None of the changes to the debt laws altered the legal situation regarding seizure for defaulture.

Ionian peasants despised this practice. It was also denigrated by elite critics of the British protectorate and by those members of the intelligentsia opposed to "feudalism" (Ioannis Moustoksidis, "Memorial to Her Majesty," Dec. 12, 1839; printed in A & P, Blue Book of the Colonial Office: Ionian Islands and Malta (London: House of Parliament, 1839), memorial 3, sections 53–59) Both of these groups pointed to the deleterious effects of imprisonment on the general economy. I would suggest, however, that it was loathed by the peasantry not only for its material consequences, but equally for its symbolic ones. Honor was the issue here: honor expressed symbolically by control of the body. On a number of occasions, rural guardsmen reported that men sought for default of rent resisted vigorously when confronted in public, only to submit docilely later in private. As numerous scholars have noted, honor is bestowed or denied by the court of public opinion through a performative discourse on social status, involving actors and an audience (Gilmore 1987; Herzfeld 1980: 339–51; 1984: 439–54; Wikan 1984). The following example vividly makes the point.

On September 13, 1853, Ioannis Markantonatos, a sharecropper from the village of Spartia on Kefallenia, was to be arrested for failure to pay his rent. When rural guardsman Ioannis Makris appeared in the village square, Markantonatos confronted him and eventually they came to blows. Markantonatos would not allow himself to be publicly arrested in his home village; to do so would have resulted in his total loss of face and honor, and so he resisted violently. Yet later on the same day, he sat docilely by the side of the road chewing on bread and cheese waiting for Makris to take him away.[6] To seize a man publicly, then, was to humiliate him; to place him in prison, moreover, was to threaten the very existence of his household. In the ways that counted in this society, therefore, to seize a man for default was to emasculate him, to shame him, to make him symbolically impotent, like the cuckold.

The conjuncture of a number of material factors—the wild fluctuations of currant prices on the international market, the rapid increase in indebtedness, the imposition of higher taxes, and the increasing competition for land due to the rising population—together with changes in law and custom, including the hardening of the conditions of tenant contracts and the increasing use of penal detention to enforce the payment of rents, all led to widespread immiseration, which in turn placed in jeopardy the ability of households to fulfill successfully their productive and reproductive roles. This "conjuncture of the structure" (to use Sahlins's phrase) had profound ramifications.

Understanding the Erotic Language of Resistance

The material bases for peasant discontent and its expression in violence are evident, but to leave the explanation here would be misguided. We need to explore the cultural basis of discontent; in particular we must explicate the peasants' language of resistance. In order to do so I will now turn to the episodes related earlier in this chapter and interpret their significance in light of the discussion to this point.

In the case of the 1819 riot on Lefkas, peasants were expressing their opposition to the intrusive, "inquisitorial" (to paraphrase Lord High Commissioner Adam) nature of the new taxes. The taxes penetrated to the very essence of the household and threatened the viability of one of its primary roles, that of production, and so by analogy it was *as if they taxed sexual intercourse*—and thus violated its other major function, that of reproduction. In their attempt to clarify in the starkest possible terms the potential impact of the new taxes on their households, Ionian peasants chose not the banal language of the ledger sheet but the evocative discourse of the household as metaphor. Their words had such resonance because they called forth a chain of cultural interpretations; one of which equated sex, reproduction, and production. Another focused on masculinity, equating head of household (*nikokirios*, literally, the lord of the house) with control of sex, control of the body (and thus reproduction and production). By this chain of reasoning, loss of control of one's body or of one's wife's sexuality brought on shame, or the loss of honor. A man who could not control his household was like the cuckold, impotent and honorless. This was the threat which the British taxes and odious census posed to Ionian men, and thus their willingness to die resisting it.

The implications of this explanation can be carried further. Erotic language is just one element in a hierarchically ordered set of social actions, and latently embedded in the use of provocative words and symbols is the threat of escalating, more violent responses. E. P. Thompson (1990: 483), for example, recounts the case of a butcher on the Isle of Wight who in 1782 gunned down three men after they had appeared in his wedding procession adorned with rams' horns on the sides of their heads. Elijah Anderson (1978: 18–27), as well, recorded episodes where verbal clashes quickly turned nasty as steel replaced words as the demanded riposte. A public confrontation between two individuals resembles a game with each player exchanging moves—in the form of words and symbolic gestures—and countermoves, each more provocative than the previous one. After each exchange, the contenders have the opportunity to stop the cycle or raise it to the next level. Erotic language plays a key role in this dialogue. The use of symbolically charged erotic terms signifies a major shift of a confrontation toward violence. The studies by Thompson and Anderson emphasize the role of erotic words and symbols as devices employed in a contentious process for status and honor, and that such contention demarcates the boundaries of in-group membership. There is, I suggest, an extremely important interclass dimension as well. David Gilmore found that members of the upper class left their community during Carnival, the period when shaming, insults, and other verbal assaults were most common, because they did not want to risk being caught up in the wars of words and because of the not-unfounded fear that physical violence might also occur (1987: 121). The "cuckolding" of landlords on Kefallenia convincingly demonstrates the inclusionary power of erotic words and symbols and shows how they have the potential to incite violent actions between groups, and especially between classes. By extending to the elite the discourse by which Greek peasants established and defended face and honor among themselves, they convinced each other that the gulf that separated themselves from their superiors could be temporarily bridged, and this opened up new avenues for action.

The episodes on Kefallenia show us how erotic language can act as an enabling factor for higher levels of interclass violence. Before open and overt violence could be taken, the cultural cocoon which surrounded patron-client bonds had to be shattered; put another way, class relations as structured in Greece had to be demystified, stripped of their aura of deference and filial submission. By hurling the charge of cuckold at a landlord, the peasants were making a direct and lethal accusation that the patron had lost his power, had lost his honor, and was thus no longer a man. Power was about control, and to be cuckolded demonstrated the loss of control over what is most important to the male-dominated household. Just as summary seizure of the peasant defaulter was to cuckold him metaphorically, so too to gain control of the landlord's body, by say crippling him, was to reverse the positions. The cloud enshrouding the asymmetrical power relationship between peasants and landlords was thus lifted by the humiliation visited on the latter by the former through the accusation of cuckoldry. Moreover, the use of sexual language eradicated the gulf between the peasant and his lord. By extending the application of such emotionally charged terms to the landlords, peasants incorporated their masters into their own, peasant realm of discourse. In this way, deference was replaced by laughter and submission exchanged for violence. Real, physical combat waged with guns and bullets was preceded by symbolic, erotic combat waged with words.

We can finally understand the laughter engendered by the rams' horns in the incident described at the beginning of this chapter. When the unnamed instigator threw down the horns, his action tapped into a reservoir of symbolic understandings which drew enormous significance from the unity they created between the material and ideal. In the interpretation I presented earlier, I argued that all of

the onlookers—tenants and bailiffs, constables and civilians alike—
were immediately able to read the horns as a symbol of the cuckold.
They connected this sign with powerlessness and impotence, and recognized it for the warning signal that it was intended to be. Symbolically the tables had been turned. No rents would be collected because
the bailiffs and the constables were not "men" enough to take them—
at least not without a major loss of life. Moreover, both sides recognized this fact. They both knew that the casting down of the horns
was an unambiguous provocation and that it signified a prelude to violence. Control was at issue: control of the rents (the production of
the household), control of the tenants' bodies (the reproduction of the
household), and control of space (the territory of the community, the
aggregate of the households). In the peasants' laughter lay humiliation, loss of face, and shame for the forces of the patrons. Through
their laughter, the peasants found honor and the resolution to resist.
The horns, and the tables, had indeed been turned between the powerful and the powerless: at least for one cold winter's day. But in the
larger scheme of things, their actions reinforced many deeply held aspects of the stereotype of the peasantry: that they were superstitious,
irrational, and ignorant. All of which reinforced the belief of the ruling groups, be they British colonial officers or Ionian aristocrats, that
rule over the subaltern was justified.

CHAPTER SIX

Dueling with Daggers

Masculine Identity and Ritual Violence

On the sweltering night of July 26, 1830, Tonia Theodoros, from the village of Agios Theodoros on the island of Kerkira, brutally slashed the face of his covillager Gioragachi Mokastiriotis. After the gruesome but nonlethal cut had been delivered, Theodoros spit on his prostrate victim and left the wineshop while five other men, including the proprietor, Panos Landates, looked on. Ten days later Constable Andreas Sallas approached Theodoros, served him with arrest warrant number 3157, and took him into custody on the charge of assault with a deadly weapon. At his trial in police court on August 28, the various versions of Theodoros's assault on Mokastiriotis were recounted. There had been bad blood between the men for some time; no one was quite sure why. That night at the bar, both had been drinking heavily when Theodoros called Mokastiriotis a fool and a braggart. Mokastiriotis loudly replied that he would rather be a fool than "the lord of a house full of Magdalenes." Theodoros erupted from his chair, drew his pruning knife, and demanded that Mokastiriotis stand and face him like a man. None of the other men in the room intervened as the knife fighters traded parries and thrusts. Finally, Theodoros with a flick of his wrist delivered a telling blow that cut his victim from the tip of his chin to halfway up his cheek. As blood flowed from his face, Mokastiriotis fell to his knees cursing his assailant. When asked by the presiding magistrate at the police magistrate's court in the town of Kerkira why he caused the fight, Theodoros sternly replied that no man would call his wife and daughters whores and get away with it. His reputation would not allow it. As a man, he would not stand for it. He was found guilty, sentenced to forty days (less time served) in the house of corrections at Fort Abraham, fined three Ionian dollars, charged for court costs, and bound over to keep the public tranquility (IAK EA 870).

This vignette captures the three themes I address in this chapter: honor and masculinity, violence, and the courts. From the moment they took control of the islands, the British were appalled at the level of violence they witnessed between Ionian men. Henry Holland, for example, noted that murders were a daily occurrence on Zakinthos. Indeed, he advised that the first step they should take when they assumed administration of the island was to introduce severe measures to curb the slaughter (Holland 1815: 23, 32). As we have already seen, the propensity of Greek men to settle their disputes with lethal action formed one element of the British perception of them as Paddies or European aborigines. Law and legal process were seen as the way to deal with this problem. One of the lord high commissioners of the islands, Lord Seaton (formerly Sir John Colborne), put it best when he wrote that it was the aim of the Colonial Office's legal system "to bring justice to the peasant's own door." (CO 136/120: Seaton to Stanley, October 10, 1843 PRO). By making law fair and the courts open, they argued, crime and violence would stop.

Of course, law was one of the main props of the British Empire, but if anything law and legal process were even more important in the case of the Ionian Islands. This was true for a number of reasons, many of which we have already touched on. One was certainly the perceived need to curtail lethal violence. Another was that the ruling process on the islands was complicated by their ambiguous status. Under the terms of the Treaty of Paris, they were a sovereign state placed under the aegis of British protection. The British occupied the islands as protectors, not rulers. That "protection," however, quickly elided into imperial rule, but with a twist. The British had to give greater institutional autonomy to the Greeks than they did to indigenous cultures in other parts of the empire.

Yet another reason law and legal process were important was that the rule of law was the central trope deployed by the British to distinguish to the islanders their dominion from the previous centuries of Venetian rule. We saw in Chapter 2 that in crafting a rationale justifying their rule over the Greeks, the British demonized the epoch of Venetian rule, and they reserved special vituperation for the Venetian justice system. The legitimacy of British dominion rested on its claim to have brought fair, evenhanded justice to the people. This meant that the criminal justice system had both Greek and British components. The British wrote the legal code and controlled the upper echelons of the police forces and the courts, but in devising the legal code they included indigenous lawyers in the process and built on the previous Venetian and Orthodox canon legal systems. The new code owed much more to the civil law tradition of the French than it did their own based on common law. Also, they left much of the day-to-day operation of the law and its enforcement in Greek hands. In this chapter I explicate one form of behavior that accounts for the high level of masculine interpersonal violence: the duel. I demonstrate that dueling among Ionian plebeian men was analogous to dueling elsewhere and that it was a practice grounded in an ethos of honor. I then show how and why, in fact, the British colonial policies did eventually contribute to a marked diminution in violence. This analysis, combined with the next chapter, shows the complexity of the relationship between legal process and human behavior, and between the intent of hegemonic colonial policies and how those policies are received and acted upon by the subaltern population. I begin with an examination of honor and violence.

The literature on honor, or that cluster of attitudes and attributes often glossed as honor, in anthropology is large and important. Ethnographers and anthropologists working in Greece have been early and critical contributors to this body of work, and consequently Greece is often considered paradigmatic of an "honor culture." While some works in this corpus indicate that honor was part of a masculine cultural code that often required displays of aggressiveness, few studies have actually discussed the role of violence in the ethos of honor. Indeed, for most of this century, Greece has manifested remarkably low rates of interpersonal violence (Gallant 1995; 1998a; 1998b).

Historians working in other areas of Europe and the world have borrowed from the rich anthropological honor literature in order to understand better the cultural logic of male violence in the past. Prominent have been studies of the duel—a form of ritual male-on-male violence that drew its cultural meaning from an ethic of esteem or honor. McAleer, in his recent study of the duel in Wilhemine, Germany, for example, explicitly connected the two literatures, stating, "I hope to challenge the conventional shibboleth of cultural anthropology that sees Mediterranean societies as far more sensitized to the *point d'honneur* than their neighbors to the north" (McAleer 1994: 5; see also Nye 1991). However, historians have by and large related honor to the duel among members of elite classes; few have tried to connect it to plebeian or peasant violence.

There seems to be a paradox: ethnographers have studied honor among peasants but did not discern notable manifestations of interpersonal violence; historians have studied interpersonal violence among elites and found it to be intimately connected to honor. One element of this dilemma has been that historians have not studied honor amongst the lower orders, and they have been reluctant to accord the same ritual status to plebeian violence as they do to upperclass dueling, even though they been more than willing to see other forms of plebeian behavior as rooted in culturally constructed rituals (Muir 1997). Another is that ethnographers have studied groups in societies where levels of interpersonal violence regardless of class have plunged to historic lows.

In one of the few works that explicitly connects the historical and ethnographical data, Frank Henderson Stewart (1994: 139–44) noted that many honor disputes among the contemporary Bedouin he studied ended in arbitration and settlement rather than in a duel, as they would have among aristocrats in medieval or early modern Europe. His interpretation is correct, but leaves unanswered the larger question of why a defense of honor in the past called for violence whereas today it does not.

This chapter aims to contribute to the existing scholarship by showing that plebeian violence in the past was highly prevalent, that it was often rooted in an ethic of honor, that these forms were as ritualized and rule-bound as the aristocratic duel, and indeed should be considered a form of lower-class dueling. It aims to move that literature forward by offering an explanation as to why honor remained an integral component of Greek men's identity while at the same time dueling violence ceased to be an important element in the cultural construction of masculinity. It also shows that the court system imposed by the British on the islands played a crucial role in the transformation of men's contests over honor and status. By explicating how

Ionian men retained honor as a cornerstone of masculinity but dissociated it from violence, this chapter furthers our understanding about the processes leading to the reduction of interpersonal violence noted so ubiquitously in the historical record.

Quick Tongues, Quicker Knives

"In many parts of this country [Greece] the knife," according to Charles Tuckerman, U.S. consul to Greece during the 1860s, "is as quick as the tongue" (1872: 340). The Ionian Islands were no exception to this conclusion. Both contemporary observers' accounts and the abundant archival sources of the criminal justice system bear this out. William Goodison, for example, noted of the Ionians that the blade was "the means of directly prosecuting their revenge" and that all too frequently they were "given over to the license to raise the dark knife and bloody stiletto against the breast of unoffending innocence" (Goodison 1822: 196). The readiness to redress perceived wrongs and slights by recourse to the dagger was commented on by nearly every other colonial officer or traveler to the islands during the period of the British protectorate (Martin 1856: 141; Kirkwall 1864: 57–60; Napier 1833: 97–98; Davy 1842: 126–27; CO 136/76: January 10, 1835; 692: August 18, 1841 PRO).

An examination of police and court records from sixteen years during the period of the British protectorate suggests that knife fighting was a relatively common occurrence.[1] Based on my analyses, the average annual homicide rate on Kerkira and Kefallenia was 12.4 per 100,000 and the combined rate for homicide/attempted homicide was 37.9 per 100,000 (Gallant 1998b). Of those recorded homicides, approximately 20 percent were the result of knife fights. Both of these figures are substantially higher than the comparable rates from elsewhere in rural Europe, like France, England, Spain, Germany, and Italy. Indeed, only mid-nineteenth-century rural Corsica manifested a higher rate (Wilson 1988: 16). For our purposes, however, the homicide and attempted homicide rates do not provide a truly accurate picture of the prevalence of knife fighting among Ionian Island men.

Most episodes of dagger fighting did not result in a loss of life, nor did the criminal justice system typically categorize or consider them as attempted homicides. Instead, knife fights were classified as simple assault or assault with a deadly weapon. A key judicial decision in 1835 set the precedent for considering the knife fight as a lesser offense. The two British members of the Supreme Council of Justice, William Blair and John Kirkpatrick, in their decision in support of a lower-court verdict that a man who killed another man in a knife duel was guilty only of manslaughter, not murder, established the legal standard. They argued that unless there was clear and equivocal evidence of premeditation, a participant in a knife fight could only be guilty of assault, assault with a deadly weapon, or manslaughter. In the case before them, the issue hinged upon whether the defendant left the wineshop after being insulted, went to his house to get his knife, and returned to fight (CO 136/76: October 2, 1835 PRO). Blair and Kirkpatrick defined in law what Ionian men already accepted: the knife fight was different. Consequently, I focused on warrants or indictments for assault or assault with a deadly weapon and recorded 2,677 in the sixteen sample years.

This translates into a rate of 134 assaults per 100,000. From this group, I selected 125 cases (5 percent) for detailed investigation, i.e., a thorough analysis of the warrant, the police report, and the trial transcript if the case went to court. Of the 125 assaults, 61 were knife fights. In other words, in 48 percent of the recorded cases of assault the offense involved dueling with knives. Assuming that this ratio characterizes the entire sample, then this would mean that during the period from 1817 to 1864 over 8,000 duels would have taken place. The figures become even more revealing if we consider only assault with a deadly weapon. There were thirty-seven of these, of which thirty-three (89 percent) were knife fights. As Peter King has suggested, historians have largely neglected to study assault and other similar forms of interpersonal violence, and so it is difficult to situate my case into a comparative framework (1996: 43–75). Nonetheless, the point that Ionian Islanders had a marked propensity to draw their blades and to use them frequently and regularly, and that violence was an integral element in masculine social discourse, seems abundantly clear.

This last is important. The distinctiveness in this case lay in the ready recourse Ionian men made to the knife fight as a primary response to a challenge to their reputation. A close reading of the narratives of these clashes allows us glimpses of the inner logic and rules of these plebeian duels. Unlike with the usual type of aristocratic or bourgeois duels studied by historians, there are no manuals to guide us in our search for the rules of knife fights. Instead the scripts and rituals that men followed can only be excavated from the tales of the fights men told to each other, the police, and the courts.

When Ionian Island men during the nineteenth century felt that they had been insulted or had some sort of grievance against other men from their group, they frequently challenged one another to settle their differences by dueling with knives. Among European aristocrats, U.S. southern elites, and other men who dueled, verbal insults or slights or symbolically charged physical gestures, like a slap in the face, inaugurated ritual combat. Greek men employed provocative insults drawn from their rich vocabulary of erotic words as their *causae belli*. Analogous to the touching of the face, once certain words were uttered in specific contexts, usually a wineshop or tavern, there was no turning back. A man had to rise to the challenge or lose face. Once the knives were drawn, the men followed a shared script. They aimed not to kill but to maim; not to slay but to scar.

They sought to cut the face of their opponents. In numerous cultures at various points in time, scarring or cutting or in some way attacking the face of an opponent was seen as a way of branding or shaming her or him (Groebner 1995: 1–15; Gorn 1985: 28; Greenberg 1996: 16; Muchembled 1989: 167–83). According to the stories told, part of the enactment compelled onlookers to refrain from interfering. They were to observe and evaluate performances, not to become actors themselves until a certain part of the play was reached or if one of the participants deviated from the script. As soon as one man drew blood, then the audience stepped onto the stage and pulled the opponents apart. The victor often would seal his triumph by spitting on his opponent or collecting a trophy, often by dipping his neck kerchief in the blood of the vanquished or by wiping the blood off his knife with it. But the drama did not end here; the story was not done with one man losing face.

In many cases, the winner remained at the scene of the fight until the constables or the village authorities arrived and took him into custody. In others, the victor would leave the exact location of the fight but make no attempt to flee the vicinity. It would appear from their behavior that these men wanted to be caught. There was, it would seem, a third act to these dramas, and it was performed in a different site: the court of law. Some examples both exemplify the essential elements of the dominant script and illustrate some of the variations it could take.

The vignette with which I opened this chapter portrays some of the key elements of the script. Both men knew one another. Animosity existed between them before the fight. The confrontation occurred in a wineshop, and thus in a male-dominated public space where both were well known to the other patrons. The clash commenced with verbal sparring, and then the words that would shift the contest from tongues to knives were uttered: erotic words that slurred the reputation of one man's female relations and that branded him as a cuckold—a *keratás;* the power of this term was great, as we saw in the previous chapter. Reputations were at stake, and in this culture those were high stakes indeed. Each man drew his blade. Based on the way they aimed their blows at each other's faces, it would seem that the intent was not to kill but to scar. So, the parries and thrusts sought to inflict the cut that would settle the contest. Once it was delivered, the observers, who had previously stood aside and assessed the fight, intervened presumably to stop the bout before further damage was done. The victor then validated his triumph by symbolically humiliating his opponent. In the aftermath of the contest, he made no effort to avoid capture. It appears that he wanted his day in court. The sentence he received of forty days, $3, and a promise to keep the peace was a common one.

This was the basic script. Though there were some slight variations on it, two basic patterns predominated. In one version, the fighters were acquaintances and a precedent cause of the contest was some previous grievance that existed between the two. These were not, however, vengeance fights or vendetta killings. As we shall see shortly, slayings of those sorts manifested their own rituals. Some additional cases portray the basic script of the plebeian duel in which an existent grievance set up a violent clash. Theodoros Kavvadis, from Fiskardo on Kefallenia, killed Gerasimos Salomon from nearby Assos. After a hard day of fishing, Kavvadis retired to a nearby tavern. Salomon, according to witnesses, shortly thereafter entered the emporium, walked up to Kavvadis, and accused him of having stolen some tackle from his boat (TIAK 873: April 24, 1835). Kavvadis warned him to be wary of whom he called a thief. Knives were drawn, and a fight ensued. Salomon lunged at his opponent, but his blow went low. Rather than slashing his foe's face, as he stated in his testimony was his intent, he severed his carotid artery. Bloody death soon followed.

Giorgios Antippas from Antippata, also on Kefallenia, on the evening of July 25, 1840, killed his cousin Athanasios with a stroke of his blade. The affray took place while the two were drinking wine in front of the house of a covillager. In small villages such as Antippata it was not uncommon for someone to obtain a license and serve wine at his home. Two days before, a person unknown had injured Giorgios's donkey with a rock. The quarrel began when he started accusing his cousin of having done the deed. As more wine was drunk, the banter between the two grew more heated. Giorgios then taunted his cousin, saying that he was not man enough to take care of his ass. Athanasios responded by "giving him the horns," i.e., making the gesture that accused the other man of being a cuckold. Enraged, Giorgios unsheathed his stiletto and demanded that his cousin fight him. In the midst of their fight, Athanasios tripped over a chair leg, and while off balance he fell forward at the same time as his cousin thrust forth his blade. The fatal blow entered his neck just below his Adam's apple (TIAK 1454: July 25, 1840).

Ioannis Pelemedis from Kerkira learned the hard way that it was best not to mess with a man who made his living working with knives. Red-faced with anger, he stormed into a wineshop on Gavia Street and approached a table at which Evstathis Sklonias, a butcher, was seated with some friends. Standing before the watchful group in the bar, he accused the butcher of having cheated his wife on a sale of meat. Sklonias nonchalantly replied by sniffing the air and announcing to the assembled group of men that he "smelled a horned one [i.e., a cuckold] in the room, and as a butcher, he knew the stench." Pelemedis drew his dagger and demanded a fight. The duel was brief. With his second stroke, Sklonias cleanly severed his opponent's left ear from his head. He then added insult to injury by asking Pelemedis if he "wanted this piece of meat [the ear] added to the bill as well?" (IAK EA 1119: January 10, 1856). Numerous other stories also adhered to this script. A grievance existed between two men. One confronted the other with it in a public place. They exchanged insults, almost invariably of a sexual nature. The knives came out, and the fight ensued.

In most cases, the precedent grievance involved not the world of praxis and material goods, but cultural capital in the form of reputations. When Alexandros Salamis from the village of Agios Theodoros on Kerkira in 1847 slew Ioannis Bassianis, it was because the victim had insulted his sister by approaching her in public and slapping her spindle and distaff out of her hands. When the brother learned of the slight, he confronted Bassianis on the main road leading into the village. In front of some other peasants who were coming home after working in their fields, he challenged him to fight. The knives were drawn and used. Bassianis died from the cut he received on his face. Presumably he succumbed to an infection (CO 136/748 PRO). This case is different from the norm in that it was not one of the duelists who was directly insulted. The following cases were more typical.

Ioannis Tsoudis entered the tavern of Spiridon Briotas in Argostoli and demanded that Panagis Magdalios stop calling him a cuckold. According to the police report, Tsoudis believed that Magdalios was the source of the gossip about him, gossip that Tsoudis's wife had made known to him. When confronted with the accusation, Magdalios simply laughed. Beside himself with fury at being mocked, Tsoudis swore to make him eat his words. After a fight that the witnesses all agreed was a good and fair one, Tsoudis needed thirteen stitches to close the wound on his face (TIAK 658: March 4, 1835).

On the night of April 23, 1835, Giorgos Koidan entered a billiard parlor in the town of Kerkira and demanded satisfaction from Ioannis Deninzzando. Koidan had just learned that Deninzzando had been overheard calling his wife a Magdalene in public. Having tracked down his wife's slanderer, Koidan walked up to him and while standing nose to nose with him announced to the assembled group that "No man insults my *onoré*." He then drew his dagger. In the subsequent fight he cut Deninzzando on the face and the ears (IAK EA 1317: April 23, 1835).

Theodoros Kirinaris did not like his paternal cousin Spiridon, and, according to elders in their village of Kominata on Kerkira, had not since childhood. Spiridon, it seems, was a bully. On December 18, 1854, matters came to a head. Theodoros had heard that his antagonist had been telling other men tales about his wife. According to the constable's report, when confronted Spiridon said to his cousin, "It's a shame that your hen won't stay in the yard." Stilettos were unsheathed. Neither man fought well, and the affray ended with Theodoros receiving a cut on his left arm. When the night patrolman arrived on his rounds, he took statements from the two fighters, who had remained

at the wineshop, and the witnesses. On the constable's recommenda-
tion the next day, the police magistrate issued warrants for the arrests
of both men for assault. Four days later, after hearing testimony, he ac-
quitted both men with the admonition that they should behave like
kinsmen and not fight (IAK EA 215: December 18, 1854).

In these and numerous other examples, gossip in the form of
sexual insults about one of the men or his wife (or another kinswoman) was the root cause of the fight. As we saw in chapter 4, the
most direct challenge to another man's reputation was to call him a
cuckold. It was an insult that cut to the quick because it called into
question a man's capacity to fulfill in the ways prescribed in this society the duties of a man. Most frequently, however, men chose indirect
means of making the accusation. The butcher in the story recounted
above humiliated his foe with a pun revolving around his own occupation. By "horned one," he alluded both to a goat or ram, the smell of
which he would know from being a butcher, and a cuckolded man.
The insult was sufficiently ambiguous so as to leave the offended party
with an out if he wished to avoid a fight. But the consequence of
doing so would have been a diminishment of his reputation as a man
who could protect what was his, i.e., his honor.

Another well-represented variant of the script involved men who
were strangers or, if they were acquainted, men who seemingly held no
grudges against one another. The participants were often drunk, and
almost invariably erotic taunts were exchanged leading to the onset of
a fight. Ioannis Kousaris from Kerkira and Athanasios Merkouris
came to blows in the wineshop of Sathi Nikieravatos when one questioned the other's paternity: "*Sappiamo ch'e la vostra madre, ma suo padre
il Dio sa* [We all know your mother, but your father God only knows]."
The onlookers intervened only after Kousaris had drawn first blood by
slashing open Merkouris's cheek (IAK EA 1317: December 8, 1835).

Spiros Petrolides was a well-known forty-two-year-old barber in
the town of Kerkira. On the night of July 17, 1860, he fought a duel
with a twenty-three-year-old laborer from the village of Velonades.
The latter had challenged his manhood and honor by calling his wife
a Magdalene. No one knew what started the trouble before that word
that could not be borne was uttered. The *consensus opinio* was only that
the two men, after some heavy drinking, had taken a dislike to one another. The unfortunate barber received a vicious cut across his chin

before the men were separated (IAK EA 1334: July 17, 1860). In these cases, strangers clashed in a public setting. Though unknown to each other, because they came from the same social class and culture, they performed the rituals of violence according to the same culturally inscribed script.

The Vendetta and Other Forms of Ritualized Violence

An examination of some other forms of masculine violence amply confirms the degree to which the knife fight was ritualized and rule-bound. It could be argued against my interpretation that men simply fought with what was literally to hand, and since, until the imposition of strict weapons-possession laws in 1830s, most men in this culture carried edged weapons with them—such as *pslithia* (pruning knives), daggers, stilettos, etc.—they instinctively drew them when necessary. In addition to the more obvious point that the same script was followed so frequently and thus it is unlikely that men were acting wholly without intentionality, an examination of those episodes in which a quarrel took place but did not end with a knife fight indicates that indeed participants knew their roles in preexisting narratives.

On March 2, 1843, Athanasios Diavatos, a fishmonger in the central market of Kerkira, confronted Antonios Avella, a twenty-three-year-old laborer, in a wineshop by the pier and accused him of having stolen his scale. They exchanged insults. Everything, it would appear, was in place for a knife fight, but instead of knives they fought with fists. The deviation from the script, I would suggest, related to the fact that Avella was not a native. He was a foreigner from Malta, and as such he was not rooted in the same cultural system as Diavatos and the other Kerkirans (IAK EA 679: January 1, 1835). In another case from Kerkira, instead of fists a man used a clay pot to smash the skull of his antagonist. Once again, the man was an outsider (IAK EA 1421: June 9, 1832).

In another episode, where the dominant script would usually have called for knives, fists were used. But here the sexual taunts were exchanged between a British soldier and a local Greek peasant (IAK EA 1610: July 27, 1835). A fight at the wineshop of Panagis Lefkaditis at the fort of Agios Giorgios on Kefallenia in 1832 had all of the requisite elements for a knife fight. But instead Sisifos Romanos put Chimachi Kantouzza in *"pericolo di vita,"* as the medical examiner put it, not with a knife but with a pistol. Instead of cutting him with a blade, he pistol-whipped his Maltese foe with a gun (TIAK 217: July 27, 1832).

In the majority of those episodes which had all of the elements that usually resulted in a knife fight but did not, one of two differences was evident: either one of the participants was a *xenos*—a foreigner—or one was not a social equal. Knife fighting, then, was reserved for insiders, for men who were anchored in the same social milieu. The seemingly scripted nature of the fights was not a coincidence but the result of a purposeful adherence to a shared cultural practice. An examination of another type of violence prevalent among Greek men, the vendetta homicide, further highlights the distinctiveness of the knife duel.

During the customary afternoon perambulation at the village square of Pilaros on Kefallenia on September 11, 1835, Spiridon Kallihias, a farmer, approached Theodoros Maridas, an auxiliary constable, pulled a pistol from beneath his belt and fatally shot him in the head. Many in the hushed crowd were not surprised at the killing. A few people even nodded their heads in grim-faced satisfaction. Some of the dead policeman's kinsmen ran to get their guns; others hastened to the church to ring the mourning bell. His kinswomen gathered around the body, singing ritual laments, and began the funeral rituals. Within hours a posse of ten armed constables arrived from the district capital. Questioning of the forty witnesses elicited only stony silence: no one had seen anything. Even the deceased's kinsmen professed no knowledge of the assailant's identity. After seventeen days of quarantine during which time no one could leave the village, the killer's identity was anonymously revealed. He was captured by the posse three days later at his agnatic cousin's house in a nearby village. A week after that Kallihias stood at the bar in the hall of justice in the island's capital. Kallihias, his lawyer argued, was merely defending the reputation/honor (*timi*) of his family by killing a man who had shamed the Kallihias patrigroup. Maridas had earlier that year arrested the younger brother of Kallihias for violating the British quarantine laws, leading to the youth being sentenced to life in prison. Justifiable homicide based on the notion of blood revenge was thus Kallihias's plea, and his covillagers supported it. In order to prevent a "perversion of justice" and to restore the "public tranquility," however, the tribunal rejected this line of reasoning, and found him guilty of murder. Kallihias was duly executed, his corpse dipped in tar and hung in the city square for ten days (TIAK: 847: September 11, 1835).

For sheer audacity, few men can match Bernardo Leftachi. He was the coxswain of the *sanita* boat on the island of Zakinthos. While accompanying his patron, the wealthy and powerful Dr. Dimitrios Lombardos, on a visit to one of the villages attached to the former regent's estate, Leftachi learned that his younger brother had just been killed in a fight with a man named Glassi. Having ascertained that the contest had been unfair, the coxswain returned to the island's capital and went to the main police station. There he confronted Glassi's brother, who was a constable, and in front of the desk sergeant and two other officers, he shot Glassi once in the head and then stabbed him through the heart. Before the shocked constables could act, Leftachi bolted out the door. In spite of an islandwide manhunt, the avenging brother was never captured. It was widely rumored that his *padrone* had given him refuge and helped to engineer his escape from the island (*Dispatches from Her Majesty's Consuls in Corfu, Zante, and Cephalonia* [London, 1867], dispatch from Consul Wodehouse to Consul-General Saunders, February 13, 1865, enclosure 13, 12).

The scion of a noble house on Kefallenia was seated alone in the upper dining chamber of his family's country estate. Two rifle shots broke the summer evening's silence. The youthful count was instantly killed as both bullets hit home. A full staff of servants was on duty and numerous peasants were working in the vicinity of the house, yet no one claimed to have seen the assassins. During the course of their investigations, the police learned that the young aristocrat recently "had paid his addresses to, and then abandoned" a maiden from one of the villages under his family's control. On account of the widespread belief in blood revenge, the police automatically assumed that her brothers were the ones who went to the house that night, climbed on to the arbor outside of the dining-room balcony, and killed the man. Though "universally given credit" by the authorities for having "really done the dark deed," the brothers were never charged because "none of the peasantry could be induced to come forward to present evidence which many of them, it is believed, were able to supply" (Kirkwall 1864: 70–71).

These three cases typify vendetta killings on the Ionian Islands and demonstrate some of the key differences and similarities between this type of violence and knife dueling (vendetta violence in Greece resembles the practice as recorded elsewhere in the Mediterranean. See, for example, Wilson 1988; Boehm 1984; Koliopoulos 1987: 251–53; Gallant 1988; Campbell 1992: 137). Both were related, ritualized forms of violence, but with different rules of engagement. Honor was the key to both. But it is the differences that require emphasis here. First, the intent of a vendetta was to kill; in the duel, the intent was to maim or scar. Second, the weapon of choice in a vendetta was usually a firearm rather than a knife. Third, stealth or ambush was acceptable in a vendetta. Fourth, there was no sense that a vendetta fight had to be a fair one. On the contrary, none of the victims discussed above had a chance to respond to their assailant. Fifth, the cause of the vendetta conflict stemmed from actions, not words. Insults alone did not initiate a vendetta. Moreover, the provocative act had to be seen as a violation of communal norms. Note the very different responses of Leftachi and the kinsmen of Theodoros Maridas. Leftachi believed that his brother had died in an unfair fight, and so the act called out for blood vengeance; Maridas's patrigroup accepted his fate as just and so felt no need to cleanse their honor in Kallihias's blood. Sixth, the victim of a vendetta did not have be the one who committed the act; any of his kinsmen was fair game. Seventh, vendetta killers vigorously sought to elude apprehension and trial. Unlike duelists, who welcomed their capture, the men discussed above tried to escape apprehension—even when they had committed their crime in a police station. As many scholars have noted, vendetta killers often could never return to their homes and so took to the hills to become brigands. Eighth, contrast the loquaciousness of the witnesses to knife fights with the stony silence steadfastly maintained by those who saw vendetta killings. The Greek code of silence pertained to certain types of violence but not others. This last point especially requires attention. Men wanted to tell tales about knife fights, and they seemed to relish the opportunity to recount them in court. We shall see in chapter 8 that breaking the code of silence surrounding other forms of crime was a central concern of the Colonial Office.

Courting Reputations

Where knife fighting was involved, Ionian Island men incorporated the British colonial criminal justice system into their masculine discourse of honor. Cases of assault or assault with a deadly weapon could be inaugurated by the victim as a private prosecutor or by the advocate fiscale on behalf of the state. Acting as the presiding magistrate in the police court, he would hear testimony from the participants and the constables and other officials. His role in these cases was to determine if there was a case to be answered. In the 125 cases I examined, in only 29 of them did he determine that the case should not go forward to the correctional court, the lowest rung of the criminal justice system that had a public trial. In the cases that he did not set forward, the magistrate determined that either no party was legally at fault or that the wounds sustained were negligible. In some cases, he ordered that the victim be awarded a sum of money. The vast majority of cases, however, went before the correctional court, where a panel of three Greek jurists would hear the case. All parties attended, and witnesses gave evidence.

In their testimonies, Ionian Island men talked about the fight: what it was over, what was said, etc. But they also rendered an evaluation of the contest, and the judges paid heed to their assessments. Men talked about how well the fight went. Whether or not the two were equally adept. Was one man drunker than the other? Did one aim to kill rather than to maim? The judges seem to have taken these factors into account. If the fight was fair and the provocation unbearable, they occasionally imposed a light, noncustodial sentence, but as we shall see later, this became increasingly less so. Magistrates sought to learn whether or not there had been preexisting bad blood between the fighters. If there had, then they usually imposed a stiffer sentence. They inquired about the course of the fight. If one man had taken advantage of the other, i.e., not played by the rules, then a term in the house of correction was in store for the guilty. If one of the fighters had died as a result of wounds received in the fight, then the judges focused on the question of intent: did the killer intend to inflict a mortal blow? The fate of the defendant hinged on how the witnesses responded to this crucial question. Intent distinguished accidental death from homicide and assault from attempted homicide. Initially at least, jail time awaited only those convicted of the latter two offenses. As time went on, however, regardless of how men answered these questions or if intent was or was not manifested, it became ever more probable that incarceration would result for anyone caught knife fighting.

The courtroom provided the site for the third and final act of the drama of the knife fight. It was there that the final verdict was rendered on the duel and the duelists, but witnesses, not judges, rendered it. Courts, then, were co-opted, and legal ritual was subverted to serve the needs of the contestants. Reputation, not truth, was on trial, and disputes that started with words that cut ended with words as well.

The trial provided the loser with an opportunity to try and salvage his reputation. He could claim that he was drunk and taken advantage of. Or that his opponent had tricked him or that the fight had in some other way been unfair. The winner got a public forum in which to heap scorn on his opponent. In spinning out his tale of triumph he redoubled his assault on the public reputation of the loser. As the man in my opening vignette crowed, no man would insult his reputation and get away with it. The most often-heard refrain from the victor was that he made the other man "eat his words."

Just as important, I suggest, were the stories by the witnesses. Even more than the participants, they framed the discourse for public assessment. In their narratives men commented on every aspect of the fight: who fought well; who did not; who instigated; who got what he deserved. The discursive power of the duel to damage or salvage reputations stemmed from the comments of the witnesses, which acted to formalize the narrative. While the knife fights were usually high drama, men could and did die in them: the witnesses' assessment could reduce them to farce as well, meaning that the reputations of both the scarred man and his unblemished foe were damaged. In the case of Andreas Magiras and Nikolaos Bamboulis in 1835, the onlookers heaped scorn on both because they were so drunk that they did not fight well. As one man told the court, "This was not serious, they fought like fools" (TIAK 724: July 14, 1835).

The narratives told in court also tell us what the fights were really about: honor. Repeatedly in their stories men talked of *onoré* and *fama*, insults and *villania insolenza*, *timi* and *diko mou*. As Tuckerman observed, the single most prevalent cause of interpersonal violence among Greeks was honor: ". . . a wound of honor or a family insult," he remarked, "burns and did so till soothed by the blood of the insulter" (Tuckerman 1872: 240). Nineteenth-century Ionian Island men were as sensitive to their reputations and status as their later-day kindred whose preoccupations with honor have been so well documented by ethnographers. As we saw in the previous chapter, certain words had extremely evocative power in this society because they tapped into a set of core metaphors through which men made sense of their world. The combat with knives was part of the same discourse in which men fought with words. Men walked a very fine line in their struggles for honor and status. The banter and verbal sparring, so well described by Herzfeld and other ethnographers in contemporary Greece, was a part of men's discourse in nineteenth-century Greece as well (Herzfeld 1985: 126–29). But Ionian men were fully cognizant that there were certain words and certain phrases that once uttered could lead to violence. These words challenged a man's honor and reputation. Ionian men literally put their faces on the line in order to save face figuratively. If we accept that Greek knife fighting was a plebeian form of dueling, in what ways then was it similar or different from dueling among the higher orders of other societies as studied by historians?

Comparisons and Contrasts

In a number of respects, Ionian knife fights were remarkably similar to duels conducted among U.S. southern aristocrats (Bruce 1979; Wyatt-Brown 1982; Greenberg 1996; Ayers 1985), British soldiers (Simpson 1988; Kiernan 1988; Morgan 1995; Andrew 1980), French bourgeoisie (Nye 1993), Italian liberals (Hughes 1998), and German students (McAleer 1994; Frevert 1985; 1993). This is not, of course, to imply that dueling everywhere and at all times was identical. There were variations in style and form both between cultures and over time. Some general characteristics, however, are apparent.

First and foremost, the Ionian knife fight and the canonical duel were ritualized single combats fought by men in the name of honor. Witnesses were central to the ritual, but their role was by and large a passive one. Unless a rule of combat was infringed or until a certain point in the ritual was reached, they were to act as observers only. The Greek duel was fought to first blood, as was the duel with swords in France and Italy. Moreover, in Greece as elsewhere, the duel acted as a boundary marker between groups and classes. Many students of the duel have emphasized that a man restored his honor and good name simply by entering the arena of combat. Dueling was not about winning or losing but about playing the game. Thus, the German students who participated in the *mensur* proudly displayed their facial scars. Indeed, according to McAleer, the tactics of the sword fight developed in such a way that exposed the participants' "faces to the jagged lacerations on which every student duelist plumed himself" (1994: 123). Among the Greeks, a man who refused combat lost the respect of his peers, but how they regarded the loser is problematic. Based on their courtroom narratives, it appears that they considered the facial scar of a bested fighter as a mark of defeat, and so they held him in lower esteem. The one who was cut did not suffer shame but rather, as the Greeks put it, *systoli*—a word the root meaning of which is "diminution." In other words, losing a knife duel did not *dis*honor a man. He kept his honor, but his reputation was diminished. By and large, then, for the Greeks, as for duelists in other societies, the true test of a man's mettle was his willingness to fight solo combat in the name of honor. Only the failure to fight would have signified a man's status emasculation.

There were a number of differences between Greek plebeian knife fights and dueling elsewhere. First, Greek peasants and workers had no written *code duello*. There were no equivalents to the dueling codes published in Germany and France. This, however, is a rather minor distinction due to class-based differences in literacy. The more important differences were these. First, there was no or only a slight delay between the utterance of an insult and the duel among the Greeks. Combat followed hot on the heels of the attack on a man's honor. A key part of the upper-class duel was the time delay between affront and affray. Second, Greek plebeian duelists did not seek to elude capture and, as suggested earlier, an appearance in the courtroom was a vital component of their ritual. This is markedly different from the practice in Germany and France. McAleer shows that even the introduction of special "courts of honor" did little to alter duelists' reluctance to engage the state in honor disputes (1994: 86–98). And in the case of France, "both defenders and opponents of the duel agreed that a man who took his case to the courts would be perceived as a 'coward' whose sense of 'independence' was so feeble that he was willing to entrust a decision about his personal honor to complete strangers" (Nye 1993: 176). One final aspect distinguishing the Greek knife fight from the upper-class duel of Europe and the United States is that none of the explanations proposed to account for the end of dueling can explain why Greek plebeian men kept their honor but put away their blades.

For some historians, the differences in the rituals of lower-class combat and upper-class dueling are so substantive as to mark them as two distinct forms of violence. The following from Dickson Bruce captures well the argument that the time delay and the nature of the combats are enough. "The duel, unlike the street fight, was an outgrowth of the carefully cultivated style of the Southern gentry. A fit of passion may have led to the problem but duelists quickly assumed the kind of behavior of which society approved, and instituted procedures to maintain order. . . . The street fight not only admitted the passions, but brought to the fore impatience, revenge, and a rejection of order. The chapters may have been the same whether one fought for revenge or dueled for honor, but the procedures and the symbolism were very different" (Bruce 1979: 73). Others writing about dueling in the Old South also accept the distinction drawn by Bruce between honor and dueling among elite men and their absence from the social realm of plebeian men. Echoes of this view resound in the literature on the duel in Europe as well. Nye, for example, draws a clear distinction in the role of honor between the French duel and the lower-class knife fight (1993: 136). Simpson in his study of the English even more explicitly distinguishes the duel as a class boundary delimiter. In his view, "It would be impertinent to equate the psyches of the working-class brawler and the aristocratic duelist" (1988: 176). For some, then, it is the seeming absence of honor that is crucial.

For others, it is the seemingly unscripted nature of lower-class violence that is crucial. Some sociologists and criminologists, for example, have recently returned to an idea proposed by Wolfgang almost thirty years ago that much masculine working-class violence was caused by "trivial slights" over honor or reputation (1958: 188–89). Daly and Wilson, for example, have argued that "a seemingly minor affront is not merely a 'stimulus' to action, isolated in time and space. It must be understood within a larger social context of reputations, face, relative social status, and enduring relationships. Men are known by their fellows as 'the sort who can be pushed around' or 'the sort that won't take any shit,' as people whose word means action and people who are full of hot air, as guys whose girlfriends you can chat up with impunity or guys you don't want to mess with. In most social milieux, a man's reputation depends in part upon the maintenance of a credible threat of violence" (Daly and Wilson 1988: 128). In his study of over five hundred homicides involving Australian youths, Kenneth Polk concluded that the overwhelming majority of them were confrontations of honor in which young men traded insults and then blows in defense of their status among their peer group (Polk 1988: 188–205). While the sociological literature revises the historical studies of the duel by suggesting that lower-class violence is also connected to honor, it still espouses the notion that it was not ritualized or formulaic. Polk specifically distinguishes the cases he studied as "confrontational homicides," thus perpetuating the idea that plebeian violence was spontaneous, unscripted, and rage-driven (Polk 1988: 191).

Pieter Spierenburg, more than any other historian, has shown that knife fighting among lower-class Amsterdam men was rule-bound and ritualistic and that the cause of most conflicts was slights and insults to another man's reputation. As he concisely put it: "Masculinity and honor were central to the knife fighters' world" (Spierenburg 1998b: 107; see also Spierenburg 1998a; 1994. Cf. Boschi 1998). Elliot Gorn, in his examination of southern backcountry lower-class violence, argued that honor was directly implicated in such fights and that they were subject to their own rituals: "A rough-and-tumble was more than a poor man's duel, a botched version of genteel combat. Plain folk chose not to ape the dispassionate, antiseptic, gentry style but to invert it. While the gentlemen's code of honor insisted on cool restraint, eye-gougers gloried in unvarnished brutality" (Gorn 1985: 41; Ayers 1985: 21). The evidence from Greece supports the argument that certain forms of plebeian violence were rooted in an ethic of honor, were ritualized, and were therefore more akin to than different from upper-class dueling.

The role of the courts, however, was the one difference between the rituals of Greek plebeian knife duels and upper-class dueling that was truly distinctive. Ionians embraced them, others eschewed them. While this in and of itself is insufficient as a basis for drawing a categorical distinction between them, it may suggest an avenue for explaining the other major difference: the ending of the duel. Studies of the duel on the Continent are remarkably consistent in concluding that it was the carnage of the First World War more than anything else that caused the duel to fall into disuse. As Nye put it, "The duel perished in the trenches of the Western Front" (1998: 83; McAleer 1994: 201; Frevert 1995: 192; 1998: 60). Italy walked a slightly different path whereon it was the war and then the advent of Fascist rule that kept Italian liberals off of the field of honor (Hughes 1998: 74–75). Britain, as so often happened, marched to a different drummer. On Albion's isle, dueling had pretty much come to end by the third quarter of the nineteenth century. Contributing factors seem to have been the democratization of the duel, which led to the practice ceasing among the aristocracy; vigorous action of the state to curtail dueling in the military, where it had been most prevalent; and a shift in masculine sensibilities among middle-class men that transformed attitudes about violence (Simpson 1988: 139–40; Stearns 1990: 49–50). Ayers has proposed a complex explanation to account for the demise of the duel in the U.S. South. He sees the Civil War acting in much the same way that the Great War did in Europe to generate a revulsion against violence, but he also suggests that evangelicalism, and the spread and adoption of a bourgeois business ethos from the North to the South led to diminution of the importance of honor among the upper class (Ayers 1985: 271). As honor lost its saliency, dueling was diminished in importance.[2] The cultural arguments proposed by Ayers and Simpson for the duel follow along the lines proposed by other scholars attempting to explain the general decline of violence in the West which derive from Norbert Elias's idea of the "civilizing process" (1978: 447–49; Fletcher 1997; Johnson and Monkkonen 1996; Spierenburg 1996). None of these explanations satisfactorily explains why Greek plebeian men stopped dueling when they did. There was no war that rocked their world. There was no evangelical religious movement, nor a transformation of masculine sensibilities based on bourgeois values. We have to seek, like Ayers and Simpson, a complex and multicausal explanation for the demise of the working-class duel in Greece, and our explanation must account for why the duel ended but honor remained.

The literature on the duel strongly suggests that when the practice ceased honor also lost its central position in the core of masculine identity. As Peter Stearns has noted, in the new bourgeois society of the West, "honor [became] an archaic remnant" (1990: 50). But, honor has been seen as a central element in contemporary Greek and Spanish rural societies since the groundbreaking ethnographies of Campbell (1964), Pitt-Rivers (1961; 1977), and Peristiany (1968). Subsequent studies both in these countries and other regions of the Mediterranean led to the assertion that the "honor and shame complex" was a central defining element of a Mediterranean culture system.[3]

There are clusters of actions and beliefs that recur cross-culturally and historically among cultures that profess to hold dear an ethical concept regarding status and reputation that they gloss as honor. Two such recurring patterns concern us. One is that in honor cultures, status, reputation, and esteem are assessed, bestowed, or rescinded by the court of masculine public opinion. Because of this, honor acts as a cultural boundary delimiter. Second, honor is intimately connected with aggression. Manhood, because it is on public display, is always at risk, and so, a man's reputation is directly connected to his ability to be seen to be able to defend openly against all challenges. Thus, in honor cultures there develops an "agonisitic ethos [that] has deep roots in the atomized social context of Mediterranean society. The grim conflict it embodies are real and pervasive; the interpersonal aggression it spawns are not gratuitous" (Gilmore 1987: 43; 1990; Hatch 1989: 341–54). Part of being a man in an honor society is a readiness to employ physical violence to defend one's reputation.

The Mediterranean ethnographic record is replete with vivid descriptions of colorful displays of masculine bravado. But there is a paradox: for all of the macho posturing, anthropologists record very few actual acts of violence, especially lethal violence. Nor do official court and police documents record many instances of honor homicides. In other words, there is a great deal of masculine bluster but little blood. In his study of the Sarakatsanoi, a group renowned for its supposed violent propensities, Campbell noted that "knives are pulled with great bravado [only] when it is certain that others are present to prevent their use" (1964: 151). During the time period over which he studied the group, he saw many displays of aggression but few actual conflicts. Robert Paine elaborated slightly on this theme. In his view, the Sarakatsanoi construct zero-sum dramas in their contests over honor rather than zero-sum fights (Paine 1989: 667). Herzfeld, in his work on Cretan shepherds, another group with a reputation for violence, found that men competed with one another at cards and contested status by trading sung insults, a Greek type of "playing the

dozens." He also noted that aggressive displays and boisterous announced threats of violence were common, though actual conflicts
were few. He concluded what mattered to Glendiote men was to be
seen to be good at being a man (Herzfeld 1985: 47). In Spanish Andalusia, Pitt-Rivers found that assailants squared off only when they
were sure that the onlookers were prepared to pull them apart (1977:
32). In a more recent ethnography from the Iberian peninsula, Miguel
Vale de Almeida noted that when men fight "there is always someone
there to restrain the contenders just in time" (Almeida 1996: 102).

Finally, in his wide-ranging examination of aggression and honor,
Gilmore observed no cases of actual life-threatening violence; instead,
he concluded that masculine aggression in Spain had by and large
been channeled into symbolic displays of machismo (Gilmore 1987:
11). Stanley Brandes as well demonstrated how Andalusian men channeled their aggressive confrontations with other men into rituals such
as joke-telling, skits, and riddles (1980).

What we see, then, is that even among contemporary groups
known for their sensitivity to honor in Greece and elsewhere, violence
in defense of reputation has been largely reduced to ritualized, symbolic forms. This was definitely not the case in the past. There is then
a very important question that arises when we connect the anthropological literature on honor to the historical studies of violence. If
honor was an integral part of Greek plebeian masculine violence in
the past, and if honor as an ethic still pertains among rural Greek men
in the recent past but associated with symbolic rather than actual
lethal violence, then when and why did this crucial transformation
take place?

Men, Honor, Violence, and the Colonial Courts

As noted earlier, Greek knife fighters used the court systems in ways
unlike duelists elsewhere, and an examination of the role of the courts
can provide a starting point for explaining the end of the duel. As I
examine in the next chapter, the criminal justice system offered a possible remedy to Greek men with a sullied reputation: slander. Over the
course of the protectorate, thousands of men and women filed warrants, attended magistrate's tribunals, and went to the correctional

court to prosecute fellow islanders for slander. Women also used the courts in their contests over reputation, and they extended their networks of gossip to include the criminal justice system. Men's knife fighting and women's use of the slander laws served two different strategies embedded in the same discourse over the honor and reputation of the household. Could taking a man to court for slander, almost invariably involving the same erotic insults that inaugurated knife fights, restore a man's damaged reputation? Some inferences drawn from an examination of over two hundred slander cases suggest some possible answers to this query. In addition, they can provide us with an explanation that can connect the historian's world of the honor-based duel to the anthropologist's domain, where masculine honor rules but without high levels of interpersonal violence.

The first aspect that stands out is that members of the aristocracy are far more represented in slander trials than in knife fights. In just over 10 percent of slander trials, one or both of the litigants was an aristocrat, whereas no aristocrats were prosecuted for assault or assault with a deadly weapon. Unlike in the cultures most often studied by historians, the Ionian aristocracy did not duel. There were some cases of members of the *signori* killing one another, but these were rare and they were not the result of a ritualized duel. The nobility earlier and disproportionately took each other to court; I do not want to overstate this point—for the most part they neither dueled nor litigated. The reason, I suggest, is that the aristocracy on these islands was organized into relatively tight patrilineal kingroups, each of which employed gangs of armed tough guys or *bravi*. Aristocratic factions fought one another by proxy using their lower-class gangs. In addition, given that the ethos of the vendetta was prevalent, *signori* had to be very careful about instigating a confrontation because by so doing they could incite a potentially destructive feud. In certain respects, then, plebeian men had a more autonomous sense of self-identity than did their noble brethren, and as a consequence they had to defend their reputation in different ways. One very important way was the knife duel. The courts gained legitimacy as an arbiter of honor first among the aristocracy.

Plebeian men soon followed suit and flooded the court docket with their accusations of criminal slander. A statistical trend analysis of complaints and arrests for assault and assault with a deadly weapon shows a decrease over time. At the same time, the propensity of men to swear out complaints for slander rose.[4] To be sure, knife fighting persisted, but the relative balance of dueling to litigation shifted. The lawsuit, then, gradually replaced the duel. But no single element can account for why Greek men began to place less emphasis on violence and more on the courts as the means of preserving their reputation.

A number of factors contributed to this change. First, there were cultural and ideological developments that could have contributed to a "civilization" of male sensibilities to violence. Since the 1830s, pro-British Ionians, who disproportionately held the levers of local political power, used the law and public policy to transform the national character of their countrymen. They took their cue from the colonial officers, who, as we saw in chapter 2, denigrated the Ionians, comparing them to aboriginal groups like the Hottentots or the Irish. Indeed, the British frequently referred to the Ionians as the "Mediterranean Irish."

A key part of the civilizing mission launched by the Greek leadership, as we have seen repeatedly, focused on the restoration and maintenance of public order. In chapter 8, we shall see that the Orthodox Church was brought into the struggle against crime and violence through the practice of excommunicating criminal offenders. Standing before assembled communities of Greek peasants, dark-robed clerics pronounced the ultimate sanction—eternal damnation—against certain criminal offenders, and they reserved their sternest opprobrium for those who had committed acts of violence. While the policy was not a great success at either diminishing crime, especially crimes against property, or in breaking Greeks' code of silence, nonetheless the constant preaching of the clergy against violence would have resonated with some men because of the close interconnection between Orthodoxy and Hellenism. Greeks drew a distinction between the church as an institution and Orthodoxy, and Greek men held ambiguous and conflicted views about the church. Because a key element in the Ionian islanders' identity as Hellenes was the Orthodox faith, pronouncements that challenged their status as Christians would have captured men's attention.

Finally, and most importantly, after 1850 the leadership of the Ionian Greek nationalist movement changed their tactics from ones that encouraged violent agitation against the British to ones which emphasized nonviolent forms of resistance (Knox 1984). During the

1830s and 1840s, the radical unionists fomented public unrest whenever possible. Thus, public processions frequently turned into riots.
Political rallies and elections were used as vehicles to whip up anti-
British sentiments, and such events often ended in bloodshed. Nationalist fervor culminated in 1848, when violent uprisings rocked a
number of the islands. In the aftermath of 1848, the nationalist leaders
changed tactics and opted for political disruption rather than open
confrontation as the best means to drive the British off the islands
(Knox 1984). They sought to make the islands ungovernable by dis-
rupting the political process. A new rhetoric accompanied this change
in tactics. Violence now was constructed as an impediment to the nationalist struggle (Pratt 1978: 140). In sum, their political leaders told
the people that violence was "nonwestern" and uncivilized; their priests
told them that it was immoral and unchristian; their radical nationalist
leaders told them it was anti-Greek and hindered the struggle for national union. It would be surprising, then, if Greek plebeians did not
begin to internalize new values that militated against violence. Especially given that other forces were also at work that reinforced this
message.

Laws were passed which forbade the wearing or possession of
bladed weapons or implements in public. Only butchers were exempt
from these regulations. Farmers and farm laborers could only possess
pruning knives with a blade length of less than two inches. Enforcement of the laws banning possession of knives and stilettos was one of
the primary duties of the Greek police, and the strict application of
the laws acted to take weapons out of men's hands. The courts increasingly took this offense seriously. In 1823, for example, the average
sentence imposed for illegal possession of a knife was five days in the
house of correction. The same offense in 1855 could well have brought
a spell in prison of six to eight months at hard labor. A trend analysis
of arrests for illegal arms possession shows a very marked increase over
time.[5] In short, the police became ever more vigilant in arresting men
for possession of a knife in public and the courts began to impose
stiffer sentences. The end result was that fewer men had knives.

Finally, and perhaps most importantly, the courts treated knife
fighting very differently over time. The pattern of sentencing imposed
on the guilty is depicted in Table 1, which compares the sentences imposed by the correctional courts in 1823–24 and 1847.

The difference is stark and remarkable. During the 1820s, nearly one-third of cases resulted in a noncustodial sentence. Instead of prison, the guilty party was fined a sum ranging from $1 to $5 and bound over to maintain the "public tranquility." Based on the courtroom testimonies it appears that the decision whether or not to impose a custodial sentence and its length were based on the details of the fight and the nature of the wounds inflicted. Modal sentences were ten days and twenty days. By the latter part of the 1840s, however, judicial attitudes had changed dramatically. Everyone convicted received a jail term. The modal sentences in this period were sixty days (accounting for slightly over one-quarter of all cases) and two years. Indeed, almost 40 percent of those found guilty of knife fighting in 1847 received sentences of ninety days or more, whereas no one had received a jail term of more than sixty days for knife fighting in 1823 and 1824. Knife fighting, then, went from being a relatively minor offense to one that brought with it a hefty spell in the house of correction.

From the beginning of the period I examined, the courtroom discourse was an integral part of the knife duel, constituting, as I argued earlier, the third act in these narratives. By incorporating the institu-

Table 1.   Custodial Sentences for Men Convicted for Assault or Assault with a Deadly Weapon Involving a Knife Fight

Number of Days	Percentage, 1823–24	Percentage, 1847
0–5	45.2%	0%
6–10	20%	1.7%
11–15	9.8%	3.2%
16–20	10.9%	0%
21–30	6.5%	3.8%
31–40	5.4%	12.1%
41–50	0%	0%
51–80	2.2%	41.3%
81–120	0%	19%
121–200	0%	1.7%
>200	0%	17.2%

tion into their daily dramas about honor and masculinity, plebeian men bestowed legitimacy upon it. The fact that the nobility had already shown that the courts could provide a vehicle for disputing reputations through the charge of criminal slander opened up a new venue by which plebeian men could contest honor in an ideological climate that was increasingly hostile to interpersonal violence. In an act of social mimesis, some plebeian men also opted for the docket over the blade. For the reasons cited above—especially the confiscation of their knives and the stiffer sentences imposed by judges—men came more and more to contest reputations in the court of public opinion. But now, rather than being restricted solely to the enclaves of male sociability—the wineshops and taverns—the site for their contests was the Palace of Justice. To be sure, the knife fight did not disappear, and the heightened stakes may even have held attraction for men who saw greater honor in greater risks. But the tide had turned. Beginning around midcentury, more men who suffered the slings and arrows of outrageous insults took their antagonist to court rather than cut his face. By the 1880s, the assault rate on the islands had fallen from 134 to 27 per 100,000, and by the 1920s it fell even further to 8.7 (Gallant 1998b: 11–12). The Eliasian civilizing process had occurred, and the knife duel as a means of defending one's honor became a relic of the past. Honor, however, did not.

Elias argued that the culture of honor that predominated in early modern Europe was prone to violence precisely because honor and violence were causally connected. Men of honor fought, and they fought over honor. For him and for the historians who have followed his lead, the duel was a perfect manifestation of this connection. He argued further that the rise of a "bureaucratic ethos" during the nineteenth century supplanted the ethic of honor and that alternative mechanisms of dispute resolution arose. Their advent severed the connection between masculinity and violence (Elias 1978: 292–300). Studies of the changing ideas about masculinity in the West during the nineteenth century suggest that the civilizing of working-class men went hand-in-hand with industrialization and urbanization. In the factory, men internalized ideas about discipline and self-control; these were reinforced by the new civic institutions that developed in the burgeoning cities of Western Europe and the United States (Stearns 1990: 48–107; Adler 1997; Wiener 1997). New ideas about middle-class male gentility were rooted in the emerging white-collar professions (Stearns 1990: 108–54; Rotundo 1993; Kimmel 1996; Tosh 1994; 1996). In this new world, "respectable" men were assertive, not aggressive, and violence became unacceptable (McLaren 1997: 11). In the southern United States, the way of life of the aristocracy was markedly changed in the postbellum period. What we see, then, is that in the areas where the honor-based duel flourished, its demise was accompanied by radical and profound changes in the material infrastructure of the dueling class. The cultural logic that had given honor its privileged place in defining masculinity had changed, and honor disappeared with the duel.

This study of plebeian violence in nineteenth-century Greece shows that honor was a more malleable concept than has been previously allowed. In this case, the ethic of honor remained, but the intimate connection between it and violence had changed. What remained of plebeian violence and masculinity were their symbolic manifestations so well documented in mid-to-late-twentieth-century ethnographies. The Greek men studied by Campbell, Herzfeld, and other ethnographers contested status and reputation in a variety of ways, but without the high incidence of interpersonal bloodshed that I have documented in this study of knife dueling. The marked decrease in masculine violence was not associated with a shift from an ethos of honor to something else. Dueling ended, but honor remained.

There are a number of major reasons why honor persisted. First, unlike in the other cases where both honor and dueling disappeared, in the Ionian Islands, the material basis of life that undergirded honor's role in defining masculinity did not change substantially until the very recent past. The islands experienced neither industrialization nor urbanization. Men were still mostly peasant farmers, shepherds, dockworkers, and merchant seamen. Theirs remained a world of stiff competition for scarce resources, and thus the reasons why honor developed in the first placed persisted. Second, the ethical foundation of honor remained intact. The campaign waged by politicians, priests, and nationalists was against violence, not honor. No Orthodox priests decried honor from the pulpit, as Evangelical and Utilitarian clergy did in England (Wiener 1997: 210, 240; Tosh 1994: 180–81). Far from denigrating honor, Ionian radicals seeped their nationalist rhetoric in the discourse of honor. In short, no agency or group on the islands challenged the notion that honor was at the core of what it was to be a Greek man. Finally, the courts and the legal system proved central in perpetuating the importance of honor in the discourse over masculine identity. One of the unintended consequences of the British Empire's endeavor to insinuate law and the courts into the heart of colonial rule on the islands was to make the courts relatively cheap and accessible.[6] As the courts gained legitimacy among plebeian men as a venue for contesting reputations, their disputes took on less violent and more symbolic forms. Honor remained, however, central and prominent in slander trials. At each of the thousands of courtroom dramas over criminal calumny, Greek men stood in the dock and through their words reshaped what it meant to "be a man" in their society. The connective tissue between honor, masculinity, and violence was severed. Honor remained the cornerstone of Greek masculine identity, but violence did not. The transition from actual combat with knives to verbal duels with words took place, then, in the nineteenth-century courtroom. When the British relinquished the islands in 1864, the Kingdom of Greece took them over and imposed its own legal system on them. The courts ceased to be as open and prevalent, even after the major legal reforms of the 1880s and 1890s (Gallant 2000b: 403–6). With access to the rituals and formal mechanisms of the courts removed, masculine contests over honor and reputation returned to the more informal settings of the tavern or the wineshop, where they would be studied by anthropologists in the 1950s and 1960s, but with a difference. Violence and the knife duel had been dissociated from cultural concepts of honor and masculinity. In more recent times, then, men dueled over honor with words, not with stilettos. They bested one another with cards, not blades. Losing one's face increasingly became a figure of speech rather than a fact of life in the rough and tumble world of Ionian Island men. There is, however, another side to this story. It was not Greek men but Greek women who first exploited the legal space created by the British colonial court system, and it is that story I turn to now.

CHAPTER SEVEN

"We're All Whores Here"

Women, Slander, and the Criminal Justice System

Katerina Koulias was angry. As she stood in the back of the church of the Virgin Mary in the working-class suburb of Mandouka on Sunday, January 26, 1850, her ire grew. It had come to her attention that some women in the neighborhood were gossiping about her, and that the source of the lies was Anastasia Liotas. Liotas and her husband, Manolas, lived on the same block as Katerina and her husband, Mathaios. When the mass was completed, Koulias exited the church and gathered with some of her kinswomen and friends in the adjacent square. Across the esplanade, Liotas stood chatting with her clique. Unable to contain herself any longer, Katerina stormed down the stairs, walked up to Liotas, and told her to stop telling lies about her. Words were exchanged. Tempers flared. Koulias called to her friends and said, "Let's go. I'll fix her." And off they marched. Liotas and her friends followed suit. They knew the destination: the metropolitan police station. Winding its way through the narrow streets of Kerkira town, the parade of women filled the neighborhood with their din of taunts and laughter.

Constable second-class Fotis Kondis's peaceful shift as sergeant of watch was rudely distributed when over twenty-five women entered the police station. Shouts and accusations were hurled across the room. Koulias sidled up to his desk. Kondis shouted for silence and asked the distraught woman what she wanted. Though she was sobbing, she blurted out that Liotas had been telling everyone that she was a "Mag-dalene"—in Greek this could mean either a whore or an adulteress—and she wanted it to stop. The room was filled with noise as the women offered their own commentaries on the proceedings. Ringing out above the din, the shrill voice of the venerable widow Paraskevi Koutavas could be heard: "What can I say, we're all whores here." After the laughter had subsided, Kondis accepted the $1 fee and swore out an arrest warrant against Anastasia Liotas and five other women for the criminal contravention of Penal Law Title 7 Article 4 of having "committed in public in front of witnesses verbal outrage [*ingiuria verbale*] against Katerina Koulias" (IAK EA 1645: January 29, 1850).

The case against Liotas et al. went no further in the criminal jus-tice system than the brouhaha in the police station that Sunday. As in thousands of other episodes in which women filed complaints for slander against other women, the case went no higher than the bottom rung of the criminal justice system imposed upon the islands by the Colonial Office. This chapter picks up where the previous one left off and examines the ways that women used the court system in their daily struggles with other women over status and reputation in their neighborhoods and villages through the leveling of slander charges against one another.

This story contributes to or revises existing scholarship in a number of areas. First, it joins the growing ranks of works that depict the complexity of the relationship between imperialism and law. As recent discussions by Sally Merry (1991; 1995) and Nathan Brown (1995), for example, have shown, rather than being simply the hand-maiden of imperial social control, law and legal systems were more contested and their impact on indigenous society more complex and variegated. Law was not merely the blunt instrument of imperial rule, it also created new opportunities and spaces for the subject population both to resist the hegemonic designs of their rulers and to contest power, status, and reputation among themselves. As I show in the case of the Ionian Islands, the British-devised legal system opened a realm of public space that women quickly incorporated in unexpected ways into their daily social discourse.

Second, this chapter contributes to the literature by legal histori-ans on slander and defamation law by incorporating gender into the

analysis and by focusing on a civil rather than common-law legal tradition (Post 1986; King 1991; 1995; Spindel 1995; Slaughter 1992).
Third, in addition to joining the few other studies that examine
women's agency in the past through their participation in the public
discourse of the courts, I want to revise the argument put forth by
Laura Gowing (1995; 1996), Mary Beth Norton (1987), and others in
distinct ways. These scholars separate the verbal struggles of men for
status and reputation from those of women; they correctly see issues
involving honor and slander as gendered, but they then draw the inference that men's contests and women's contests constituted two
separate and distinct domains. I argue, contrariwise, that the two discourses intersected and were integrally intertwined. While the actual
practices of men and women differed and the contests tended to be
gender specific in content and in space, a unitary set of social strategies connected these seemingly disparate realms.

A household's honor and reputation was founded upon the status
of both its men and women. A challenge to one constituted a challenge to all. In their struggles for status and honor, Greek men and
women employed sexually charged insults as weapons, and through
the slander laws, they drew the police and the courts into their everyday war of words. Moreover, lurking behind this verbal sparring of
women was the very real possibility that one or more of their kinsmen
could end up disfigured or dead.

Law and Empire: Slander in a Colonial Perspective

In this chapter I focus exclusively on slander, defamation, and verbal
outrage because they were numerically the largest categories of criminal offense by both men and women, and they were at the nub of the
social conflicts over honor. It is through an examination of slander
that we can see most clearly how people used the law in creative and,
from the perspective of their rulers, in unintended ways. The British
saw slander and defamation as being especially important as well for a
number of reasons. First, even as early as the 1820s it was evident that
the Greek press could create major headaches for the Colonial Office,
and so strong laws were deemed necessary to curb the license of news-
papermen, especially anti-British, Greek nationalist newsmen. Second,

and most important for this discussion, it was abundantly clear to the British that the single most important factor accounting for the extremely high rate of male interpersonal violence was insults to a man's reputation. Strong curbs on verbal sparring could, it was hoped, lower the homicide and assault rates (Kendrick 1822: 23). Before we can understand how people used the law, we need to explicate the slander law imposed on the islanders.

Slander in English jurisprudence had a long and complex history (Starkie 1843; Newell 1923; Gatley 1967; Helmholz 1984; Manchester 1991). In the medieval period, attacks upon the reputation of another fell under the jurisdiction of both ecclesiastical and manorial courts; the former was concerned for the salvation of the victim's soul while the latter looked after his or her reputation or honor. This dual jurisdiction for slander was later joined by a third, when the Court of Star Chamber appropriated cases involving seditious libel. Until the middle of the nineteenth century, however, English law dealt with slander in two primary ways. One was through the ecclesiastical courts. Martin Ingram (1987; 1995), J. A. Sharpe (1980), and most recently Gowing (1995; 1996) have analyzed how slander cases were adjudicated in the church courts. Gowing shows how women, in particular, used the consistory court to prosecute others, usually women, for slandering them in public—almost invariably through calling them a whore. The courts sought to salvage the soul of the accuser if the imputation was false or the victim if it were true. The ecclesiastical court largely meted out symbolic punishments. In the common-law courts, slander was treated as a tort. In the early modern period, according to M. M. Slaughter, the tort of defamation was built upon a communitarian concept of identity in which slander was seen as an attack upon the very essence of an individual's identity (1992). Post refers to this aspect of a person's reputation as "personal honor" (1986: 693). Beginning in the late eighteenth century a shift occurred in the notion of reputation (Helmholtz 1984; 1987). A man's reputation became commodified as a type of property (Post 1986: 693–99; Slaughter 1992: 358–62; Hoffer 1989). In other words, the law considered that his good name possessed a quantifiable market value. Common law recognized four main areas of slanderous insults: those insults that imputed to another a criminal offense; those that imputed a disease; those that called into question one's competency in business, a trade, or a profession; and those that imputed serious sexual misconduct. In regard to each of those the accusers had to show actual, quantifiable damage to themselves because of the defamation. In the case of sexual conduct this often referred to the impact that the slander had on a person's marriage prospects. Slander could be indictable as a criminal offense if the words uttered did or could "create ill blood and provoke the parties to acts of revenge and breeches of the peace" (Starkie 1843: 210).

As the British Empire expanded, English legal traditions were exported, but in different forms depending on whether it was a settler colony or not. In colonies settled by British men and women, common law provided the backbone of the legal system. One of the best examples of this, of course, is the United States. Practices varied in the colonies and these differences became even clearer after independence, but by and large slander and defamation laws in the U.S. relied heavily on the common law. The single most important difference was that the ecclesiastical court disappeared in the New World. Most U.S. courts found, therefore, that because the English common law did not treat sexual slander against women, it insufficiently protected their reputations and so states implemented procedures to do so. In the U.S., then, sexual slander became a female tort (Starkie 1843: 205; Newell 1924: 652–55; King 1995: 73; Spindel 1995: 33; for Australia, see Edgeworth 1990; for Canada, see Coombe 1991). Slander still remained for the most part within the realm of civil law.

This was not the case in areas, like the Ionian Islands, where the British came as conquerors or occupiers and where some mix of direct and indirect rule was the norm (Merry 1991; 1995; Brown 1995; Schmidhauser 1989). The Colonial Office in this type of colony did not impose common law but instead drafted new legal codes that incorporated indigenous legal traditions. Modifying the judicial system on the Ionian Islands was a priority from the inception of the protectorate. Lord high commissioners from Sir Thomas Maitland onward made reformation of the criminal justice system a major policy issue. Even though they found the Venetian legal system "unjust" and its procedures "corrupt" they retained the essence of the Italian system, opting to modify and revise the laws and to render their application evenhandedly (Napier 1835: 326). According to the missives of the men who wrote the new penal codes, the source they drew on to revise the Venetian code was the Code Napoleon (Dixon 1969: 205–6). Not surprisingly then the law of slander drafted for the islands owed more to the French and Italian legal traditions than to English common law. The law promulgated on the islands, then, more closely resembled the modern Italian and French laws of slander (Amodio 1989; Calisse 1928: 437; Cappelletti and Merryman 1967; Certoma 1985; Del Duca and Vincenczo 1991; von Bar 1916: 266; Konzczal 1989).

As articulated in its final form, Penal Law Title 7 (first passed in 1823 as Articles 742–48, revised in 1843 and 1848) defined three categories of slander: defamation, outrage, and hurtful indiscretion. All of them were criminal offenses of one of three degrees: a *délit* (the most serious), an offense, or a contravention. The common-law delineation of slander as a tort was not adopted. The reasons for that were first the French and Italian models on which the Colonial Office's lawyers drew considered slander to be a crime because it deprived a man or woman of a right guaranteed by the state: the right to a "good name." Second, it became crystal clear to them that many of the homicidal affrays to which Greek men were so prone were the direct result of verbal insults. Thus, slander or insult fell under the common-law definition of a crime because slander was likely to lead to a breach of the public tranquility.

Defamation was committed when a person, by means of a distributed document printed or not printed, imputed to another the commission of a crime or imputed "facts . . . intended to impair or destroy the good fame or the esteem or the social consideration" which the individual enjoys (Article 2). Outrage refers solely to the spoken word. An outrage was committed when a person defamed a person publicly and orally. There were two other differences between defamation and outrage besides the medium of communication. First, an outrage encompassed the same criteria as defamation, imputing a crime or an immorality to another, but it also included all words that vilified the reputation of another. Second, malice was crucial in proving outrage but not defamation. With defamation, the law assumed malice on the part of the writer; with outrage, the victim had to show that the accused intentionally spoke so as to vilify him or her with actual malice. In both cases, the truth was a valid defense. According to Articles 5 and 6, if the facts alleged were true, this constituted grounds for dismissal of the charges. But the onus was on the accused to prove the truth of the words uttered.

If defamation was proved as a *délit*, then it was punishable "from the third to the fourth degree in the House of Correction." If it was an offense, then it warranted a second- or third-degree punishment. If it was a contravention, then it was punished by police penalties. Outrage constituted only a second-degree *délit* or contravention—if the former, then punishable with a custodial sentence of the first or second degree in the house of correction; if the latter, then it was punishable by police penalties.[1] There was an explicit class bias to the laws on defamation and outrage. Article 14: "In cases of defamation, or outrage, the high social position of the person defamed or outraged, the character and the dignity of the individual, as well as the greater gravity and publicity of the imputation, shall be considered discretional aggravations of the offence. The judge must consider such circumstances in fixing the punishment within the limits determined by law." We shall see shortly that judges and magistrates also took gender into account when meting out punishment for outrage.

In defining the slander law in this manner the British had two main goals in mind. The first was to provide a mechanism for British officials and pro-British Greeks to combat the machinations of the nationalist popular press. Through the defamation laws, it was hoped that the worst excesses of the press could be controlled without having to resort to the very illiberal measure of actually denying the Greeks a free press. Second, the very broad nature of the law against verbal outrage was intended to provide a means for men to contest honor and reputation without recourse to violence. The new law produced an unintended result: women by the thousands began to incorporate the courts into their disputes over reputation. It is this realm of activity that this chapter examines.

Slander by the Numbers

The rich archival materials left by the Anglo-Greek criminal justice system allows us to analyze its operation in detail. As a sampling strategy, I selected sixteen years from the forty-eight during which the British controlled the islands. I introduced an element of stratification to ensure coverage. So, three to four years from each decade were selected, but which years in each decade were determined randomly. In order to examine the operation of the system in its entirety, I recorded data from all levels: complaints and warrants, constables' reports, arrest registers, court proceedings from all levels of the judiciary, sentences and convictions, prison records, and correspondence inside the criminal justice system and between its functionaries and the colonial officers. I employ data from all of these levels in this examination of slander cases. However, only two of the seven islands are included: they are Kerkira, the largest island and city, and Kefallenia, the second largest.

Ionian islanders lodged with the police 2,605 formal complaints for slander, including both *délits* and contraventions, during the sixteen sample years (this would suggest that the total number of complaints would have been close to 8,000 for the period of the protectorate). The overwhelming majority of cases involved the lesser offense of a contravention; the exact ratio was 92 percent contraventions and 8 percent *délits*. I recorded aggregate data on each of these complaints, and then selected a subset of 2 percent of them for detailed examination of the police logbook, and the police and magistrate's court proceedings. Since a large but as yet undetermined portion of cases never went beyond the complaint stage, the 2 percent sample is larger than it appears at first glance. Before discussing the data in detail, let me make some generalizations about them.

Table 2.   Distribution of Arrest Warrants for All Crimes and for Slander in Ten of the Sixteen Sample Years

Year	All Crimes	Slander	% Slander
1823	370	70	19%
1830	1,565	281	18%
1835	2,507	369	15%
1843	1,539	238	15%
1844	953	61	6%
1845	604	60	10%
1850	724	58	8%
1851	424	24	6%
1856	1,495	366	24%
1859	2,032	454	22%

r squared = 0.91

It seems apparent that the propensity of Greeks to complain officially to the police varied significantly over time, as did the rate at which they filed charges for slander. However, we cannot infer that there was a change in regard to slander per se because the rates for slander accusations and all crimes was highly correlated. Thus, when people availed themselves of the criminal justice system, they filed charges for slander at approximately the same rate as they did when they were utilizing the system to prosecute other offenses. I am not in a position to argue convincingly why the pattern varied so markedly over time. Some factors that I would suggest are:

1. During the liberal reform phase of the 1830s, British and Greek authorities endeavored to use public institutions as a mean of legitimizing British rule, and a crucial aspect of this policy was to make the criminal justice system far more easily accessible than it had been before (Gallant 1990).
2. Part of the reform package involved the introduction of "ethnic policing" in the form of imported Albanian and Corsican constables, and this policy seems to have made Greeks more inclined to involve the authorities because the Albanian police were seen as standing outside of the local social network and so it was thought by some that they would act as "honest brokers" (Giffard 1837: 54).
3. At the same time, in order to defray the administrative costs, the British instituted a policy whereby policemen were paid a fee for each warrant they served. This led to the police being far more amenable to issuing warrants for somewhat frivolous charges (CO 136/1254; Ansted 1863: 468). By the mid-1840s these policies had fallen into disrepute, and the fall in complaints was related to the new policies implemented between 1845 and 1854.[2]

We can turn now to an examination of the gendered difference between men and women regarding slander. First, it was the crime that more than any other brought women into contact with the criminal justice system. I should point out that women, even including slander cases, were largely absent from the historical record of crime: women appeared in the archives either as victims or perpetrators in only 10 percent of the cases recorded. When they did appear, slander was often involved. They were present in some capacity in 37 percent of all slander cases. In two-thirds of the cases in which women were the victims of crime, the charge was slander. The next highest category was rape, which accounted for 24 percent. When women were accused of a crime, 72 percent of the time it was for slander. We are, therefore, dealing with a pattern of behavior that brought thousands of women into the public eye. If we extrapolate from the 2,605 complaints recorded in the one-third sample, then over the course of the British imperial period over 7,815 cases would have been recorded, of which approximately 2,100 would have involved women as the accuser. This produces an annual rate of 478 slander complaints per one hundred thousand women. Considering further that 95 percent of the time when a woman brought forth an accusation of slander it was against one or more other women, we must increase our estimate of the number of women who came before the courts. Adding this additional estimate to the figure cited above means that over 4,000 women entered the formal police and court records either as victims or perpetrators of slander. Even this figure underestimates the involvement of women in the courts because (*a*) in many cases there was more than one plaintiff, and (*b*) on numerous occasions, a man filed charges against a woman or group of women on behalf of his wife, mother, or daughter. Thus, a more accurate figure for women's involvement in slander cases would be closer to 6,000. How do these figures compare with other documented historical cases?

The consistory court records of early modern England have provided the raw material for a number of studies of women and slander. In the recent contribution, Gowing observed that while women were largely absent from the common-law courts they were present in large numbers in the ecclesiastical court records. She examined 230 cases involving women in the early seventeenth century. By 1633, 70 percent of the traffic in the consistory court involved slander, and women were involved in 85 percent of those (Gowing 1995: 27). Overwhelmingly the slander uttered involved some slur on the sexual behavior of another woman, invariably calling her a whore or some cognate phrase imputing that she was a prostitute. Most of the cases involving women never reached the stage where a verdict was rendered—80 percent were dismissed or resolved; when the magistrate did render a judgment, 81 percent of the time it was for the plaintiff (Gowing 1995: 41; 1996: 62). So far the similarities with the Greek case are marked.

One crucial difference does emerge, however. Gowing states that in seventeenth-century London, "Evil words lead [only] to more evil words" (1995: 39). As we shall see shortly, this was certainly not the situation in nineteenth-century Greece.

Mary Beth Norton has examined civil trials for slander in colonial Maryland. She found that women were largely absent from the courts and that when they did appear slander or defamation was the action that brought them before the bench (Norton 1987: 4–5). The single most prevalent slur was "whore," and as in Greece and England the courts usually found in favor of the plaintiff (1987: 37). Donna J. Spindel examined slander and defamation further in North Carolina, and she found a slightly different pattern. Statutes in this region of the South made criminal prosecution of slander more readily accessible than in other colonies. Women, she discovered, were almost completely absent from criminal prosecutions for slander (approximately 4 percent of cases), but they were far more active in civil suits: 63 percent of civil suits involved, 51 percent of the time as plaintiffs and 49 percent as defendants. The most common slur once again was "whore." Different from everywhere else studied so far, Carolinians did not bring each other to court to solve disputes over reputations; slander or defamation constituted only 17 percent of the criminal docket and 1 percent of the civil-court caseload (Spindel 1995).

The cases from the Ionian Islands fit well with a couple of patterns evident in the comparative data. First, slander was the crime or action that more than any other brought women into the legal system. Second, whether the cultural setting be early modern Italy (Cohen 1991; 1992; Cohen and Cohen 1993; Burke 1987), colonial and postrevolutionary America (in addition to Norton and Spindel, see King 1995a: 69; 1995b: 75–76), early modern England, or eighteenth- and nineteenth-century Canada (Moogk 1979: 535; Coombe 1991: 17), the single most common insult that constituted the slander was "whore." One aspect of the Greek case, however, does stand out, and that is the sheer volume of slander cases involving women. No place else studied to date witnessed the large number of female litigants and criminal defendants seen on the Ionian Islands. To explain why, we must examine the role and status of women in nineteenth-century Greece, and in particular we have to see the role that gossip played in women's lives.

Women and Gossip on Nineteenth-Century Ionian Islands

"I had stayed forever in the house. Forever in the house! Ah! . . . Trapped inside day and night, not being able to go out either to church or to walk" (Moutzan-Martinengou 1989 [1881]: 53). So wrote Elizabeth Moutzan-Martinengou, the daughter of a wealthy aristocratic family on Zakinthos in 1828. Frequently throughout her memoirs she wrote deploringly about the strict segregation of women from the public eye. Her assessment of the position of women in Greek society is amply supported by other sources. One Greek aristocrat explained to Viscount Kirkwall as she took him on a tour of a townhouse that the holes he saw cut into the bottoms of some of the bedchamber doors were so that women could be fitted for slippers by the cobbler without exposing themselves to the sight of a nonkinsman (Kirkwall 1986: 55–56). Other colonial officers and British travelers commented on the segregation of women (Kendrick 1882: 15; Davy 1842: 112–13, 142–43; Ansted 1863: 56–58).

Greek sources as well suggest that an ideology of gendered separate spheres flourished on the islands. In his poem "The Women of Zakinthos," Dionisios Solomos critically commented on the status and treatment of women on his home island (1944 [1823]). His views were benign compared to the scathing excoriation of Greek men's treatment of women penned by Andreas Laskaratos in his satire *The Mysteries of Kefallenia.* Women, he noted, moved from the anonymity and seclusion of their father's house to the dwelling of their husbands, where their new job was to bear children and to guard their good name. In his view, men treated women little better than servants (1981 [1836]: 11–12).

Primary sources devoted to the lives of nonaristocratic women are scarce. One of the few views we have pithily described the status of women thusly: "Young girls are pretty, but it quickly fades and they become old crows. When young and good-looking, they are shut-up; when married, their husbands are at first foolishly jealous and then cruelly indifferent. They [women] have to take a full share of all house and field work" (Ansted 1863: 57). A woman long resident on the islands gave Davy a more nuanced, insider's assessment. She told him that women's roles were sharply distinguished by class. "Those [women] of the higher order [live] in independent circumstances;

those of the lower, having no objection to go out and be employed in service; and an intermediate class, supporting themselves in part or entirely by needlework and embroidery, and who, like the upper class in these islands, lead a very secluded life" (Davy 1842: 141–42).

Recent studies of women's roles and the ideology of gender in the nineteenth century suggest that the situation of women as related by Davy held true for the rest of Greece as well (Sant Cassia 1992: 227; Bakalaki 1994; Gallant 2001: 105–7). The image of women's roles that I inferred from the sparse nineteenth-century sources is highly reminiscent of the one presented in ethnographic studies of "traditional" Greece in the recent past.

Two aspects about women's roles in society and the ideology of gender apparent in the ethnographic studies conducted in Greece are important to our examination of slander in the past. The first relates to the connection between honor and gender. Recurrently one of the crucial elements of a man's status in the community of men was the reputation that the women of his household enjoyed. A woman's reputation, moreover, was founded upon the public perception of her as being chaste, modest, subservient, and a good housewife (Bottomley 1986; Campbell 1964; Dubisch 1974; 1986; Friedl 1986; Herzfeld 1983; Lazaridis 1995; Salamone 1987; Salamone and Stanton 1986). The second point refers to the ideology of gendered separate spheres. Numerous commentators have observed that there is a marked demarcation of activity spaces between men and women that roughly corresponds to a division between public and private realms, between the domestic and outside world (Dubisch 1974; Friedl 1986; Herzfeld 1986; Antman 1990).

These two points are connected: a woman's reputation, in theory, rested on her abiding by this cultural code of gendered space. Transgressors risked having their "good" name sullied. Many have pointed out that the appearance of gender roles in Greece and the reality of women's lives were different. Strict segregation and absolute adherence to the rules were never fully enforced. But those who violated the ideal without good cause risked their reputation. The question, then, is how and by whom was "good cause" determined? The mechanism by which this occurred was gossip. "The character of gossip at Ambéli," du Boulay observed, "is determined by the various features of the society—the nature of the value system, the importance of a limited number of roles which express these values and which provide ideal standards of behavior, the privacy of the home, the publicity of communal life, the intense relevance of every member of the community to every other member, and the unceasing competition for reputation. It is consistent also with these conditions for gossip that it is an activity indulged in pre-eminently by women" (1974: 204). Women in Greece used gossip as a means of enforcing conformity to society's proscribed roles and of punishing those who violated them (du Boulay 1974; 1976; Campbell 1964; Dubisch 1986; Friedl 1986; Herzfeld 1983; 1986; 1991; Lazaridis 1995; Zinovieff 1991; see also Gilmore 1979; Mintz 1997; Murphy 1985).

Given the other similarities between rural Greece during the twentieth century and the Ionian Islands during the nineteenth century, we would expect that gossip would have been important in the latter just as it is in the former. And there is limited evidence that indicates that it was. Solomos's touching poem "The Poisoned Girl" (1826) relates the story of a young woman from Zakinthos who was so wounded by the gossip circulating about her that she took her own life. The plot of Antonios Matesis's (1981 [1836]) bitingly satirical play *The Basil Plant* hinges in part on the backbiting and gossiping that goes on among women. Almost invariably in their statements to the police or in court for slander trials, women talked about gossip and how the case now before the magistrate stemmed from the talk of women. British commentators concurred (Spencer 1853: 222; Ansted 1863: 49; Kirkwall 1864: 8). These statements echo the sentiments Greek men expressed to du Boulay in 1965 that "women . . . do nothing but gossip" (1974: 205). But a paradox arises when we compare the situation on the Ionian Islands during the British occupation with the contemporary one depicted by anthropologists. The practice of gossip seems very similar, but women in the present do not go to court to contest reputations. Indeed, the very cultural rules that regulate gossiping pretty much preclude women from intruding into the masculine domain of the courts. How, then, do we explain why at one specific moment in the past the discourse about reputation among women moved from the doorways of their houses, the fountains where they collectively gathered to get water, or the communal ovens where they baked bread to the magistrate's chamber at the police station and the decorous halls of the Palace of Justice?

Slander in Action

We can begin to formulate such an explanation by examining the types of slander cases women brought before the criminal justice system. I emphasize again a point made earlier: in the Ionian system of justice slander was a crime, not a tort, and it was tried in the criminal, not the ecclesiastical or civil, courts.

Clementina Atavatis accused Andreoulla Karella, both residents of the town of Kerkira, of calling her a Magdalene in public. Atavatis, with a full entourage in tow, paraded to the police and duly swore out a warrant. After collecting the requisite fee, a constable third class served Karella with a summons. Unlike in most cases, both women appeared before the police magistrate's court on September 23, 1835. Atavatis produced five witnesses, all women from the same neighborhood, and Karella produced two of her own to rebut them. The truth was on trial. Each side told its tale of gossip and slander. Moreover, compromise was impossible. The insults exchanged had pushed the matter too far for that. Unlike most cases, then, the case proceeded to a verdict. After hearing the testimony, the magistrate found Karella guilty. In the magistrate's view she had not met her burden of proving the truth of her statement that Atavatis was a whore or an adulteress. He fined her $2, charged her with court costs, and bound her over to hold her tongue—at least with reference to Atavatis's alleged promiscuous ways (IAK EA 1317: October 5, 1835).

Age seemed little impediment to women determined to protect their good names. A 110-year-old widow from the town of Argostoli gambled and lost when she prosecuted her neighbor for calling her a whore. The magistrate decided that, though the words uttered by the accused were patently false, no damage had been done to the accuser's reputation because the slander was totally unbelievable. So, he found the defendant not guilty: leaving the elderly widow, of course, liable for court costs of £1 3s 10d. Only an emergency resolution of the Ionian senate, in which the legislators voted to expend money from the public purse to pay her court costs, kept the aggrieved geriatric out of prison (CO 136/748/15, enclosure 131: local Director of Police John Stevens to Captain N. P. Lawrence, October 20, 1847 PRO).

Dionisia Chiliakis sought to silence the vicious tongue of Konstantina Konderas. On November 9, 1843, she made her way to the capital town of Kerkira from her tiny village of Valanio, accompanied by six friends and kinswomen. Upon arrival in town they went to the police station, where she swore out a complaint in which she alleged, and her witnesses affirmed, that Konderas was a liar when she gossiped about Chiliakis being a Magdalene. Her reputation, she argued, must be above reproach, and so she wanted the police to make the insults stop. In the column of the warrant logbook reserved for comments regarding the disposition of the complaint, the scribe has left his comment on the case: he drew a thick, black diagonal line across the entry, meaning, I would argue, that he knew the case would go no further (IAK EA 1154: November 20, 1843).

On November 18, 1834, Violetta Markopoulos confronted her opponent even more daringly. On her own, she made the arduous journey from the village of Lakithra to the capital town of Argostoli on the island of Kefallenia and filed a complaint against her sister-in-law Paraskevi Markopoulos. She accused Paraskevi of spreading lies about her by telling other women that she was a Magdalene and that she had not been a virgin when she married her husband, Spiros. Violetta told the desk sergeant that she wanted Paraskevi to "eat her words" before it was too late. She feared that unless she did so "blood will flow, and God will not forgive it." What she meant was that the Markopoulos brothers, Spiros and Efthemios, were likely to come to blows or worse if the gossiping did not cease, and she, like all Greek Orthodox people, knew that fratricide was an affront to the almighty. She was thus asking the court to put the lie to her sister-in-law's poisoned words (TIAK 154: December 2, 1834).

These episodes, along with the one that opened this chapter, exemplify those cases in which women filed slander complaints against other women. In every instance, the insult involved a slur on a woman's reputation based on an alleged transgression of socially accepted sexual behavior, and invariably *Magdalene* was the preferred term of approbation. This fits exceedingly well with the comparative data. As noted earlier, in every study conducted on women and slander, the single most prevalent insult was "whore." In the first case in this section, both of the women resided in the same working-class neighborhood in the town of Kerkira. As in the chapter-opening vignette, they were ensconced in the same network of female sociability. Given the relatively restricted occupational opportunities in this port town, both were probably the wives of laborers, and may even have had jobs themselves as domestic servants or vendors—the two largest categories of female workers in the town. Thus, both would have been quite accustomed to operating on the fringes of the supposedly male public spaces, and indeed transgressing them when necessary. These women fit well with the groups studied by Gowing in London, Garrioch in Paris, and Cohen in Rome.

The last two cases present some important differences. In both of them, village women made the difficult and drastic decision to travel to the town in order to file a complaint. The rich ethnographic and historical record from rural Greece suggests that it was in the countryside that the strictures of the separate-spheres ideology of gender relations were most rigidly enforced. For women, either in a group or, even more significantly, singly, to violate such a central value as the prohibition of contact between women and nonkinsmen or strangers suggests just how important a social act the trip to town and the invasion of the male enclave of the police station or the court would have been for them. The third example represents about 15 percent of the cases in which kinswomen, usually affinal rather than consanguineous kindred, were the ones exchanging insults. All the cases cited indicate what it was the women sought from the swearing out of a complaint: they wanted the insults and the gossip to stop. The Markopoulos case provides a clue as to why cessation of the sexual slander was so important. The blood of kinsmen could well be shed if the slander did not stop and the woman's reputation restored. I shall return to this last point shortly.

There was another category of cases involving women as victims or slanderers that is different from those discussed above. In almost 40 percent of the cases in which a woman was accused of slander, a man on behalf of an aggrieved woman filed the complaint—invariably a kinswoman of his. On August 11, 1830, for example, Dino Fachiolas from the village of Krinias on Kerkira filed charges against Elena Fachiolas, the wife of his cousin Anthony, and her daughter Anna for insulting his wife by calling her a Magdalene in public (IAK EA 1318: August 11, 1830). This episode exemplifies the normal case of this type: a man goes to the police on behalf of his wife. The second most frequent category involved fathers going to court on behalf of their daughters, as in the case of Vincenzo Astanitas vs. Carola Vlacchos from Kerkira in May 1830 (IAK EA 1318: May 17, 1830). His reasoning was clear: if the gossip about his daughter being a whore did not stop, he would never find her a husband. The third type of case involved adult men acting on behalf of their widowed mothers. There were few of these. In most instances, widows actively took the lead in publicly confronting their defamers.

I want now to compare and contrast slander cases involving men from those of women. Ninety percent of the time men slandered other men. Moreover, as with women, it was invariably men from the same social milieu. I have not finished completing my reconstruction of neighborhoods in the town, and so this inference is based on the residential pattern manifested by those who lived in a village and who filed a complaint. Invariably, they accused covillagers. Also similar to the cases involving women, erotic words were the weapons of choice. In 85 percent of the complaints the insult that cut the most was *keratás*, or "cockold." I have shown elsewhere that this word had enormous evocative power (Gallant 1996; 2000). The next most common insult was to call a man a liar. There were other cases that I have characterized as nonerotic but which are problematic. In one episode, for example, a man complains that another man persists in calling him "shitty pants" (IAK EA 853: November 14, 1840). In another, a man swears out a warrant against another man whom he thinks urinated in his doorway (IAK EA 425: August 1, 1846)! That provocatively pissing in public could be considered an act of slander suggests just how broadly men deciphered acts as insults. Overwhelmingly, men clashed over insults regarding the sexual behavior of their women. Unlike in the war of words among women, however, in which insults were most often leveled indirectly through gossip, men usually confronted one another. Often it occurred in taverns and wineshops or other all-male venues. In some cases, the exchange transpired in public space. There are numerous examples in which groups of men paraded after a chosen victim and sang dirty ditties about his wife's promiscuity and his wearing the horns of the cuckold. What is clear is that the discourse among men and the one among women were integrated; each of them drew from the same taproot of meaning: women's sexuality. I return to this point in my conclusion, but first we need to examine how the criminal justice system handled slander cases based on gender.

Slander in the Criminal Justice System

One aspect stands out with startling clarity when we analyze how the criminal justice system dealt with cases involving men and those involving women: for women the crucial social act was the swearing out of the arrest, because they could have no realistic expectations that the case would be taken to a higher court. If we look at the full data set, it appears that 75 percent of the formal complaints for slander or defamation were made by men and 25 percent were made by women. Both

Table 3.   Slander Cases of Men and Women in 1823, 1835, and 1843

	Men		Women	
	Accused	*Convicted*	*Accused*	*Convicted*
1823				
Warrants Served	52		18	
Total Tried	44	39	7	5
Police Magistrate	12	11	4	2
Correctional Court	28	24	3	3
Criminal Court	4	4	0	0
1835				
Warrants Served	323		46	
Total Tried	303	287	17	14
Police Magistrate	137	127	13	12
Correctional Court	154	149	4	2
Criminal Court	12	11	0	0
1843				
Warrants Served	202		36	
Total Tried	179	165	13	11
Police Magistrate	62	58	12	10
Correctional Court	109	101	1	1
Criminal Court	8	6	0	0

groups were thus regularly using the system. Table 3 presents data on slander cases from three of the sixteen sample years: 1823, 1835, and 1843.

In 1823, seventy arrests warrants were issued for slander: fifty-two (74 percent) against men, and eighteen against women (26 percent). Only seven of the cases involving a female defendant went before any branch of the court system. Sixty-one percent of the cases did not even proceed to the stage of a preliminary hearing before the police magistrate. Of the seven cases that did go forward, four were determined to be contraventions of outrage in the second degree punishable by police penalties, three were first-degree contraventions brought before the correctional court, and none constituted a *délit*. Contrast this with cases among men. Forty-four of the fifty-two cases of slander went before a tribunal of some sort. The police magistrate dealt with twelve second-degree contraventions, the correctional court heard twenty-eight more serious ones, and the criminal court adjudicated on four defamation *délits*.

The data from 1835 and 1843 tell much the same story but in greater detail. In 1835, 369 slander accusations were recorded. Men were the accused in 323 of them and women in 46. Only 17 (37 percent) of the cases involving women went before the courts, whereas 303 (94 percent) of those involving men did. Women's cases were overwhelmingly dealt with in the lowest tier of the court system, whereas once again those in which men were on trial went before either the correctional or the criminal courts. The same pattern emerges with the 1843 data as well. Women's accusations then were far more unlikely to result in a hearing of any form; on average, two-thirds of cases where a woman was the defendant never made it past the stage of swearing out a warrant. Of those cases that did go forward, most were considered minor contraventions and were dealt with by the police magistrate. Rarely was a woman prosecuted for criminal outrage or defamation: all female offenses were treated as contraventions, not *délits*. This was not the case with men. Approximately 90 percent of the episodes involving men went to the courts. Between 50 and 60 percent of men's cases were heard by the correctional court, and only men's slanderous words were considered criminal offenses. The gatekeepers of the criminal justice system, then, treated slander very differently when women rather than men were involved.

The courts treated men and women differently when it came to sentencing as well. Where it was evenhanded was in finding the accused guilty better than 90 percent of the time. In the police magistrate's court, when a man was found guilty of slander, on average, he was fined $4 and made to pay court costs. For women, the average fine was $2 and court costs, and in a considerable number of cases, she only had to pay court costs. Accompanying the police penalties was the practice of making the convicted person swear to desist slandering the defendant. Among cases heard by the correctional court, men received custodial sentences in the house of correction ranging from one to sixty days, with the average sentence being seven and a half days and with three, four, and six days being the most frequently imposed sentences. Among women, the average sentence was four days; the stiffest one meted out was twelve, and the most common sentence (accounting for one-quarter of the cases) was two days. The criminal justice system treated men's and women's slander cases differently. Most episodes involving female litigants never went further than the swearing out of a complaint. The overwhelming majority of men's cases routinely went forward to the police magistrate's or the correctional court.

Women, Men, and Slander

In the way of a conclusion, let me draw together some of the points made so far and explicate further their social and cultural significance. At a basic level, my study reinforces the observation made by Gowing and others that, rather than being passive victims of a male-dominated legal system, women in the past were active agents in their own right. This conclusion may have even greater saliency in this case given that the system of patriarchal control and male dominance was greater in Greece than in early modern London, Paris, or Rome. In the rush to redress a long-standing lacuna by writing women into the historical narrative, there has been a tendency to create an artificial division between the contests of men and women over status. Gowing, for example, though she at some points recognizes that they are connected, still sees the trading of insults and the leveling of defamation charges of women against women and men against men as separate discourses (Gowing 1994: 30). It is this conclusion that requires revision.

Honor manifested as status, reputation, and esteem was the central constitutive element of nineteenth-century Greek society. For a man, honor equated to public, collective recognition that he was in control of those things that mattered most: women, property, and prowess. This last refers to his ability to defend and protect the first two. For a woman, status was predicated on her perceptible abilities as a *nikokyria*, or manager of a household, and on her reputation as a chaste, modest sexual being—to use a local idiom, that she possessed *dropi* (shame). The honor of both men and women was a collective, shared commodity. The esteem in which one was held reflected upon the other, and together they determined the honor of the household. Thus, a threat to the reputation either of a husband or his wife constituted an assault on both. Ionian islanders believed that honor was a limited good and that contests for it were a zero-sum game. And, a vitally important element in the everyday struggle for status was the exchange of verbal insults.

Men and women in this culture wielded words as weapons in the struggles for status. Rather than being distinct, the trading of insults and slanders by men and women were integral parts of the same discourse. But there were two different gendered sets of strategies. In the domain of men, any challenge to reputation mandated an aggressive response. Theirs was a masculine ethos in which the restoration of status was linked to violence, or at least the willingness to rebuff provocations with violence. As I have shown elsewhere, no insult cut deeper than to call a man a cuckold. Symbolically, the cuckold was the antithesis of a real man. To be cuckolded meant that a man had lost control of those things considered most important in this culture. Moreover, in theory at least, the man had to act autonomously to restore his status. In chapter 6, we saw through an examination of over five thousand assaults, attempted homicides, and homicides that, almost invariably before a knife fight took place, the last word uttered before the daggers were drawn was *cuckold*.

The langauge of insult among women and men, then, drew on the same metaphor: sexuality. Moreover, women's sexuality was at the heart of the matter. *Keratás* and "Magdalene" were two sides of the same erotic coin. In spite of Solomos's powerful invocation of the killing power of women's gossip, when a woman called another woman a whore/adulteress, she initiated a contest that rarely resulted in a woman's death but could easily and frequently did end with her husband being mutilated, killed, or imprisoned. Just as when men waged their wars of words, so too did women walk a fine line. They could challenge the reputation of another woman through gossip, and by extension put at stake the honor of her kinsmen, by slandering her as a Magdalene. But as Bergman has noted, "In contrast to other communicative genres, gossip seems to admit no internal terminating mechanism" (1993: 138; Merry 1984; Tebbutt 1995). Men confronted offensive speech by escalating the contest to violence; in the masculine domain, the knife was the terminating mechanism. This was not so with women. There are very few cases in which women resorted to violence. But failure by the opponents to respond to slander diminished their reputation, and could even eventually lead to male violence. Women filed slander complaints as an integral strategy in these contests. The involvement of a formal, public institution, the courts, could provide a terminating mechanism to women's gossip. How then did women use the system?

For women, the crucial social act seems to have been the lodging of a formal complaint with the police. This was so for a number of reasons. By violating the culturally defined male space of the police station, a woman demonstrated the seriousness with which she took the insult. She thus challenged the veracity of the claim by opening herself up to the very types of gossip she was seeking to halt. Note the fanfare that often accompanied the visit to the police station in the episodes recounted earlier. Women were in fact drawing attention to their flagrant violation of society's proscribed boundaries of gendered space. As has often been noted, honor and reputation require risk-taking. Ideally in Ionian Island Greek society, a woman was not to be seen in public unaccompanied either by kinsmen or other women. To do so would have provided grounds for gossip about her modesty and decorum. In this case, by invading the male domain of the city police station, the offended woman purposely exposed her reputation. But by doing so, she also challenged her insulter to step out into the public limelight. Moreover, she had to stand exposed in public and recount her slander, and provide some facts to support her allegations. In essence, the offended party dared her opponent to confront her in public, to repeat her gossip before an audience of men, and to risk her own reputation by being found herself to be a liar.

In addition, by paying the hefty sum of $1 (the equivalent of two days' wages for a dockworker), she exposed her reputation as a *nikokyria* to public scrutiny. Moreover, a woman had to be sure and pay for the warrant. If she did not, she risked being fined or even imprisoned—as Maria, the wife of Leo Moraitis, from Klismata found out. She swore out a warrant for slander against another women, but was delinquent in paying for it. A fine of six shillings and ten pence was added to the initial fee. When she failed to pay that, the police magistrate issued a warrant for her arrest (TIAK/Correspondence Books/1832–33). Moreover, she would stay in prison until she worked off debt to the state; the rate of recompense was one shilling per day.

For women, therefore, it was unnecessary for the dispute to be taken to the next level in the judicial system. It was not the decisions of the court that restored a woman's reputation, but the public act of her putting it all on the line by filing the complaint that did. Above all, restoration of reputation entailed risk-taking. Women's cases did not go farther in the court system because to do so would have increased the risks disproportionately for both the accuser and the accused. If the plaintiff pressed the charges, then she exposed herself to profound shame. An acquittal signaled the total humiliation of the plaintiff. The court verdict transformed gossip into fact. She would be socially branded as an adulteress and, if nothing else, her reputation would have been irredeemably sullied. Her husband could possibly prosecute her for adultery, avail himself of the unwritten law and kill her, or turn to canon law and divorce her (CO 136/1306/2. Barton to Lane, January 3, 1862 PRO). Likewise the defendant sought compromise. A conviction could ruin her. She would have publicly been forced to eat her words; she would have been branded by an impartial agent as a liar; she would have called into question her own reputation as a *nikokyria*. Often the women agreed to desist gossiping and the case would be dropped by mutual consent. So plaintiffs failed to appear for a hearing and the case would proceed no further. Defendants received an admonishment and scolding from the magistrate and swore never to gossip about the plaintiff again (TIAK 1324/12: May 7, 1843). In return the plaintiff dropped the charges. The aggrieved party felt that her reputation was recouped and so the case went no further. In sum, by swearing out a warrant, a woman accomplished two things: she restored her reputation by turning the bite of slander back on the defamer, and she acted preemptively to stop the gossip about her being a Magdalene. The defendant avoided possible humiliation and punishment, but because her words were never proven false, the truth of her accusations remained ambiguous. Each side could claim partial vindication. In addition, and just as importantly, by acting in this way both prevented their contest over reputation from entering the male domain. Because in that domain, words might wound but knives could kill.

How do we account for the paradoxes referred to earlier? Why did so many more women on the Ionian Islands than elsewhere use the courts to prosecute slander, and why did the practice flourish for only a discrete moment in the past? The answer to both questions lay in the criminal justice system developed on the islands by the British. In their endeavor to enshrine law as the core mechanism of social control and as the ideological justification for their rule, the British democratized the criminal justice system in significant ways. It was meant to provide a mechanism that would enable men to resolve disputes in nonviolent ways, and eventually it did. But their policy also had an unintended result. Women utilized the new system in ways and in numbers that were totally unexpected by the British. Women saw in the slander laws and the easy accessibility of the lower court system possible weapons to be wielded in their contests over reputation. Gossip moved from the usual enclaves of women to the male public spaces of the police station and the courts. My data on a related issue are sparse, but preliminary analysis suggests that women saw the potential of the slander laws well before men and that they employed them in large numbers well before men did. As the potential of the courts to act as an arbiter in disputes of honor became apparent and as other policies made male dueling more difficult (Gallant 2000a), men turned to the courts. We see then an increasing masculinization of the courts during the period of the protectorate. The crucial change came in 1864, when the islands were ceded to the Kingdom of Greece. The Greek criminal justice system supplanted the Anglo-French-Venetian hybrid, and one major consequence of this transition was that access to the police and the courts became far more restricted. Women's wars of words moved back to where they had taken place before the British and where they would through the twentieth century, and where they have been observed by ethnographers: in homes, streets, and other "female" spaces.

There was, however, one comparatively brief moment when women intruded into the male-dominated public space and seized upon a new opportunity created by the actions of a hegemonic government and used the formal institution created by the state creatively and purposefully to achieve their own ends.

CHAPTER EIGHT

"We Are the Christians"

Religion, Identity, and Colonial Rule

Two images, one verbal and the other visual, capture some essential elements of the dynamic processes of rule, resistance, accommodation, and identity in the peculiar situation of the Ionian Islands. The first, while initially a drawing, now is only accessible to us from a verbal description by a British official. In an angry missive to the Colonial Office, George Bowen (1862: 335) described with great outrage a depiction in the radical newspaper *Rizopastis* on May 6, 1850, which showed Queen Victoria standing to one side and the personification of the Ionian Islands on the other. Her Majesty was portrayed in the guise of a Temptress, while the demure female depiction of the islands appeared as the Tempted. The caption above her head has Victoria saying "Fall Down and Worship Me." The threatened Hellenic maiden turns her head away and with an extended arm rebukes her overture with the words "Get thee behind me Satan!"

The second image is a watercolor painting (see next page) by an unknown artist to commemorate the unification of the islands with the Kingdom of Greece in 1864. This is an extremely powerful image. It presents the symbolic joining of the islands to the Kingdom of Greece. Dominating the center of the picture is the Ionian Islands personified as a demure maiden standing before the Motherland. Mother Greece extends a hand above her head, preparing to crown the maiden with an olive wreath. The central scene of unification is framed by two sets of pairs. Standing behind the Ionian Islands is Ioannis Kapodistrias, the first son of Kerkira, first president of Greece,

Figure 2. "Union of the Ionian Islands with Greece, 1864,"
artist unknown, the National Historical Museum, Athens, Greece.

and arch-foe of the British. Behind Mother Greece stand Patriarch Gregorios and Bishop Germanos, two clerical heroes of the Greek Revolution. Gregorios was the leader of the Orthodox Church at the time the revolution began and was killed in Istanbul by the Ottoman authorities; Germanos was the priest whose actions were instrumental to the start of the conflict. Forming the other axis is the figure of Ilias Zervos-Iakovatos, a leading nationalist radical from Kefallenia whose actions led to the British departure. Standing opposite him and dominating the right side of the picture is the personification of the British Empire. Note how the figure is draped in the crimson cloak and miter of the western Christian faiths and how the cloak of religion conceals the figure of a military man whose boots and sword peek out. Religion permeates the entire scene. The nationalist struggle for unification is symbolically connected to the Greek War of Independence. But of especial importance is the way that the British Empire is depicted: here we see the cloak of religion masking the hard reality of the coercive force of colonial rule as symbolized by the sword.

Religion shaped and informed the ways that both Greeks and Britons experienced dominion during the period of colonial rule. Both cultures considered themselves to be "Christian" peoples, and each believed that the other lacked the virtues that accrued to a Christian nation. Yet each appreciated the centrality of religion for the other.

Religion and British Identity

"In [a] broad sense, then, Protestantism lay at the core of British identity." (Colley 1992: 369). As Linda Colley demonstrates in her analysis of the formation of a British national identity during the eighteenth and early nineteenth centuries, Britons came to see themselves as the chosen people, and a crucial element of that status was related to the establishment of the empire. "For most Victorians, the massive overseas empire which was the fruit of so much successful warfare represented final and conclusive proof of Great Britain's providential destiny. God had entrusted Britons with empire" (Colley 1992: 368). That religion was central to Anglo-Irish relations needs no elaboration (Wolfe 1994). It also formed a key cog in imperialism as well (Miller 1994).

"May Greece henceforth advance on firmer ground under the enlightened banner of Christianity. For Christianity has power, not only to raise up fallen nationalities, but to bear them onwards to the highest pinnacle of freedom, of virtue and of happiness" (Kirkwall 1864: 177). So Viscount Kirkwall opined in his final speech to the Ionian Senate, placing an apposite coda on the forty-eight years of British colonial rule. His words aptly capture what was a central goal of the Colonial Office on the Greek isles: that the duty of the protectorate was to bring Christian enlightenment to the Greeks (Ansted 1863: 449). Forcing conversion, however, was never British policy on the islands. They did not challenge the Orthodox Church directly, though they did regularly mock church rituals and beliefs as base superstitions and idolatry, as "empty ceremonial and cunning priestcraft" (Mure 1842: 33; Kendrick 1822: 107; Williams 1820: 167). The following from Charles Tuckerman is typical of the vituperation heaped on the practice of religion on the islands: "While the simple-minded peasant of Corfu continues to believe that the body of St. Spiridon rises from its precious casket, where it is daily worshipped, and daily parades the cornfields and walks the sea on certain nights to bless the work of the husbandmen, their faith will be as dry and repulsive as the mummified remains they ignorantly bow down to" (Tuckerman 1872: 195–96). The British blamed the moral failings of the Greeks not on Orthodoxy per se but on the clergy. Drawn from "the scum of the earth" (Hennen cited in Martin 1856: 140), the priests were directly responsible for the moral failings of the Greeks. Only by breaking the hold of the clergy could moral enlightenment be brought to the Greeks.

The vehicles for doing so were to be education of the masses, reform of the church, and co-optation of the "respectable people" (CO 136/1318: Sutherland to Fraser, May 27, 1841 PRO). Representatives of the London Missionary Society arrived on the islands soon after the establishment of the protectorate. Under the leadership of the Reverends Lowndes and Croggan, Methodist Lancastrian schools were set up on all of the islands with the explicit purpose of spreading both literacy and religious education. By 1828, over thirty such schools had been established. For the teaching of young Greek girls, the Ladies of Scotland sent Miss Goddard, Miss Anderson, and Mr. and Mrs. Dickson (Wilson 1839: 215–21). On the government's side, successive administrations from Thomas Maitland onward endeavored to cultivate and promote clerics who were pro-British. As we shall see shortly, all of these measures contribute to the complicated contest over religion, identity, and colonial rule.

Religion and Greek Identity

Orthodoxy provided a crucial, if not *the* crucial, element in Greek identity. This was the case on the Ionian Islands even though they had not been incorporated into the Islamic Ottoman Empire, where the millet system of rule had categorized the subject peoples of the empire according to religion (Runciman 1985). The Millet-i Rum, or Roman Millet, legally and practically collapsed all members of the Orthodox faith into a single category, regardless of their natal language and culture. Ionian Islanders already existed in a society under the Venetians in which religion was a primary cultural marker, distinguishing the Catholic rulers, the sizeable Jewish community, and the Orthodox majority. During the Greek Enlightenment of the late eighteenth century, an identity that conflated being Orthodox with being "Greek" developed, largely in the writings of diaspora intellectuals, including some prominent islanders. In the years leading up to the Greek Revolution of 1821, the sense that religion and ethnicity were one and the same became even stronger among the islanders, and when the war broke out, as we saw in chapter 1, thousands of Ionians flocked to the banner of Greek liberation, and thousands of others supported it from afar. The war forged ever stronger the connection between Orthodoxy and Greekness in the minds of the islanders. In other words, being Orthodox meant that they were Greeks. The foundation of a free Greek Orthodox polity just across the narrow straits that separated the islands from the mainland only heightened their awareness of their identity as Greeks. Increasingly then, for the Ionian Islanders in the nineteenth century their being Orthodox and their being Greek were one and the same.

We can come to grasp the centrality of religion to the way that Greeks and Britons experienced dominion through an examination of how the Colonial Office tried to use the Orthodox Church to construct a mechanism of social control and by how the Greeks responded to the initiative to curb crime through the application of excommunication for secular crimes.

Religion and Rule, Religion and Resistance: Excommunication

Every bone in his body ached. Spiridon Apostolatos had already been awake all night, and, after twelve hours of backbreaking labor on a small caique in the freezing cold and rain, he wanted nothing more than to return to his village of Koulourata and have a hot meal before going to bed. As the youngest member of the crew, he was often stuck with the dirty jobs (TIAK Excommunication Decree 121; hereafter the decrees are cited as TIAK ED plus the number). So, instead of going home, he found himself standing on the cold sand of the beach at Sami, Kefallenia, tying the heavy baskets filled with fish to the wooden saddle on his donkey's back. Securing the ropes was proving to be a hard task. Plus, he was in a hurry. Before sunrise, he had to be well on his way to Argostoli, the capital of the island, and he had at least a four-hour trip ahead of him (Napier 1833: 12). His boss, Master Ioannis Floratos, had made it quite clear that he wanted the fish in the market and ready for sale as soon as possible. It was not a great catch, just some bonito, red mullet, and gunnard, but it would bring in a good profit because prices were high (Gallant 1985: 61, 64, 66). All in all, it had been a good night's work for him and the crew.

In order to reach the main road, Spiridon had to travel the length of the beach, skirt the edge of the village, and then cross the "Great Breakwater," which protected the inner part of the harbor. As he walked along leading the donkey, he kept scanning the underbrush for movement. After all, two months ago during the Festival of the Presentation of the Virgin, bandits had attacked one of his mates. After soundly thrashing his friend, they had made off with his donkey and the baskets of fish it was carrying. As Spiridon approached the breakwater, he sensed that something was amiss, but before he could act nine people surrounded him. Some were armed with *psilithia*, or pruning knives—a lethal weapon carried by all peasants—and others with clubs. Even in the dark, he could see their garb well enough to know that they were peasants. As they spoke, he began to recognize them. They were all from Haliotata, a village of about five hundred people not far from his own: the brothers Fioravandes, Yerasimos and Panayis, the sons of Vangelis; Yerasimos's wife and their teenage son Evangelinas; Yersimos Vasilias and his wife; Konstantinos Rasias; Spiridon Solomos; and Panayis Andrutsos Spathis. They demanded that he give them the donkey. When Spiridon refused, they attacked him. As he lay in pain on the sand, he caught a glimpse of them as they led the beast off into the morning mists. Spiridon knew that it was going to be a long day.

The robbery of Spiridon Apostolatos took place on the morning of January 12, 1863. It was neither a particularly vicious nor audacious crime. Indeed, we are struck by its seeming triviality. Numerous crimes far more serious than this one—indeed, far more violent than this one—occurred daily on Kefallenia. Certain events in its aftermath, however, render it historically significant. In particular, the episode provides us with an entry point to examine how the British attempted to use religion as a means of exerting social control over Greek society.

The crime was reported in the normal manner. Each tier in the highly centralized administrative hierarchy of the British-designed criminal justice system had an opportunity to read the report of the local constable and decide as to the disposition of the case. Until it reached the desk of the chief of police, all was as it should have been with the case of piscatorial pilfering. Then, something peculiar happened. Rather than leaving it with a lieutenant, who would have written to Sami with instructions, or with the advocate fiscale, who would have opened a criminal prosecution, the chief of police took the affair into his own hands. After consulting with the regent, the highest Ionian civil official, as well as with the advocate fiscale, the attorney general, and the resident, the official representative of the British Colonial Office on the island, he wrote to the highest religious figure in the land, the Metropolitan Spiridon Kondomihalis. He requested that the metropolitan issue a decree of excommunication against the bandits and anyone who had knowledge of them or in any way aided or abetted them. Kondomihalis agreed. On January 24, he placed his seal on the one hundred and fourth excommunication decree issued by his office since he came to power in 1841.

The following Sunday, January 27, Protopapas Panayis Kavalieratos, the archbishop of the deme (county) of Sami, somberly attired in black vestments and holding a crucifix draped in black, stood in the church of Agios Spiridon before the congregation of Haliotata and officially proclaimed the decree of excommunication against the hungry fish thieves. After this, bathed in incense at the head of an icon-laden procession of clerics, he made his way down to Sami, chanting the excommunication proclamation as he went. Why should a decree of excommunication have been issued for such a banal crime? Eternal damnation for the snatching of a few baskets of fish seems rather severe. Moreover, what can this episode and others like it tell us about the place of religion in the imperial encounter between Britons and Greeks on the Ionian Islands?

This chapter aims to contribute as well to the wider historiographical debates about peasant resistance and hegemony. I argue that Greek peasants were not passive receptors in the process of defining culture, values, and ideology. Nor were they "apolitical" or "mystified" when confronted with a hegemonic ideology, as has frequently been argued (Gramsci 1971: 179–212). Instead, they actively participated in the dialogue through which power relations are mediated by constantly assessing and passing judgments on the words and deeds of those who would endeavor to rule them. As James Scott put it, ". . . subordinate groups develop their own interpretations" (1985: 338). His work, along with Michael Herzfeld's on the village of Glendi in Crete, poses powerful and persuasive arguments against the orthodox view (Scott 1985: 304–50; Herzfeld 1985: xiii) The only drawback to their studies is that in each case their data were drawn from only one village. Recently Steve Stern and Ranajit Guha, among others, have critiqued the "hegemony" hypothesis utilizing historical data on peasant revolutions from Peru and India (Stern 1987: 3–25; Guha 1983).

This chapter aims to contribute to the debate raised by these works and in general supports their conclusions, but because the unit of study is larger than a single village yet more manageable than a macroregion, like India or the Andes, it allows us to analyze in more intimate terms the interplay between peasants and elites, between crime and religion in a peasant society, and between a colonial power and indigenous culture. The response of the Kefallenian peasants to the introduction by the British Colonial Office of a policy of issuing excommunication for secular crime provides a case study of how peasants can create an ideology and then use it as a basis for action or resistance. But I want to move beyond the resistance model that has become so popular recently. Basing their arguments on Gramsci, Scott, and some of the others listed above, historians and anthropologists have produced a whole genre of resistance studies. Many of these have been extremely valuable; others have turned the study of resistance into a morality play with bad rulers, usually Europeans, and good, clever natives who find ingenious ways to resist. Resistance, like Foucault's notion of power, is in danger of becoming so ubiquitously present that it becomes unsusceptible to analysis. Resistance, like power, is analogous to the air we breathe: everywhere yet imperceptible.

Specifically in the case of the British in the Ionian Islands, I want to examine one of the main themes of this book, that of identity and culture, through the lens of religion. Religion was central to how both the British and the Greeks experienced colonial rule. During the 1820s and 1830s, the British colonial officers and their Ionian counterparts were made repeatedly and painfully aware of the centrality of religion in the life of the peasantry.

As we have seen already and shall touch on again, religion was a central element of the clash of cultures between the British and the Greeks. With alarming regularity, religious festivals turned into violent demonstrations against British rule, and, almost without exception, the lay clergy played prominent roles in them (Adams 1819; Ansted 1853: 448–50; Holland 1815: 41, 273). While these sporadic outbursts of violence received higher visibility, there was another, more pervasive, everyday form of resistance which highlighted the government's increasing loss of power and authority in the villages: crime and the inability of the authorities to obtain testimony from peasants against criminals (Scott 1985: note 6, 28–39). Once it became clear that the terror tactics employed by the Anglo-Ionian authorities since 1817 were singularly ineffective in ensuring the "public tranquility," to use the Colonial Office buzzword for peaceful acquiescence to British rule, the British authorities entered into a struggle with the nationalists and other anti-British factions for the hearts and the minds of the peasantry. At the center of this contest stood popular religion. In some crucial ways the assumption that religion was the best way to control the Greeks was predicated on the British identification of the Greeks as the "Mediterranean Irish," as discussed earlier. As a consequence of this belief, one of the most critically important elements in British strategy for establishing their claim to be the sole source of legitimate authority through religion was the practice of excommunication for crime. The British, then, saw religion as a mechanism of social control. The way that many Greeks responded to this attempt to manipulate their religion shows the complexity that may lay behind what we often call resistance. In this case, Greeks did not resist hegemony overtly; instead, through their reaction to a policy initiative they inadvertently articulated a language of resistance.

The public performance of the rituals of excommunication was susceptible to a number of different readings, each with its own internal logic and sets of meanings. We can identify and analyze several such variant readings at two different levels of social discourse. At the level of high politics, the policy as conceived by the Colonial Office was a failure. Manipulated by the pro-British members of the elite as an instrument of patronage, it merely reinforced peasant notions concerning class distinctions and concerning the fundamental injustice of British rule, and both of these further incited their yearning for union with the Kingdom of Greece. There had always been a cleavage in the church hierarchy between the higher orders, almost exclusively manned by members of the aristocracy, and the lay clergy in the villages, almost exclusively members of the peasantry. The policy of excommunication for crime exacerbated this rift. According to canon law, only those from the highest echelons of the church, basically bishops and those above them, could perform excommunication. Thus, in order to operationalize the policy of excommunication for crime, these officials had to "intrude" into peasant villages, places where by class and by culture they were already outsiders, aliens. Excommunication, by putting on display the complicity between the high church and the British protectorate, sealed the divorce within the church in the eyes of the peasants. In response to the question "Who speaks for the church?" the answer from the peasantry was unequivocal: it was the priest of the village, not the bishop of the state. Thus, in their revised ideology, only the village priest could legitimately lay claim to authority in the community. In the end, the result of the British attempt to employ religion as a means of communal control had exactly the opposite effect from what they had intended (Appadurai 1981: 19; Adas 1982; 1987; Davidson 1990).

At the level of local politics and society, this same policy had other ramifications unforeseen by the authorities. Because the elite and their followers transformed excommunication into an instrument of patronage, it acted to strengthen the existing personal power relations in Greek communities. Yet simultaneously, it reinforced peasant notions of group identity and the moral superiority of that group vis-à-vis "outsiders"—the designation of which was determined by cultural context. The public performance of religious rituals, like excommunication, enabled peasants to perceive these identity distinctions more clearly. The erosion of the legitimacy of state authority inherent in this revised ideology allowed for more militant actions against British rule.

The Historical Context

During the negotiations about the islands after the demise of Bonaparte, the Ionian Greek clergy supported vigorously the British position that the islands should be granted independence but placed under the protection of the English monarchy (Tumelty 1953: 15). Their support was based partly on their very negative experience of French rule during the first decade of the century when the church had come under attack by Greeks inspired by the French Revolution and partly by their belief that the British would maintain the church's privileged position within the ruling structure and its independence as an institution. The bloom of cooperation soon faded from the rose of church and Colonial Office relations. Within two years of the protectorate's foundation, Britons and Greek clerics clashed.

The Colonial Office's first taste of civil unrest and the role of the local clergy in it occurred on Lefkas in 1819 (CO 136/12; A & P, June 1820 PRO; Goodison 1822: 4, 81; Mahairas 1940: 13, 50–61; Jervis 1852: 213–14). In consultation with the local municipal council, it had been decided to dredge a canal through the narrow salt flats on the northeastern part of the island; the cost of the project was to be covered by a special tax to be levied on the islands. In order to determine the level of payment, a detailed census of all peasant households was necessary. When the assessor and his bodyguard of Maltese and Albanian constables approached the village of Sfakiotes, the first on their list, they were greeted by hundreds of armed peasants, at the head of which stood Papas Yioryios Asproyerakas. Because the islanders considered the taxes to be an assault on their way of life and an insult to manhood, for the reasons discussed in chapter 6, they were determined to stop them from being levied. Their actions are reminiscent of peasant responses to state taxes elsewhere (Tilly 1982; Scott 1976: 91–98; Dickson 1983). The rioters attacked and drove the police back to the town of Lefkas. They then turned their attention to the municipal hall and tried to burn it down. The regent fled to the Fortress of Saint George.

The fighting continued for two more days. After the arrival of British troops from Kerkira the fate of the peasants was sealed: they were simply no match for trained troops. Just before the final battle, Papas Asproyerakas stood before his flock and shouted at Colonel Stove, the commander of the British troops: "Colonel, Colonel, you may have better guns and cannons, but we have our flintlocks and our hearts, and we shall fight you" (Mahairas 1940: note 13). They did, and lost.

In the ensuing investigations no fewer than nine village priests were arrested for treason (CO 136/12: Maitland to Barthurst, Oct. 20, 1819 PRO). Indeed, at one point, the archbishop himself was detained on suspicion that he was withholding evidence. The central charge against the priests was that they, in conjunction with some devious village headmen, were inciting the peasants to riot by filling their heads with nonsense. The British, the priests had announced from their pulpits, intended to tax the peasants into poverty; plans were being made to tax window doors, and even sexual intercourse. To the Colonial Officers such talk was absurd. All they saw was a naive and gullible peasantry being led by sly and devious priests. What they failed to appreciate was that the grievances of the peasants were deep-seated and real; all the priests did was to articulate and vocalize these feelings. After some difficulty, Asproyerakas and two other men were hanged. Charges against twenty-five others, including eight priests, were dropped; nevertheless, their property was confiscated, their houses burned, and they were exiled (CO 136/1258–59: Penal Law Code, Chapter 2, Title 5 PRO). This incident was just the harbinger of more to come.

With the archbishop of Zakinthos's death in the summer of 1820, the lord high commissioner for the first time exercised his constitutional prerogative to appoint the head of the church on each island. This amendment had been controversial from the start, and it had created bad feelings between the church hierarchy and the Colonial Office at the time of the constitutional convention of 1818. The objections of the church at the convention were met with assurances from

Maitland that he would not appoint archbishops without approval of the church council. His selection of Ioannis Theovasaris for the post on Zakinthos violated this pledge. The public response to the investiture of a British-appointed prelate was as unexpected as it was violent (CO 136/17: Maitland to Barthurst, Sept. 12, 1820 PRO).

Within the first few months of his tenure, the new archbishop was expected to traverse the island and to visit the churches in every village. But Theovasaris never completed his rounds. All of the villages in the island's rugged interior refused to receive him. Open gunfights with the police and with British troops ensued. Two attempts were made on his life, and plots abounded. The following passage from the testimony of Theodoros "Kukli" Koliva, a well-known *bravo* in the employ of Count Montegrino, explains why: "Everyone knew why he [the archbishop] was coming. He wanted to take our church, you know what I mean, to steal our icons, to take what was ours. For weeks Papas [Ioannis] Petsas, and all the priests, and even his Lordship Count Montegrino, had been telling us that he [the archbishop] was sent by the British to close our churches. I told my friends, 'sure, we let him come, but the minute he touches the icons I'll throw a rock at him.'" This was to be the signal for everyone to throw rocks (CO 136/17: Trial Transcript deposition 4, Mar. 13, 1821 PRO).

The British blamed the entire affair on Montegrino, who was indeed its mastermind. But more to the point was the way in which the peasantry defined their church and contrasted it with the church of the state, the church of the archbishops. They believed that the "leader" of the church, their "spiritual Father," had come to take "what was theirs" and to steal their village church. Events over the next twenty years only served to exacerbate this rift in the church and further convince the peasantry that the village church and its priest deserved their allegiance.

As we have seen, the creation of the Kingdom of Greece and the intense sentiments of nationalism that it spawned split the church. Throughout the course of the Greek War of Independence, the British strove mightily to keep the Ionian Islands neutral (Wrigley 1978; 1987; 1988). They did so only with difficulty. Numerous Ionians, including many priests, crossed over and joined the fighting. Many of those who stayed behind actively agitated for inclusion of the Ionian Islands in the struggle for independence. Those who did faced stiff opposition from the British. On one occasion, for example, Colonel Travers, an aide to Sir Charles Napier on the island of Kefallenia, arrested a priest in the village of Liksouri for preaching rebellion. Rather than prosecuting him for sedition, Travers dragged him into the public square and before the assembled community he shaved the priest's beard, cut off his hair, and flogged him (Napier 1857: 47; Kirkwall 1864: 39). Across all of the islands, priests preached to their plebeian flocks that the ongoing struggle taking place on the shores opposite their islands was a religious war of liberation that they should join in. Unification with Greece was a dream shared by peasants and priests alike. Therefore, the Colonial Office's policy of strict neutrality drove in even deeper the wedge between the British and the Orthodox clergy.

The critical rupture inside the church came in July 1833, when the Holy Synod of Athens established an autocephalous Orthodox Greek Church and severed all relations with the patriarch in Constantinople. This new entity was inseparably linked to the Greek nation-state. Thus its name: The Orthodox Eastern Apostolic Church of the Kingdom of Greece (Sherrard 1973; Frazee 1977). "In a land where religious and national feelings had become almost identical" (Bowen 1862: 317), clerics and laymen alike were being asked to choose sides: unification with the Greek nation-state and its church, or with the British protectorate and the patriarch of Constantinople. The metropolitans, archbishops, and bishops of the Ionian Islands chose the latter; the priests of the village, the former (Herzfeld 1982: 59). The struggle for unification with the Kingdom of Greece completed the unification of nationalism and religion.

Moreover, it was apparent that the local priests were among the most important characters in village society. This was so for three reasons. First, because they were themselves peasants, covillagers considered them to be culturally insiders, members of the same group. Second, because of their higher level of education, they could interact better with outsiders like tax collectors, notaries, and landlords; villagers often turned to the priest for assistance when confronted with these outside forces. Third, in their capacity as spiritual shepherd and mediator with the supernatural, priests could speak with authority on communal affairs (Holland 1815: 9, 41, 273: CO 136/1249: Jun. 21, 1841; Debono 1985: 27–35; Kondoyiorgis 1982: 277–98; Tsotsoros 1986: 165–75; for comparative material from Italy, see Sabetti 1984: 88; Silverman

1975: 149; Sarti 1985: 77–78). Furthermore, many had deep roots in the communities they served; 72 percent of the village priests whose careers can be reconstructed resided in their natal village.

Two examples vividly portray the extent of the influence local priests wielded. In 1813 Major De Bosset, the temporary governor of the island, attempted to introduce the cultivation of the potato as a means of breaking the peasants' dependence on imported wheat. The experiment failed dismally. The peasants refused to grow potatoes, much less eat them, after the priests told them that it was "the very apple with which the serpent seduced Adam and Eve in Paradise" (Holland 1815: 41). As was noted earlier, the British established a comprehensive school system that was placed under the control of various missionary societies. The plans for public education foundered from the lack of pupils as the priests flamed the peasants' suspicions that their children were being converted to "Methodism" (*Blue Book*, Mustoxidi Memorial 1839: 39; CO 136/1316: Parsons to Gilpin, February 21, 1836 PRO). Since the schools were being run by bible societies, their fears were not baseless. From 1833 onwards the issue of proselytism and conversion became an explosive one, sometimes boiling over into public unrest, as on one occasion on Zakinthos in 1850. In this case, a mob of over five hundred plebeian men marched through the streets of the town attacking the houses of Greeks who had converted to Protestantism and who taught at the Lancastrian schools. No one was seriously injured, but hundreds of books were burnt in the streets in this spontaneous demonstration of religious fervor (CO 136/783/3: Hill to Fraser, July 18, 1850 PRO). In spite of repeated assurances to the contrary, Greeks would not believe that converting them to Protestantism was not a central goal of British rule. To lose their Orthodox faith would be to lose their identity as Greeks, and this they would not stand for.

The case of Papas Horsi Tsipallo demonstrates just how politicized the local clergy was becoming. He was arrested and exiled in October 1840 because he "used under the guise of religion to preach revolt" (CO 136/1249: Fraser to Mackenzie, January 10, 1840 PRO). The final proof against him came when letters from the exiled priest Papas Eusebios Parsi were found in his house. In the letters, Parsi exhorted Tsipallo to join with the other priests and act. "That from the nobles and the gentry no help is to be expected as they are corrupted

by money and care nothing about the preservation of the church. That
the lower classes of the people and particularly the peasantry must
raise their voices from the religion of their ancestors against its perse-
cutors and destroyers" (CO 136/1249: Parsons to Gilpin, October 8,
1838 PRO). Religious sentiment and nationalism had become wedded,
and together they formed a volatile mixture (Knox 1984). Every outburst of nationalist unrest was to some degree instigated, controlled,
or led by members of the clergy. Thus, the Anglo-Ionian authorities
perceived the need to "do something" about religion.

One additional factor of relevance remains to be identified: crime
and its control. Despite proclamations by the Colonial Office to the
contrary, crime and violence were serious problems on the islands
(Ansted 1863: 450; Bowen 1853: 324). In chapters 6 and 7 we analyzed in
some detail certain aspects of the operation of the criminal justice
system. I am currently engaged in a large project which focuses exclusively on crime, violence, and dispute resolution on the islands during
the protectorate. During the 1830s and 1840s, nearly every aspect of
the criminal justice system—from policing, the courts, and even the
law code—was revised or reformed. For the purpose of this discussion,
I want to focus on just one element of the crime question: its legitimacy in the eyes of the lower classes. The Anglo-Ionian authorities
were hampered in their endeavors to deal with crime by the stony silence maintained by the villagers regarding certain types of violence
when questioned by the police. As the following examples illustrate,
even in the face of brutal violence plebeian Greeks refused to cooper-
ate with the police. Even the kin of victims of lethal violence kept
their silence when questioned by the authorities. In the world of
Ionian Greek men, shame or *dropi* defined the moral obligation of villagers to exclude outsiders and to solve conflicts internally.

A sharecropper in the village of Poulata had failed to pay his rent.
One night two men from a neighboring village came to talk to him
about it. They were *bravi* attached to his landlord. They urged him to
look to his affairs and give them something to take back to their lord.
After some heated words were exchanged, the farmer tried to calm
things down, and so following the social dictates of hospitality, he asked
them to stay and break bread with him. As we saw in chapter 6, commensality was a key element in male sociability on the islands. After the
evening repast was completed, the leader of the *bravi* once more asked

that the man give them the rent. When the sharecropper refused, they shot him dead. Not satisfied that a powerful-enough message had been sent to the other villagers, they attacked his family, poking out the eye of his pregnant wife and stabbing his eldest son repeatedly. Charles Napier, the resident at the time, thought that he knew the identity of the culprits and arrested them. But they had to be released because no one would testify against them (Napier 1833: 97–98).

On the night of July 10, 1835, a gang of men brutally gunned down the widow of Ioannis Kapsikoli in the village of Makriotika. The next day eight men were arrested; all were well-known members of a gang controlled by the Dellaporta family. But again no one would give evidence: "From all that I have been able to learn the party Dellaporta, to which the eight arrested belong, is held in such terror in the village of Makriotika that even should any of the inhabitants have it in their power to throw light on this barbarous act, fear and dread of future vengeance will prevent them coming forward" (CO 136/1313: Parsons to Gilpin, July 15, 1835). The offer of a reward and even a special plea from the archbishop failed to elicit testimony. To my knowledge, this was the first time that a member of the church was called upon to perform such a service.

In another case that we have already discussed, the killing of Theodros Maridas by Spiridon Kallihias in September 1835, the kin of the victim refused to give evidence against the slayer even though his identity was known to everyone because he had committed the murder in broad daylight in the public square (TIAK 847: September 11, 1835). The code of silence held a powerful sway over the people.

On hundreds of occasions, in the face of harsh retribution, Ionian islanders kept their silence, preferring to redress wrongs with blood. In fact, the only category of violence in which silence was not mandated was the knife duel, as discussed in chapter 6. The authorities had tried unsuccessfully to break the silence of the peasants with a variety of stratagems, such as billeting soldiers in their homes or quarantining their villages. These measures failed. By 1840 it was time to try a different approach.

The decade of the 1830s proved crucial for the British in the Ionian Islands and elsewhere in the empire (Beames 1983, 1987; Donelley 1983; Guha 1983: 2–3). In India and Ireland for example, there had been violent public demonstrations and riots, and in many of them religion had played a role. The lord high commissioner, Sir Howard Douglas, had experienced such riots when he was in Canada. He saw the need for change: the police forces were reorganized, the courts were revamped, and the religious leaders were definitively integrated into the ruling structure. He ensured that all the major posts in the church were filled by pro-British clerics, and he instituted the policy of employing excommunication for secular crime. This practice was continued by his successor, Lord Seaton, who, on the death of the metropolitan of Kefallenia, Panayis Makris, appointed Spiridon Kondomihalis to the position (Moschopoulos 1984: 105; Debono 1985: 38–42). The application of excommunication was, then, part of a concerted effort by the Anglo-Ionian authorities to reclaim control of the peasantry.

The Decrees

Between 1840 and 1864 the office of the metropolitan of Kefallenia issued 131 excommunication decrees (TIAK Excommunication Degrees: loose-bound in marked volumes). A detailed analysis of the information contained in these documents leads to the conclusion that the primary factor determining the selection of crimes for excommunication was the ability of the victims to call on their own connections or the connections of someone in their network of social relations to influence the decision-making process in the Anglo-Ionian government.

The structure of the decrees is predictably formulaic. They are divided into three sections. The first is a ritual salutation in which the metropolitan first presents himself as the head of the church ("Metropolitan by the Grace of God"), then links himself to the saints, and finally, reaffirms that he is the peasants' spiritual father (he refers to them as "dearest children of our Humbleness"). There follows a long description of the crime. The victim is identified and in many cases the criminals as well. The length of the account and the amount of detail provided vary. In one case, for example, we are simply told that Stefanos Alexandratos was killed by his nephew, but neither the reason nor the method is made clear (TIAK ED 85). In other cases, the metropolitan states that he was asked by the authorities to issue the decree; "For this crime they have been charged formally by the Police of Liksuri" (TIAK ED 112). More often, he merely notes that he had been asked officially to issue the document (TIAK ED 121). It is the information contained in this section of the documents that provided the evidence on which the following analyses are based.

The next section was usually preserved for an outburst of righteous indignation: "Such a heinous, monstrous, and awful deed disturbs and shocks all sensitive Christian souls; in order that such a foul deed may not remain unpunished, it has been brought to the attention of the proper criminal authorities. Consequently, this horrible act of infanticide is seen as a blow against the Church as well" (TAIK ED 112), or "Such a foul and sacrilegious deed disturbs and shocks all Christian souls, and in order that the monstrous and polluted perpetrators of such horrible, terrible and sacrilegious deeds do not remain unpunished, the Church has been roused to action against these fearful and impious wrong-doers" (TIAK ED 143). The notion of pollution dominates these passages. But note that all members of the Christian community and not just the perpetrators were touched by the odium of pollution. This concept had powerful resonance in rural Greece (Herzfeld 1982: 183, 228; Campbell 1966: 155; see also Vodola 1986: 2). And for that reason it was considered a "moral lever" which could compel people to step forward and testify.

The last section always begins thus: "Therefore on behalf of this holy congregation, paternally and consultatively each orthodox christian, be they man or woman, young or old, regardless of age and class, whomsoever has any information pertaining to [the crime] is advised that they must immediately and without shame step forward and report to the police." There then follows the formal declaration of excommunication:

> Anyone who has such information and who makes it known to the proper authorities, will receive the blessing of almighty God and the prayers of us all. If, however, either through fear (*fovon*) or shame (*sistoli*) they do not appear and tell the truth, then let it be known that we hold them in a state of excommunication from the Father, the Son, and the Holy Spirit, from the One, Holy, Catholic, and Apostolic Church, and from the 318 Spiritual Fathers. Let them stand trembling

and lamenting on the earth like Cain; may the Earth split and swallow them like Kore, Datha and Aviron; may they inherit the leprosy of Gieza and the gallows of Judas; let iron and stones be dissolved, but not them; may they [their body] remain indissoluble and distended for eternity. [Let this happen to] each and every person who had a hand in this evil and inhuman act, and equally to each and every person who has knowledge of this [crime] or information about it and who does not come forward and tell the truth: all of these people are henceforth excommunicated.

Three elements require comment. First, at a mundane level, the church offered protection from physical harm. By appealing to "fear" it recognized that one of the reasons why peasants refused to testify was fear of reprisals by the gangs. The reference to "shame," like pollution, would have struck a deep-seated chord in Greek society (Herzfeld 1982: 233–34; 1980; Campbell 1964: 144; du Boulay 1974: 109, 111–17). The word used in the document that I translate as "shame" is *sistoli*, rather than the more common word *dropi*. The word is regularly used twice in each document. First, in the passage where people are exhorted to come forward and testify, they are told to do so "*aneu sistoli*" [without bringing on shame]. The second usage occurs in the passage in which people are told that they will not be forgiven for failing to testify even if they did so "*dia fovon i sistoli*" [on account of fear or shame]. The root meaning of *sistoli* is "diminution" or "contraction." I suggest *sistoli* conveys here the sense of loss of reputation. The implication of the word was that failure to come forward to testify would bring on reproach.

Second, at a celestial level, the sanction held out against the recalcitrant was eternal damnation. According to Greek beliefs, in order for a person's soul to enter heaven it has to be clean of flesh, and thus the curse cited in the excommunication document would bar one's entry into heaven; moreover, it would turn one into the living dead, sentenced to remain forever corporally intact and to rise periodically from the grave and plague mankind (Danforth 1982: 48–49; Campbell 1964: 164).

Third, anyone with information about the crime who did not come forth, as well as the criminals, was excommunicated. If taken seriously, practically everyone in a village could be an excommunicate. Freedom from fear, the risk of incurring shame, and the threat of eternal damnation were, then, the promises held out to the peasantry by the church: all were hollow. First, those promising protection were but a fleeting presence in the village and simply incapable of ensuring protection. Moreover, they were from the same class and kin groups as the landlords and so, in peasant ideology, automatically suspect. Second, shame, like beauty, resides in the eye of the beholder. Shame could only exist if there was a consensus amongst the villagers that an act was shameful. But if the entire village was touched by excommunication, then there could be no shame in noncompliance. Indeed, if anything, the policy only increased the honorableness of maintaining silence. Third, the threat of eternal damnation could be taken seriously only if those delivering the threat had credibility; for reasons to be discussed shortly, they did not.

The way in which excommunication was practiced in the Ionian Islands differs considerably from elsewhere. For a start, the form of the excommunication does not fit into any of F. Donald Logan's categories of medieval excommunications (1968: 15). Unlike in *ab homine* or *ferendae sententiae* excommunication, it was often proclaimed before anyone was even charged with a crime. It was not *latae sententiae* because, as I shall demonstrate shortly, specifically selected crimes, not previously defined categories of crime, incurred excommunication. Nor was it *a iure* because secular as well as religious crimes were involved, and thus both secular and canon law were involved. As both Logan (1968: 48–49) and Vodola (1986: 34–38) point out, in the Middle Ages it was the church which approached the secular authorities after an excommunication had been announced and the excommunicate remained contumacious. In the Ionian Islands it was the other way around: the secular authorities petitioned the church for an excommunication. Indeed, I can find no parallels for the way excommunication was employed on the Ionian Islands.

Furthermore, if we accept the following description by Logan as to the objective of excommunication, then a major distinction becomes clear: "Excommunication was a censure, its purpose medicinal. Separation from the company of the faithful was intended to induce the excommunicate to seek absolution, reconciliation to the church, and restoration to his place in society" (Logan 1968: 15). The church on the Ionian Islands never introduced an institutionalized means by which excommunicates could be absolved and restored to the body of the faithful. This is crucial: If excommunication was to be taken seriously by the peasants, then the reward of reconciliation to the church for those who broke rank and came forward to testify had to be a real possibility. It was not.

The British Colonial Office envisaged its role in the Ionian Islands as an essentially paternalistic one. As we saw vividly and repeatedly in chapters 2, 3, and 4, they considered it their role to guide the islanders down the path to "civilization." Their task, as they conceived it, was to teach, not rule. The way they intended to do this was by establishing policies and then leaving the implementation of those policies to the islanders themselves. With excommunication, the intentions of the Colonial Office were clearly manifested: to restore the "public tranquility" by both preventing crimes from occurring and solving those that did occur through the threat of eternal damnation. At the same time, by invoking the power of the church to accomplish this end, they sought to reestablish the high clergy's authority in the face of the threat posed by radical priests, like those discussed above. An examination of the information contained in the excommunication documents as a body, however, indicated that different priorities and intentions guided the implementation of this policy.

Table 4 presents the basic data on the distribution of crimes for which excommunications were granted, broken down by five-year period and category of crime. Crimes are divided into five categories: (1) theft (including breaking and entering, animal rustling, and the like), (2) violent crimes (such as homicide, attempted homicide, grievous bodily harm, and assault), (3) brigandage, (4) crimes of property or contract (e.g., arson, malicious damage, debt, usury, and breach of contract), and (5) moral crimes (incest, gambling, sodomy, and adultery). Because of the small number of cases in categories four and five, for analytical purposes I have combined them. Thefts and acts of violence obviously predominate.

The best way to decide whether such crimes were especially selected is to compare the distribution of crimes for which excommunications were rendered against the total number of crimes. As part of a larger study of crime and criminal justice on the islands I have analyzed the daily records of arrests made by the police. I also have data

Table 4. Excommunication Degrees by Type from 1840 to 1864, Five-Year Totals

Year	Theft	Violence	Brigandage	Property & Morals
1840–1844	9	10	3	2
1845–1849	9	18	1	0
1850–1854	20	17	4	2
1855–1859	11	9	1	0
1860–1864	6	8	0	2
Totals	55	62	9	6

Source: TIAK Excommunication Decrees.

on convictions, but because excommunication decrees were issued before malefactors were tried or convicted the arrest rate is the more appropriate measure. I compared the issuance of excommunication decrees with the patterns of arrests on Kefallenia in 1844, 1845, 1850, 1853, 1856, 1860, and 1862. For the purpose of this examination, I employed the same categories to the arrest records.

The first and most obvious difference was in the number of excommunications issued compared to the total number of crimes. Between 1840 and 1844, twenty-four decrees were issued; in 1844 alone, the police made at a minimum 1,823 arrests, including thirteen for homicide, 120 for assault with a deadly weapon, and 214 for robbery. It would appear that just over 1 percent of the crimes reported to the police resulted in a successful request for intervention by the church.

This selective process is evident also in the types of crimes for which excommunication decrees were issued. In four of the five categories, the percentage of crimes resulting in excommunication and the percentage of crimes committed compared to all crimes are fairly similar. Forty-seven percent of excommunications were for thefts, whereas they constituted only 40 percent of all crimes. For violent crimes the corresponding figures were 41 percent of excommunications compared to 32 percent of crimes overall. There does appear to be a major difference in the category of crimes against property or contracts and morals: Only 5 percent of the excommunications were for such acts, whereas debt and fraud and moral crimes accounted for 22 percent of all reported crimes. The intuitive impression that crimes of violence were more likely to result in excommunication than crimes against property is borne out by more rigorous statistical examination. Debt was the most common crime against property recorded in the police register, yet when selecting crimes for excommunication civil officials chose thefts and acts of violence over debt. While this conclusion is informative, it does not fully explain which specific robberies or violent deeds were selected for excommunication.

An examination of the status of the victims indicates that crimes committed against clerics and aristocrats were more likely to elicit an excommunication decree; nevertheless, most were issued on behalf of nonaristocrats. Ionian society was juridically divided into three categories. At the top of the pyramid was the aristocracy. These were individuals who were able to document their bloodlines to the stratification of a select committee sufficiently well to have their name inscribed in the *Golden Book*. Periodically, this group would open its ranks and allow in specially selected wealthy individuals. Below them came the *citadini* and *contadini* (the peasants); membership in each of these was determined by one's wealth. Because the *Libra d' Or de la Noblesse Ionienne* (Rangabes 1925–27) has been preserved and published, it is a fairly simple task to identify members of the aristocracy; the same, unfortunately, is not true for the other groups. Accordingly, the population is broken down into only three categories: aristocrats, nonaristocrats, and clerics.

In the 1840 census, 10 percent of the population was enrolled as members of the aristocracy; of the remaining 90 percent all but 1 percent were either *citadini* or *contadini*. This contrasts markedly with the distribution by status of those on behalf of whom excommunication degrees were issued. Of the 125 cases for which the status can be determined with some certainty, 58 percent of the cases involved either *citadini* or *contadini*, 40 percent involved aristocrats, and less than 2 percent referred to clerics. The impression created by these figures is that aristocrats are overrepresented in the excommunication decrees, indicating the status of the victim was a factor in determining whether or not a crime was selected for excommunication.

Crimes against nonaristocrats were less likely to result in excommunication than crimes against members of the aristocracy. But, in total, more excommunications were issued on behalf of nonaristocrats. As will be made clear shortly, these two conclusions are not incompatible. The key link lay in the observation that interpersonal connections were vitally important in obtaining a decree of excommunication.

I turn next to the consideration of a geographical bias involved in the decision-making process. The assumption here is that because both the British authorities and their Ionian counterparts resided primarily in the towns, there might be a tendency for crimes committed there or in the immediately surrounding countryside to receive excommunications. Table 5 presents the distribution of excommunications by deme (county) and provides information on the demes. At first glance, it appears that there might be a geographical clustering. The town of Argostoli, the nearby demes of Ano Livatho and Kato Livatho, and the town of Lixouri registered the largest number of

Table 5. Distribution of Excommunication Decrees by Administrative District

Deme	Male Population	No. of Decrees Issued
Erissos	1,396	3
Assos	1,436	3
Pilaros	2,036	12
Sami	2,056	8
Pronnoi	2,005	5
Elios	2,656	1
Ano Livatho	1,944	18
Kato Livatho	1,981	12
Krane	568	3
Homola	1,727	5
Faraklata	829	4
Dilinata	1,670	7
Anogi	2,700	8
Katogi	2,171	7
Lixouri (Town)	2,789	18
Argostoli (Town)	4,601	23

excommunications. But if we take into account the overall distribution of the population across the islands, this argument is weakened. Most Kefallenians lived in villages of less than five hundred people. There is, indeed, a very strong correlation between the size of the male population in each deme and the number of excommunications issued. A geographical bias is thus unlikely. The performances of excommunications, therefore, occurred all across the islands, most frequently in village churches. The target audience, then, was the peasantry. The following story helps us to perceive more clearly the underlying logic behind excommunication.

William Mure was a British colonial officer and classicist, and we have already discussed his role in shaping an identity for the Ionians. In his capacity of resident on the island of Ithaki, he had to deal with the following episode, about which he wrote at length (Mure 1852: 46–59). In 1817, a certain Monsieur Soleure arrived on the island of Ithaki from Patras and settled in the main town. He had served as an officer in the French army but for reasons unknown had fled to Greece. Though not a nobleman, Soleure was a learned man of breeding who had married the daughter of a wealthy landowner from Patras. His star in local society rose, and eventually he became schoolmaster for the island. In 1823 he helped establish a chapter of the Free Masons. The lord high commissioner, Thomas Maitland, was promoting the Masonry and encouraging all "right-thinking men" to join (CO 136/45: January 5, 1822 PRO); he saw it as an alternative to the Filiki Etairia, an organization which was playing a critical role in the Greek War of Independence (Frangos 1973). As we saw earlier, the vast majority of Ionian islanders were rabid supporters of the Greek revolution, and so, not surprisingly, the Masons' membership drive proved largely unsuccessful; only British soldiers and pro-British Ionians joined—and only a very small number of them. By casting his lot with the British and by taking a public stance against the war of independence, Soleure made numerous enemies on Ithaki.

The Masons' unpopularity continued after the Greek war had ended because the group was now so firmly associated with British rule and because it was seen as an impediment to Ionian unification with the Kingdom of Greece. In addition, during the 1830s, religion entered the picture in ways more visible than it had in the 1820s. Masonry was depicted as the tool of the anti-Christ. Local clerics preached that it was through Masonry that the British sought to destroy the Orthodox Church. Anti-Mason feelings ran high. In 1837, for example, under the leadership of the village priests and some local men of "respect," there was a public demonstration and near riot against them. Rocks and lemons served as projectiles for the angry mob, but no one was seriously injured. Anti-Mason feelings were running high here as elsewhere in the Ionian Islands, and as the leader of the Ithakan Lodge, Soleure bore the brunt of this malevolence.

The usual silence of a Greek winter's night in December 1839 was shattered by a young girl's screams. A peasant girl dressed as a maid burst into the police station and blurted out that there was trouble at her master's house. When the police arrived at the Soleure residence, they found Soleure sitting in the master bedroom in a state of shock. The walls were smeared with blood, but not Soleure's: he had not been the target of the attack. Instead, on the floor lay the mutilated bodies of his wife and son. Except for a cut on his arm Soleure appeared unharmed. At the foot of the bed was a bloody scabbard, but the sword that went with it was nowhere to be found.

When he recovered his wits Soleure professed his innocence. A group of masked men, he claimed, had entered his house, beat him, and then forced him to watch as they slaughtered his family. But all the evidence was against him. No one had seen the mysterious attackers and no physical evidence could be found in the house to indicate that they had been there. Except for the killing of the boy—few Greeks could accept that a father could kill his own son—this looked like a not very uncommon case of domestic violence. The islanders were convinced of his guilt: as a foreigner, he was capable of anything and, as a leader in the union of anti-Christ's—the Masons—he was linked to the Devil as the priests claimed. The masses were clamoring for "rough justice." The local Greek public prosecutor stalled. Soleure's British friends were convinced that he had been framed. A special British prosecutor was sent from Kerkira to handle the case, and a British colleague of his from the Colonial Office agreed to defend Soleure. Both sides believed him innocent but without additional evidence they could not prove it, and as was usually the case, no one would step forward to give evidence.

At the request of the civil authorities on Ithaki, the metropolitan of Kefallenia issued a decree of excommunication and sent his personal assistant to deliver it. A special mass was held, conducted jointly by the archbishop of the island and the bishop of the deme, at which the excommunication was proclaimed. Once the mass was over, a grand procession proceeded through the streets of the town: the archbishop, the bishop, their entourages, the members of the municipal council, the chief of police, the chief of customs, the constables, and finally the members of the Free Masons. Here was the unity of church and state on display. Compliance was demanded; eternal damnation was threatened.

Three people stepped forward. The maid testified that Soleure often fought with his wife and that, on the night in question, the only voices she had heard coming from the bedroom were those of Soleure, his wife, and their son. A barber announced that about a week after the incident he saw a man walk down to the pier and throw an object into the water. Since it was dusk, however, he could not determine what the object was, but he was sure as to the identity of the man: Soleure. Led by the advocate fiscale and some policemen, a crowd gathered at the waterfront. The barber pointed out into the water and a local boy dove in. After a few minutes underwater, the lad emerged, holding aloft the bloodstained sword. With high drama, a policeman produced the scabbard confiscated from Soleure's house. The hushed crowd watched as he slid the weapon into the sheath. The fit was perfect. Suddenly, a shopkeeper shouted out from the crowd that he recognized the sword; it was the very one which Soleure had tried to sell him six months before the murder. It looked bleak for Soleure.

Still convinced of Soleure's innocence and fearful of a riot if he should be found not guilty, the British authorities moved the trial to Kerkira. There, under intense examination, the witnesses broke. First the maid admitted that she was lying. There had been other men in the house that night. Next the barber recanted; he had been paid to lie. Finally, the shopkeeper admitted to perjury. The case against Soleure fell apart and all charges were dropped.

Two points are vital in this tale. First, from the onset of employing excommunication for secular crimes, the enactment of the ceremonies and rituals associated with it presented a public display of the unity between the church hierarchy and the secular Anglo-Ionian authorities. In the minds of the peasants, the two became inextricably intertwined. Second, and more importantly, the sole pressure for excommunication stemmed from Soleure's very strong connections with the Anglo-Ionian authorities. This suggests that an examination of the social networks of the victims on whose behalf excommunications were granted might prove informative.

The web of kinship and patronage connections for thirty-six of the victims recorded on the excommunication decrees has been traced to this point in my research. If we subtract from the main body of documents crimes against church property and personnel and British citizens on the grounds that the rationale for their selection is self-evident, this figure represents 35 percent of victims. It must be stressed that this is merely the number of people for whom we have detailed information and so must be taken as a minimum. In thirty-five of the thirty-six cases, it can be documented that either the victim personally had connections to the Anglo-Ionian government, or to kinsmen or patrons who themselves had such connections. Some further examples make this clearer.

I begin with some cases where the victims themselves or their relations in cases of homicide could influence the course of justice. On January, 21 1874, the house of the brothers Dr. Ioannis and Dr. Baptista Anninos was broken into; Ioannis was a member of the Ionian Senate at the time and their cousin was deputy chief of police. Excommunication followed (TIAK ED 244; Rangabes 1925–27: vol. 1, 27; Debono 1985: 262, 267). Furthermore their cousin, Ioannis Katasitis, was the husband of Susanah Karouso, daughter of Count Karouso, the most powerful pro-British Ionian nobleman. Similarly, an excommunication was issued when the house of a senator and former high court judge, Dr. Anastasios Metaksas, was burglarized (TIAK ED 52), as well as in the case of burglary at the house of the chief medical inspector, Dr. Marinos Svoronos (TIAK ED 54). In the former case, the victim was a client of Count Karouso, having once served as his personal secretary. When Dr. Metaksas was murderd, Karouso wrote his obituary (*Horikos*, May 26, 1851). In the latter case, the victim's cousin was a high-ranking member of the clergy (Debono 1985: 280–81). After he had recovered from the shock of the traumatic assault he had suffered, Dr. Ieronimus Tipaldo-Pretenderi could have called on his "friends" in the ministry of justice for assistance; he had himself been director of public prosecutions for eight years and was the mastermind behind the reorganization of the police force in the early 1830s

(TIAK ED 115; Napier 1833: 313; Debono 1985: 126–28). There are more examples of this nature, but these should suffice to make my point.

More frequently it was the victim's kinsmen who were connected to the government. Ioannis Floratos, the master whose fish were stolen in our opening tale, could call on assistance from his brother in the ministry of justice in Argostoli and his brother-in-law in the rural guard. When the house of the brothers Ioannis and Spiridon Tipaldos-Alfronsatos was attacked, they could speak to Ioannis's brother-in-law, the Deputy inspector of the executive police, or their own cousin Daniel, eparch of Lefkas, or any other of their four cousins who served in the Anglo-Ionian government (TIAK ED 31; Rangabes 1925–27: vol. 2, 177, 607–8). When the home of Dr. Timotheos Tipaldos-Haritatos was robbed, he could easily have turned for assistance to his father-in-law, Signor Konstantinos Inglesis, the regent of Kefallenia (TIAK ED 35; Rangabes 1925–27: vol. 2, 616; Debono 1985: 465). Dr. Dimitrios Pignatore in his time of need had one cousin who was the overseer of religious affairs on Kefallenia, and another who was the regent of Zakinthos (TIAK ED 124; Rangabes 1925–27: vol. 2, 521). The grieving widow of Yerasimos Likiardopulos could presumably expect help in avenging the murder of her husband from her two brothers-in-law, both members of the police force (TIAK ED 86). Finally, when someone had the temerity to rob the venerable widow Maria Gendili-Horafa, they risked incurring the full wrath of her impressive circle of kinsmen: her son was well on his way up the ladder in the health department; her husband's brother was a senator and an ex-member of the municipal council; the husband of one of her sisters was Anastasios Kondomihalis, the cousin of the metropolitan; her other sister was the widow of Marino Liseo Metaksas, former chief justice of the appellate court, and her nephew was the chief counsel to the court (TIAK ED 98; Rangabes 1925–27: vol. 1, 67, 282; Napier 1833: 499; Debono 1985: 466).

In other cases, patronage seems to have been the key. The relatives of Panaysi Makri-Anastasatos could turn to their patrons, the powerful Delladechima and Valsamachi families, after he was gunned down while out for a walk (TIAK ED 62). After all, no less than five members of this family had been involved in the gang war of February 1833 in the pay of the Delladechima family and under the leadership of Paolo Valsamachi (CO 136/77). Before his brutal slaying in June 1850,

Panayis Kaloyiratos had been the cousin of a trusted agent and gang leader for Count Karouso, regent and senator (TIAK ED 55; Debono 1985: 460).

The conclusion to be drawn is clear: The handful of crimes selected each year to receive special treatment and to be granted a writ of excommunication were those whose victims either personally or through personal associations had links to members of the government. These kinsmen and "friends" were the ones who influenced the decision-making process. The policy of using excommunication as a means of establishing social control was manipulated and transformed by members of the Ionian aristocracy into a tool of patronage.

Peasants, Patrons, Priests, and Ideology

The policy of co-opting the religious elite and employing excommunication for crime was a failure. Throughout the 1840s and 1850s, lower-class clerics continued to lead popular protest. Perhaps the best example of this is Papas Yioryios Nodaros, the infamous Papas Listis, or "Bandit Priest." He was the leader of a group of rioters which in 1849 wreaked havoc in the region of Skala on Kefallenia until their defeat at the hands of the British army (Paximadopoulos-Stavrinou 1980; Tsouganatos 1976; Hannell 1987). On seventeen occasions during the final twenty-four years of the protectorate, Lenten Carnival celebrations erupted in violence. Moreover, excommunication proved no more successful in breaking the code of silence in the villages than any of the other stratagems employed earlier. In 85 percent of the cases where bishops recorded the response their excommunications elicited in a village, they stated that they had had no effect, and, without exception, in the 15 percent of the cases where they had an impact church property was involved.

In fact, the few cases that were successful usually involved theft of church icons or holy relics, as the following example demonstrates. While cleaning the church at Mandzivinata, Papas Ardavani was forced to watch while Panayis Pankalis robbed it. The local constable, Spiridon Vounis, came when he heard the news, but he was too late. Pankalis had already fled. Letters were sent to the police station and to the archbishop in Lixouri. Three days later the archbishop, accompanied by

Police Lieutenant Valendis, arrived in the village. A special mass was said and an excommunication issued (TIAK ED 86; see also file TIAK 110: September 27, 1854, for the testimony of the witnesses). Afterwards, Valendis and Vounis conducted interviews, on the basis of which they learned the identity of the kinsmen from whom Pankalis would most likely seek shelter. As many villagers made clear, the only reason they were speaking was because Pankalis had stepped over the line by stealing the icon (see Herzfeld 1989; Kenna 1985 for discussions about the importance of icons in rural Greek society). Exceptions like this one only highlight the more usual case where excommunication had no impact on local society.

An examination of the reasons for this failure can provide insights into the ways Greek peasants defined group identity, constructed their own ideology, and employed it to either confirm or deny legitimacy to those who would exert authority over them. Furthermore, we can see how the failure on the part of an imperial power to comprehend the rules that structured power relations in the society they were attempting to rule could lead to disaster.

At this point, we face a paradox. Excommunication clearly was not deterring crime, was not compelling peasants to testify against criminals, and was not stopping them from militancy. And yet, the practice of issuing excommunications continued for over twenty years. The rate at which the metropolitan penned excommunications obviously varied from year to year. The average number issued by his office was five, but it could vary annually by as much as 64 percent. Three peaks of activity stand out: 1848–1849, the years of the great riots on Kefallenia; 1854; and 1863. In the last two cases there is not a neat one-to-one correspondence between excommunications and any single event. On the whole, however, there is not a distinct chronological pattern. The explanation lay in our appreciating that the commissioning of an excommunication was in certain contexts more important than the actual performance of the rite itself.

The public performance of excommunication had a multiplicity of meanings. Each of the actors and viewers involved could read something different into these episodes of street theater. Depending on their expectations and the role they played in them, the policy of excommunication was either a dismal failure or simply another weapon to be wielded in the struggle for power.

At the realm of high politics, the policy of excommunication was a failure. In the villages, the legitimacy of the church sprang from the bottom up, not the top down. The peasants accepted the authority of the archbishops and the church because of the village priests, not the other way around. As we have seen, the innate division within the church hierarchy based on class was exploded by the advent of fervent nationalism. In peasant ideology two contraposed sets of associations were drawn: on one side were the village priests and the idea of unification with Greece, and on the other were the church leaders and the ideas of allegiance to the patriarch in (Ottoman) Constantinople and of obedience to the alien British protectorate. The policy of excommunication enabled peasants to perceive these basic distinctions even more clearly.

As demonstrated earlier, the threats and promises contained in the excommunications were hollow. Critical concepts were touched upon, but in a garbled manner. The authorities tried to manipulate the peasant perspective by imposing their own version of categories like "religion," "crime," and "morality," but in each case they misunderstood an essential element. Actions slotted into these categories had variant meanings to the peasantry depending upon their social context. Acts like killing an adulteress or stealing food when hungry or vengeance homicide, which the state deemed immoral and illegal, were, as we saw earlier, often not considered such in local context. Indeed, just the opposite was frequently the case. Even where extreme brutality was involved, as in the case of Yerasimos Prokopi Tzpirata, who in 1836 disemboweled his adulterous, pregnant wife, people kept their silence (CO 136/1316: Parsons to Gilpin, August 18, 1836 PRO). Numerous examples of vengeance homicides committed in front of witnesses who remained mute to the authorities attest to the power of the unwritten code of silence (Kirkwall 1864: 71–72 presents an excellent example of this phenomenon). But the cultural stereotypes that the British colonial officers brought with them obstructed their capacity to grasp this vital point.

As we saw in Chapter 2, the British constructed an identity for the Greeks as the "Mediterranean Irish," and we can see in the case of excommunication how the application of the stereotype led to faulty policy decisions. In spite of their transparent loathing for popular religion, the colonial officers believed that through it they could get at the

"truth." Orthodoxy to the Greeks, they believed, stood in the same relationship, as they perceived it, as Catholicism to the Irish. They
thought thus that the church could provide the lever that could give
them some control over plebeian culture. What they failed to appreciate was that the peasants would as easily conceal information from the
church as they would the secular authorities. By having the high clergy
proclaim excommunications for acts that most villagers did not consider illegal, immoral, or even wrong, they accelerated the process of
alienation. This, in conjunction with the other readings of excommunication, sealed the fate of British policy. Legitimate theological
moral authority became vested in the village priest, and the church of
the state, because it was seen to be actively cooperating with outside
forces, lost all claims upon the villagers' obedience.

As legitimacy for the regime waned, overt peasant resistance
waxed. The pace of opposition to British rule accelerated during the
twenty-four years after 1840. The ideological foundation of this unrest
was not imposed on an unthinking peasantry from above; rather, as
this chapter has demonstrated, it resulted from an ideology constructed by peasants which gave meaning to their world. At one level
then, the attempt to maintain and even to expand cultural hegemony
by the English authorities failed as the peasants imposed their own interpretation of the government's actions and then used this understanding as a basis for action. Moreover, this development also gave
greater salience to the village priests' pleas for Greek men to resist
British rule (see page 196).

At the level of local politics and society, a related, yet more subtle,
dialogue was occurring. To illustrate it, we return to the incident with
which this chapter began. When Protopapas [Archbishop] Panayis
Kavalieratos performed the excommunication on the wintry Sunday,
he sent out a powerful message, the meaning of which would have
been clear to everyone in the rugged villages around Sami: Ioannis
Floratos was not a man to trifle with. By obtaining a decree of excommunication, he demonstrated to his supporters and foes alike that he
had patrons and protectors in the government, and he had the ability
to bend those men to act on his behalf. To his supporters, he signaled
that he could provide protection and services. To his enemies, he
showed that he could be a malevolent foe, capable of using his network of connections to deny them, for example, such vitally important

commodities as transit visas or any of the numerous licenses issued by the central authorities. Excommunication, then, became an additional card to be played in the game of power mediation.

Still another reading of excommunication occurred. By compelling the "alien"—by both locality and ethnicity—bureaucratic state and its lackeys, the aristocracy and the official church hierarchy, to act on their behalf, those obtaining excommunication decrees simultaneously enhanced their own prestige and reinforced indigenous notions as to the moral superiority of village society. When peasants such as Andreas Pefani (TIAK ED 5), Liksurioti Moschonas (TIAK ED 31), or the relatives of the slain Theodoratos Melisianatos (TIAK ED 76) petitioned and procured a decree of excommunication, they exploited the state by using its power for their own purpose. In a sense, they fooled the authorities and, thus, demonstrated by this inverse exploitation not only their own "cleverness" (in Greek, *poniria*) but that of their fellow Ionian/Greek/peasant/covillagers as well. And as we saw in chapter 2, *poniria* was a core element of Greek masculine self-identity. The public performance of excommunication provided symbolic confirmation of group identity and support for the ideology on which their claim to moral superiority was based.

The three broad sets of meaning read into the public performance of excommunication intersected and were mutually reinforcing. The boundaries and dichotomies between Us-Them, Greek-British, high church–low church, village-island, patron-client, legitimate authority–illegitimate authority all came into sharper focus when placed on public display by excommunication. Moreover, the integral connections between religion, identity, and legitimacy were made manifestly evident. By analyzing the genesis, implementation, and responses to the policy of excommunication for secular crime, then, we can gain penetrating insights into the complex interplay between a colonial power, local elites, and indigenous peasants in the process of mediating power and legitimizing authority. Each of them experienced dominion differently. Religion, all sides claimed, was the basis for their actions. "We are the Christians," they cried, and from this slogan followed manifold consequences. From this examination of religion and the policy of excommunication I hope to have shown the complex and multistranded connections between culture, identity, colonial rule, and resistance.

CHAPTER NINE

The Imperial Encounter
on the Ionian Islands

A Summary

In our discussion of the imperial encounter between Britons and Greeks in the Ionian Islands, we have examined a very wide variety of topics, from Mediterranean Irishness to carnival masks, from excommunicating clerics to knife duelists, to women who call each other whores. Since the case studies presented in this volume all have their own individual conclusion regarding where they fit into their respective literatures, the purpose of this brief concluding chapter is to discuss what I think are the threads that tie the chapters together. And there are, it seems to me, a number of elements that connect them. There are three themes that do so, and they represent the major conclusions we can draw from the studies presented here.

The first of these deals with identity. So much of the imperial encounter was shaped by the perceptions that the colliding cultures had of one another. We saw that through the application of stereotypes drawn from their experiences in Ireland and in other parts of the empire, the British colonial officers created a number of different identities for the Greeks. Based on a series of stock tropes and stereotypes, they believed that they had discovered the essential core of the Greek national character, and it was based upon this assessment that they created the policies and institutions of colonial rule. As we saw on numerous occasions, the actions that they took had unintended consequences largely because of the flawed vision of Greek identity that they had created. Be it in the area of peasant unrest, aristocratic privilege, the nature of civil society, or the role of the church in people's lives, the image of the Greeks as swarthy Irishmen or pale-skinned aborigines led the British to make assumptions about the Ionian islanders that led to misguided policies. Complicating the process further were the very different ways that colonizers and colonized had of speaking and thinking about the world. In addition there was a cultural divide among the Greeks that was based on differences of class and status. Finally, we saw how the Greeks crafted an identity for the British and how that shaped the ways in which the Greek elite both found accommodation and resisted imperial rule. Perceptions of identity, then, played a crucial role in determining how Greeks and Britons experienced dominion.

The discussion of identity presented here also makes a contribution to the literature on empire and identity generally. One of the powerful seductions of Orientalism is that it can lead us to suspect that *all* observations and evaluations of other cultures by Europeans are nothing more than reflections of the stock tropes that together constitute Orientalism. In other words, it is as if we are viewing a reflected picture of the world that is itself nothing but a reflection of a reflection. For example, a critic of the article on which chapter 6 is based chided me for falling prey to the trap of Orientalism by citing observations by colonial officers as if they were "true" (*American Historical Review*, 105, n. 5 (2000): 1868–69). What I hope that the studies in this volume have shown is that there was a tangible, perceptible reality to the imagined identities that both rulers and ruled created for one another. Aspects of Greek culture that the British honed in on—cunning, disingenuousness, and violence, for example—were in fact present and readily celebrated by the Greeks as central props of their national culture. In like vein, the aspects of British culture that the Greeks focused on were real. The crux of the matter was not that each side incorrectly observed key aspects of the other's behavior, but that each of them read the culture of the other in very different ways and made widely divergent evaluative judgments about it. In short, the bipolar, oppositional model of cultural understanding that Said's Orientalism can lead to can actually impair rather than enhance our understanding of imperialism. We need an analytical framework more attuned to nuances, complexity, and ambiguity.

A second, related observation we can draw from these studies refers to the ways that colonial initiatives, based on perceptions of national character, produced unintended consequences. Take, for example, the Colonial Office's endeavors at reform of the law and the judicial system. We saw that the British elevated legal reform so as to make it the centerpiece of their administration. Legal reform would both transform the character of the Greeks and legitimize British rule. The result, as many of the studies presented here have shown, were mixed. The endeavor to use the lower courts as a means of decreasing the rates of interpersonal violence did eventually achieve that goal, but only after a long and complicated history. Initially, it was plebeian women who exploited the opportunity presented by the new court system. Only after the courts had become masculinized did men start to settle their disputes with lawsuits rather than stilettos. And at that, even when they did avail themselves of the courts, it was not for the reasons that the British hoped. Greek men did not see the court as an impartial arbiter of the truth, but rather as a public forum in which they contested reputations and honor: thus the perennial problem of perjury that, at least for the British, impaired the operation of the courts throughout the period of the protectorate.

Even when pro-British Greeks embraced the reformist imperative of the Colonial Office, the results could be very different from what those in power expected. In chapter 3 we examined how the city fathers of Zakinthos endeavored to use municipal statutes as a way to "westernize" the Greeks. Many of the laws they passed dealt with the leisure activities of the plebeian class—drinking, gambling, prostitution—and with domestic behaviors and practices that were based on deeply held popular beliefs. So when the police used their discretionary prerogative to enforce these unpopular laws selectively, it undercut the legitimacy of the police and of criminal justice generally. This legitimacy, of course, was precisely what the British were hoping to achieve with legal reforms. Finally, as with so much else, the police as an institution continually became embroiled in the partisan disputes of the Greek elite. As the story of police chief Valsamakis and the foundlings suggests, could it have been otherwise given the very different understanding of the role of the state held by Greeks and the colonial officers?

My third observation is related to the other two, and it refers to the issue of hegemony and resistance. Both are useful concepts for examining the imperial encounter, but we need to analyze them with a keener eye toward their complexity and ambiguity. Was the British initiative in the area of law, policing, and punishment a hegemonic enterprise? The answer would have to be an affirmative. Was their attempt to co-opt the Orthodox Church one as well? Again, we must answer, yes. Yet, as we saw, the reality of how these policies worked was complex, the impact that they had was mixed, and the results they produced were often very different from what the British intended. Much the same is true with resistance. Did the Greeks resist the imperial enterprise of the British? In some ways they did and in many others they did not. In fact, many members of the Greek elite embraced the British initiatives, but they did so not as an attempt at collaboration or even accommodation with their imperial masters. They did so as a means of gaining the upper hand in their struggles for power with other Greeks. In Greek eyes, they were exploiting their colonial rulers and not the other way around. This is not to deny the hegemonic intent of colonial polices nor that Greeks occasionally openly and violently resisted them. They did. Instead, what these studies have done is to move the discussion away from an emphasis on a simple polarity between hegemony and resistance, and to suggest that the shared interaction between colonizers and colonized, rulers and ruled, foreigners and locals was complex, variegated, and filled with ambiguity. By emphasizing contingency and historical agency, intentionality and unintended consequences, this study has helped us to come to a better understanding of the processes of accommodation and resistance that shaped the shared experience of dominion between Britons and Greeks on the Ionian Islands during the nineteenth century.

NOTES

Preface.

1. Each chapter has its own introduction that contextualizes it in the relevant literature. Therefore, in this brief preface, I shall only summarize what I hope is the overall contribution of the book.

Chapter One.

1. J. J. Tumelty's 1957 University of Cambridge dissertation on the British administration of the islands is still the best starting point for any study of the topic. Michael Pratt's study of the subject (1978), for example, relies heavily on Tumelty. The major drawback with the piece is that it relies exclusively on Colonial Office records, and so the picture drawn is terribly one-sided.

Chapter Two.

1. Bowen was against either ceding the islands to Greece or granting them independence. He wrote a number of pieces in the popular press in Britain on the subject. Over time, he became less and less able to reconcile his love of the classical with his loathing of the contemporary (even though he married the daughter of the most important pro-British Ionian Islander of his time, Count Roma of Zakinthos) and so, in the end, espoused an argument that denied the Ionians any connection to the Golden Age: "The townspeople of Corfu are half Italian and half Albanian, and the whole population of at least that island is probably as far from the ancient Greeks as the mass of our own countrymen from the ancient Britons" (1862: 349).

2. Every traveler and colonial officer who wrote about their visit to the islands included descriptions of ancient monuments.

3. The best discussion of the relationship between European notions of "civilization" and self-control is to be found in the work of Norbert Elias (1978). See also the works of Peter Gay (1993) and Peter and Carol Stearns (1986) on this topic.

4. Others commenting on the laziness of the islanders were: Davy (1842: 140, 199, 203–4), Kirkwall (1864: 74), the Earl of Carlisle (1855: 217), Ansted (1863: 48, 55), and Bowen (1862: 317).

5. On this topic see Kirkwall (1864: 33, 74), Spencer (1853: 217), Kendrick 1822: 17), Martin (1856: 141), and Davy (1842: 130–31).

6. There has been intense debate about whether the Irish were a colonized people. The best summary of this literature is by Joseph Ruane (1992). He examines historical and anthropological materials on both sides of the issue and concludes that they were. My discussion is predicated on his conclusions.

7. Common in both Ireland and the Ionian Islands were stereotypes of the village priests as drunken, licentious, and venal (Taylor 1990; Kirkwall 1864: 32). In Greece, there is a long tradition of ribald humor aimed at priests for such behavior (Orso 1979: 90–114); for Spanish Catholic comparisons, see Brandes (1980) and Gilmore (1984).

8. The image (and the reality) of the violent Irish has been repeated so often in the historical literature so to be almost a truism. Some of the better discussions of Irish violence and the reasons for it can be found in Beames (1983), Clark and Donnelly (1983), Cornish (1978), Curtis (1968 and 1971), Lebow (1976), McEldowney (1991), and Palmer (1988).

9. I am not suggesting that lethal violence between Irish peasants did not occur or that it was not more common than assassinations. Nor am I arguing that Greeks did not kill landlords who violated communal norms. They did, and I analyze one especially prominent episode of interclass violence. My point here is that the English colonial officers comprehended Greek violence almost exclusively through a comparison with Whiteboy behavior.

10. See Andrew (1980), Frevert (1993: 210), Perkin (1969: 227, 274–76), Simpson (1988: 99); see Wyatt-Brown (1982: 55–59) and Greenberg (1996: 3–23) for a similar argument with reference to honor in the southern U.S. Greenberg, in particular, argued that lying was the most fundamental affront to a man's honor, and he found that among southern men of honor, of all possible insults the charge of lying was the one that would most directly escalate a dispute to violence (1996: 8).

11. Recent psychological studies cited by Barnes (1994: 103–8) suggest that in fact children are not prone to telling lies and part of their socialization into adulthood is learning to lie. This would further suggest that Victorian ideas about children and mendacity had more to do with cultural notions of stages of development than it did with adolescent behavior.

Chapter Three.

1. The municipal statutes were compiled and published as a pamphlet in 1869, *Diaphora Astinomikon Diataksis tis Dimotikis Astinomias Zakinthou* (Zakinthos: Rosolimou, 1869). The purpose of the publication was to revalidate those statutes that had been kept in force after the unification of the island with the Kingdom of Greece. Consequently, each statute was identified with

two dates: the initial date of passage during the protectorate and the date on which it had been revalidated. The laws are not labeled with sequential numbers and are arranged on the basis of the second of the dates provided. I have numbered them 1 through 136, and so in my numbering system, a law passed in 1835, for example, may have a higher number than one passed in 1836.

Chapter Five.

1. Sidney Smith Saunders (Consul-General) to Erskine, Jan. 29, 1867, *Dispatches from Her Majesty's Consuls in Corfu, Zante and Cephalonia containing Information in the State of Those Islands since the Withdrawal of British Protection, and Their Annexation to the Kingdom of Greece* (London: House of Parliament, 1867), enclosure 1, 36. This document is hereafter cited as *Dispatches*.

2. Government Press, *Esame di un progetto di legge per abolire in contratti di colonia parziaria perpetua nell' isola Corfu* (Kerkira: State Press, 1846); CO 136/585: Ward Memorandum, Oct. 1830, "On the Colono System" PRO; Kosmetatos (1972); David Hannell (1989).

3. On the question of discourse analysis in social history, see Palmer (1990).

4. Testimony by Anastasios Lambinato Bomboti at his trial on Oct. 11, 1849; A & P, *Dispatches from Sir H.G. Ward to Earl Grey regarding the recent disturbances on the island of Cephalonia* (London: House of Parliament, 1850), Oct. 19, 1849, enclosure 7, 29-35.

5. A & P, *Dispatches from Sir H.G. Ward to Earl Grey* (London: House of Parliament, 1850), Sept. 7, 1849, enclosure 3, 8-16.

6. The episode recounted here is derived from the correspondence of the chief of police preserved in a bound, unnumbered volume labeled "Petizioni, Suppliche, Demande, Requisizioni, 1853" (TIAK shelf 195, row 7). There are volumes for each year from 1821 to 1869 containing copies of all correspondence reviewed by or emanating from the office of the chief of police.

Chapter Six.

1. I introduced an element of stratification in selecting the sixteen sample years in order to ensure coverage. So, three to four years from each of the four decades of British rule were selected, but which years in each decade were determined randomly. In order to examine the operation of the system in its entirety, I recorded data from all levels: complaints and warrants, constables' reports, arrest registers, court proceedings from all levels of the judiciary, sentences and convictions, prison records, and correspondence inside the criminal justice system and between its functionaries and the colonial officers. I employ data from all of these levels in this examination of knife fighting.

2. Richard E. Nisbett and Dov Cohen assert that contemporary southerners are more prone to violence than other Americans because of the persistence of a "culture of honor" in the South. However, neither in the national-level surveys that they used nor in the social psychological tests that they conducted on University of Michigan students was any coherent definition of honor employed. In fact, they seem to conceptualize honor very differently from historians of the Old South, and so their work does not convincingly challenge the view that honor and dueling ebbed simultaneously (Nisbett and Cohen 1996).

3. The heated debate over whether or not there is such a cultural system need not concern us here. I am very aware of the dangers of reducing the varieties of contextually shaped behaviors down to a single gloss of honor. Nor do I argue that honor, as an ethical concept among Greek men, has remained constant through time. What I do contend, however, is that there is a connection between honor as ethnographers have recorded it in Greece during the recent past and the set of attitudes and behaviors that men during the nineteenth century described as honor. The literature on honor in the Mediterranean is vast. The major works consulted were: Davis 1977; Blok 1984: 51-70; D. Gilmore 1987. Those arguing against such a view include: Herzfeld 1980; 1984; Llobera 1986: 25-33; Goddard 1994: 57-92.

4. The formula describing the trend for assaults is $Yt=2297 + 3.04^*t$, while the equation for slander is $Yt=113.3 + 1.93^*t$.

5. The formula for arms-possession arrests is $Yt=2.1 + 1.25^*t$. The arrest rate rose by a multiple of six between 1820 and 1858.

6. One of the lord high commissioners of the islands, Lord Seaton (formerly Sir John Colborne), put it best when he wrote that it was the aim of the Colonial Office's legal system "to bring justice to the peasant's own door." Colonial Office 136/120 Public Records Office. Seaton to Stanley, Zakinthos, October 10, 1843.

Chapter Seven.

1. Hurtful indiscretion occurs when a person who because of their profession—physician or midwife, for example—learns secrets about a person and reveals those secrets to the detriment of the person's honor or property. It was treated as a contravention and punished by either a first- or second-degree incarceration or a fine of between £1 and £10.

2. I examined the pattern of complaints for slander by month in 1830, 1835, 1845, and 1856 and found no significant variation. Unlike some crimes, arson for instance, people reported slander fairly evenly throughout the year.

Abrahams, Roger D. 1972. Joking: The Training of the Man of Words in Talking Broad. In *Rappin' and Stylin' Out: Communication in Urban Black America,* ed. Thomas Kochman, 215–40. Urbana: University of Illinois Press.

Abrams, Philip. 1982. *Historical Sociology.* Ithaca: Cornell University Press.

Adas, Michael. 1982. Bandits, Monks, and Pretender Kings: Patterns of Peasant Resistance and Protest in Colonial Burma, 1826–1941. In *Power and Protest in the Countryside,* ed. Richard P. Weller and Scott E. Guggenheim, 75–105. Durham: Duke University Press.

————. 1987. *Prophets of Rebellion: Millenarian Protest Movements against the European Colonial Order.* Cambridge: Cambridge University Press.

Adler, Jeffrey S. 1997. "My mother-in-law is to blame, but I'll walk on her neck yet": Homicide in Late Nineteenth-century Chicago. *Journal of Social History* 31, no. 1: 253–77.

Alatas, Syed Hussein. 1977. *The Myth of the Lazy Native: A Study of the Image of Malays, Filipinos and Javanese from the 16th to the 20th Century and Its Function in the Ideology of Colonial Capitalism.* London: Frank Cass.

Allen, Theodore. 1994. *The Invention of the White Race.* New York: Verso.

Almeida, Miguel Vale de. 1996. *The Hegemonic Male: Masculinity in a Portuguese Town.* Providence: Berghahn Books.

Althuser, Louis. 1976. *Essays in Self-Criticism.* London: New Left Books.

Alvanas, P. H. 1984. *Peri ton Kerkyron Titlon Evgenias kai peri ton Timarion.* Athens: privately published.

Amodio, Ennio. 1989. An Accusatorial System in a Civil Law Country: The 1988 Italian Code of Criminal Procedure. *Temple Law Review* 62 (winter): 1211–24.

Anderson, Elijah. 1978. *A Place on the Corner.* Chicago: University of Chicago Press.

Anderson, Michael. 1988. *Population Change in North-western Europe 1750–1850.* London: Macmillan.

Andreades, Andreas. 1914. *Peri tes Oikonomikes Dioikises tes Eptanesos epi Venetokratias.* Athens: privately published.

Andrew, Donna T. 1980. The Code of Honour and Its Critics: The Opposition to Duelling in England, 1700–1850. *Social History* 5: 409–34.

Angelomatis-Tsougarakis, Helen. 1990. *The Eve of the Greek Revival: Travellers' Perceptions of Early Nineteenth-century Greece.* New York: Routledge.

Ansted, D. T. 1863. *The Ionian Islands in the Year 1863.* London: William H. Allen.

Antman, Mari-Elizabet. 1990. *Via and Poniria: Andres kai Yinaikes s'ena Ellinko Horio.* Athens: Kastanioti.

Appadurai, Arjun. 1981. *Worship and Conflict under Colonial Rule: A South India Case.* Cambridge: Cambridge University Press.

Archer, John E. 1985. "A Fiendish Outrage": A Study of Animal Maiming in East Anglia 1830–1870. *Agricultural History Review* 23: 2–27.

———. 1989. Under Cover of the Night: Arson and Animal Maiming. In *The Unquiet Countryside,* ed. G. E. Mingay, 65–79. Boston: Routledge.

———. 1991. *By a Flash and a Scare: Incendiarism, Animal Maiming, and Poaching in East Anglia, 1815–1870.* New York: Oxford University Press.

Asdarchas, Spyros I. 1994. The *Anagraffi* and Their World. In *Corfu: History, Urban Space and Architecture, XIV–XIX cent.,* ed. Ennio Concina and Aliki Nikiforou-Testone, 85–94. Kerkira: Cultural Society "Korkyra."

Augustinos, Olga. 1994. *French Odysseys: Greece in French Travel Literature from the Renaissance to the Romantic Era.* Baltimore: Johns Hopkins University Press.

Aya, Roderick. 1975. *The Missed Revolution: The Fate of Rural Rebels on Sicily and Southern Spain, 1840–1950.* Amsterdam: Universiteit van Amsterdam.

Ayers, Edward L. 1985. *Vengeance and Justice: Crime and Punishment in the 19th Century American South.* New York: Oxford University Press.

Bailey, F. G. 1991. *The Prevalence of Deceit.* Ithaca: Cornell University Press.

Bakalaki, Alexandra. 1994. Gender-Related Discourse and Representations of Cultural Specificity in Nineteenth-Century and Twentieth-Century Greece. *Journal of Modern Greek Studies* 12, no. 1: 75–112.

Baker, John Hamilton. 1990. *An Introduction to English Legal History.* Third ed. London: Butterworths.

Banfield, Edward C. 1958. *The Moral Basis of a Backward Society.* New York: The Free Press.

Barnes, J. A. 1994. *A Pack of Lies: Towards a Sociology of Lying.* Cambridge: Cambridge University Press.

Beames, Michael R. 1983. *Peasants and Power: The Whiteboy Movements and Their Control in Pre-famine Ireland.* New York: St. Martin's Press.

———. 1987. Rural Conflict in Pre-famine Ireland: Peasant Assassinations in Tipperary, 1837–1847. In *Nationalism and Popular Protest in Ireland,* ed. E. E. Philbin, 264–83. Cambridge: Cambridge University Press.

Bergmann, Jorg R. 1993. *Discreet Indiscretions: The Social Organization of Gossip*. New York: Aldine de Gruyter.

Blair, William. 1834. *The Scottish justices' manual: being an alphabetical compendium of the powers and duties of justices of the peace within Scotland, and of those points of law which they are most frequently called upon to decide.* Edinburgh [Scotland]: T. Clark.

Blayo, Y. 1980. Illegitimate Births in France from 1740 to 1829 and in the 1960s. In *Bastardy and Its Comparative History*, ed. Peter Laslett, Karen Oosterven, and Roger M. Smith, 278–83. Cambridge: Harvard University Press.

Blok, Anton. 1984. Rams and Billy-goats: A Key to the Mediterranean Code of Honour. In *Religion, Power and Protest in Local Communities: The Northern Shore of the Mediterranean*, ed. Eric R. Wolf, 51–70. The Hague: Mouton.

Boehm, Christopher. 1984. *Blood Revenge: The Enactment and Management of Conflict in Montenegro and Other Tribal Societies.* Philadelphia: University of Pennsylvania Press.

Bolt, Christine. 1984. Race and the Victorians. In *British Imperialism in the Nineteenth Century*, ed. C. C. Eldridge, 126–47. New York: St. Martin's.

Boon, James A. 1990a. *Affinities and Extremities: Crisscrossing the Bittersweet Ethnology of East Indies History, Hindu-Balinese Culture, and Indo-European Allure.* Chicago: University of Chicago Press.

———. 1990b. *Other Tribes, Other Scribes: Symbolic Anthropology in the Comparative Study of Cultures, Histories, Regions and Texts.* Cambridge: Cambridge University Press.

Boschi, Daniele. 1997. Homicide and Knife Fighting in Rome during the Nineteenth and Twentieth Centuries. In *Men and Violence: Masculinity, Honor Codes and Violent Rituals in Europe and America, 17th–20th Centuries*, ed. Pieter Spierenburg, 73–94. Columbus: The Ohio State University Press.

Boswell, John. 1988. *The Kindness of Strangers: The Abandonment of Children in Western Europe from Late Antiquity to the Renaissance.* New York: Pantheon Books.

Bottomley, Gillian. 1986. A World Divided—Studies of Gender Relations in Modern Greece. *Mankind* 16: 181–89.

Bourdieu, Pierre. 1991. *Language and Symbolic Power.* Translated by Gina Raymond, Matthew Adamson, and John B. Thompson. Cambridge: Harvard University Press.

Bowen, George F. 1862. Ionian Administration. *Quarterly Review* 91: 315–52.

Brandes, Stanley. 1979. *Metaphors of Masculinity: Sex and Status in Andalusian Folklore.* Philadelphia: University of Pennsylvania Press.

———. 1985. Women of Southern Spain: Aspirations, Fantasies, Realities. In *Sex and Gender in Southern Europe: Problems and Prospects*, ed. David D. Gilmore and Gretchen Gwynne, 111–28.

Breckenridge, Carol Appadurai, and Peter van der Veer, eds. 1993. *Orientalism and the Postcolonial Predicament: Perspectives on South Asia.* Philadelphia: University of Pennsylvania Press.

Brettell, Caroline B. 1986. Nineteenth Century Travellers' Accounts of the Mediterranean Peasant. *Ethnohistory* 33, no. 2: 159–73.

Broeker, Galen. 1970. *Rural Disorder and Police Reform in Ireland, 1812–1836.* London: Routledge.

Brown, Michael F. 1996. On Resisting Resistance. *American Anthropologist* 98, no. 4: 729–34.

Brown, Nathan. 1989. The Conspiracy of Silence and the Atomistic Political Activity of the Egyptian Peasantry, 1882–1952. In *Everyday Forms of Resistance,* ed. Forrest D. Colburn, 94–121. New York: M. E. Sharpe, Inc.

———. 1995. Law and Imperialism: Egypt in Comparative Perspective. *Law and Society Review* 29, no. 1: 103–25.

Bruce, Dickson D. 1979. *Violence and Culture in the Antebellum South.* Austin: University of Texas Press.

Burke, Peter. 1987. The Art of Insult in Early Modern Italy. *Culture and History* 2: 68–79.

Calisse, Carlo. 1928. *A History of Italian Law.* Boston: Little, Brown, and Company.

Calligas, Eleni. 1994. The "Rizopastai" (Radical-Unionists): Politics and Nationalism in the British Protectorate of the Ionian Islands, 1815–1864." Ph.D. diss. University of London.

Callincos, Alex. 1988. *Making History: Agency, Structure and Change in Social Theory.* Ithaca: Cornell University Press.

Campbell, J. K. 1964. *Honour, Family and Patronage. A Study of Institutional and Moral Values in a Greek Mountain Community.* Oxford: Oxford University Press.

———. 1992. The Greek Hero. In *Honor and Grace in Anthropology,* ed. J. G. Peristiany and Julian Pitt-Rivers, 129–49. New York: Cambridge University Press.

Cappelletti, Mauro, John Henry Merryman, and Joseph M. Perillo. 1967. *The Italian Legal System: An Introduction.* Stanford: Stanford University Press.

Carrier, James G. 1992a. Approaches to Articulation. In *History and Tradition in Melanesian Anthropology,* ed. James G. Carrier, 116–43. Berkeley: University of California Press.

———. 1992b. Occidentalism: The World Turned Upside Down. *American Ethnologist* 20, no. 1: 195–212.

———. 1995. Introduction. In *Occidentalism: Images of the West,* ed. James G. Carrier, 1–60. Oxford: Clarendon Press.

Certoma, G. Leroy. 1985. *The Italian Legal System.* London: Butterworths.

Chapman, Malcolm. 1982. "Semantics" and the "Celt." In *Semantic Anthropology,* ed. D. Parkin, 132–47. New York: Academic Press.

Clark, Anna. 1989. Whores and Gossips: Sexual Reputations in London 1770–1825. In *Current Issues in Women's History,* ed. Arina Angerman, 231–48. New York: Routledge.

Clark, Samuel, and James S. Donnelly Jr., eds. 1983. *Irish Peasants: Violence and Political Unrest, 1780–1914.* Madison: University of Wisconsin Press.

Cohen, Elizabeth S. 1991. "Courtesans" and "Whores": Words and Behavior in Roman Streets. *Women's Studies* 19, no. 2: 201–9.

———. 1992. Honor and Gender in the Streets of Early Modern Rome. *Journal of Interdisciplinary History* 22, no. 4: 597–625.

Cohen, G. A. 1978. *Karl Marx's Theory of History: A Defense.* Princeton: Princeton University Press.

———. 1982. Reply to Elster on "Marxism, Functionalism, and Game Theory." *Theory and Society* 11: 483–96.

Cohen, Thomas V., and Elizabeth S. Cohen. 1993. *Words and Deeds in Renaissance Rome: Trials before the Papal Magistrates.* Toronto: University of Toronto Press.

Colburn, Forrest D., ed. 1989. *Everyday Forms of Resistance.* Armonk: M. E. Sharpe, Inc.

Colley, Linda. 1992. *Britons: Forging the Nation, 1707–1837.* New Haven: Yale University Press.

Colquhoun, J. C. 1836. *Ireland: Popery and Priestcraft the Cause of Her Misery and Crime.* Sponsored by the Glasgow Protestant Society. Glasgow: William Collins.

Constantelos, Demetrios J. 1991. *Byzantine Philanthropy and Social Welfare.* New Rochelle, N.Y.: A. D. Caratzas.

Coombe, Rosemary J. 1991. Contesting the Self: Negotiating Subjectivities in Nineteenth-century Ontario Defamation Trials. *Studies in Law, Politics, and Society* 11: 3–40.

Corbin, Alain. 1990. *Women for Hire: Prostitution and Sexuality in France after 1850.* Cambridge: Harvard University Press.

Cornish, W. R. 1978. *Crime and Law in Nineteenth Century Britain.* Dublin: Irish University Press.

Corsini, C. 1976. Materiali per lo studio della famiglia in Toscana nei secoli 18–19: Gli esposti. *Quaderni Storici* 11: 998–1052.

———. 1983. L'enfant trouvé: Note démographique différentielle. *Annales de Démographie Historiques* 18:103–24.

Counihan, Carole. 1984. Bread as World: Food Habits and Social Relations in Modernizing Sardinia. *Anthropological Quarterly* 57: 47–59.

Couroucli, Maria. 1985. *Les oliviers du lignage: Une Grèce de tradition Venitienne*. Paris: Maisonneuve et Larose.

————. 1993. Heroes and their Shadows: The Hungry, The Humble and the Powerful. *Journal of Mediterranean Studies* 3, no. 1: 99–115.

Curtis Jr., L. P. 1968. *Anglo-Saxons and Celts: A Study of Anti-Irish Prejudice in Victorian England*. First ed. Bridgeport, Conn.: Conference on British Studies.

————. 1971. *Apes and Angels: The Irish in Victorian Caricature*. Newton Abbot, UK: David & Charles.

Dallmayr, Fred. 1996. *Beyond Orientalism: Essays on Cross-cultural Encounter*. Albany: State University of New York Press.

Daly, Martin, and M. Wilson. 1988. *Homicide*. New York: A. de Gruyter.

Dandolo, Andreas. 1851. *Les Iles Ioniennes sous les protection Britannique*. Kerkyra: privately published.

Danforth, Loring M. 1976. Humour and Status Reversal in Greek Shadow Theatre. *Byzantine and Modern Greek Studies* 2: 99–111.

Daunton, Martin, and Rick Halpern, eds. 1999. *Empire and Others: British Encounters with Indigenous Peoples, 1660–1850*. Philadelphia: University of Pennsylvania Press.

Davidson, Allan K. 1990. Colonial Christianity: The Contribution of the Society for the Propagation of the Gospel to the Anglican Church in New Zealand 1840–80. *Journal of Religious History* 16, no. 2: 173–84.

Davis, J. 1977. *People of the Mediterranean: An Essay in Comparative Social Anthropology*. London: Routledge and Kegan Paul.

Davy, John. 1842. *Notes and Observations on the Ionian Islands and Malta*. London: Smith, Elder and Co.

De Bono, Angelos Dionisios. 1985. *I Pitharkiki Prostasia: Apo tous Laou tis Kefallenias*. Argostoli: Epitropis Kallitechnikon kai Politistikon Dimou Argostoliou.

Del Duca, Louis F., and Vincenzo Zeno-Zencovich. 1991. An Historic Convergence of Civil and Common Law Systems—Italy's New "Adversarial" Criminal Procedure System. *Dickinson Journal of International Law* 10 (fall): 73–92.

Delasselle, Claude. 1978. Abandoned Children in Eighteenth-Century Paris. In *Deviants and the Abandoned in French Society,* ed. Robert Forster and Orest Ranum, 47–82. Baltimore: Johns Hopkins University Press.

Dietz, Peter. 1994. *The British in the Mediterranean*. London: Brassey's, distributed in North America by Macmillan Pub. Co.

Dimitriou-Kotsoni, Sibylla. 1995. Dramatization and De-Dramatization: Conflict and Joking in an Aegean Island. *Journal of Mediterranean Studies* 5, no. 1: 33–49.

Dixon, C. Willis. 1969. *The Colonial Administrations of Sir Thomas Maitland*. New York: Augustus M. Kelley.

Donnelly Jr., James S. 1983. Pastorini and Captain Rock: Millenarianism and Sectarianism in the Rockite Movement. In *Irish Peasants: Violence and Political Unrest, 1780–1914,* ed. Samuel Clark and James S. Donnelly Jr., 102–42. Madison: University of Wisconsin Press.

Dörpfeld, Wilhelm. 1927. *Alt-Itahka.* München: Verlag Richard Uhde.

du Boulay, Juliet. 1974. *Portrait of a Greek Mountain Village.* Oxford: Clarendon Press.

———. 1976. Lies, Mockery and Family Integrity. In *Mediterranean Family Structures,* ed. J. G. Peristiany, 389–406. Cambridge: Cambridge University Press.

———. 1986. Women—Images of Their Nature and Destiny. In *Gender and Power in Rural Greece,* ed. Jill Dubisch, 139–68. Princeton: Princeton University Press.

———. 1991. Strangers and Gifts: Hostility and Hospitality in Rural Greece. *Journal of Mediterranean Studies* 1, no. 1: 37–53.

Dubbini, Renzo. 1994. Between Myth and History: Views of the Ionian Islands in the Romantic Era. In *Corfu: History, Urban Space and Architecture, XIV–XIX cent.,* ed. Ennio Concina and Aliki Nikiforou-Testone, 113–18. Kerkira: Cultural Society "Korkyra."

Dubisch, Jill. 1974. The Domestic Power of Women in a Greek Island Village. *Studies in European Society* 1, no. 1: 23–33.

———. 1986a. Introduction. In *Gender and Power in Rural Greece,* ed. Jill Dubisch, 3–41. Princeton: Princeton University Press.

———. 1986b. Culture Enters Through the Kitchen: Women, Food, and Social Boundaries in Rural Greece. In *Gender and Power in Rural Greece,* ed. Jill Dubisch, 195–214. Princeton: Princeton University Press.

Dunbabin, J. P. D. 1974. *Rural Discontent in Nineteenth Century Britain.* New York: Holmes and Meier.

Durkheim, Emile. 1960. *The Division of Labour in Society.* London: The Free Press.

Edgeworth, Brendan. 1990. Defamation Law and the Emergence of a Critical Press in Colonial New South Wales (1824–1831). *Australian Journal of Law and Society* 6: 50–82.

Eldridge, C. C. 1969. The Myth of Mid-Victorian "Separatism": The Cessasion of the Bay Islands and the Ionian Islands in the Early 1860s. *Victorian Studies* 12: 331–46.

Eley, Geoff, and Keith Nield. 1980. Why Does Social History Ignore Politics? *Social History* 5: 249–72.

Elias, Norbert. 1978. *Power and Civility: The Civilizing Process.* New York: Pantheon Books.

Elster, Jon. 1982. Marxism, Functionalism, and Game Theory: The Case for Methodological Individualism. *Theory and Society* 11: 453–82.

————. 1985. *Making Sense of Marx*. Cambridge: Cambridge University Press.

Empson, William. 1834. Tyler on Oaths. *The Edinburgh Review* 59: 446–74.

Esmein, Adhemar. 1913. *A History of Continental Criminal Procedure, with Special Reference to France*. Boston: Little, Brown, and Company.

Fabian, Johannes. 1983. *Time and the Other: How Anthropology Makes Its Object*. New York: Columbia University Press.

Fairchilds, Cissie. 1980. Female Sexual Attitudes and the Rise of Illegitimacy: A Case Study. In *Marriage and Fertility: Studies in Interdisciplinary History*, ed. Robert I. Rotberg and Theodore K. Rabb, 163–203. Princeton: Princeton University Press.

Feierman, Steven. 1990. *Peasant Intellectuals: Anthropology and History in Tanzania*. Madison: University of Wisconsin Press.

Feingold, William L. 1984. *The Revolt of the Tenantry: The Transformation of Local Government in Ireland, 1872–1886*. Boston: Northeastern University Press.

Finlay, George. 1971. *History of the Greek Revolution and the Reign of King Otho*. London: Zeno Reprints.

Fitch, Nancy. 1986. "Les petits parisiens en Provence": The Silent Revolution in the Allier. *Journal of Family History* 11: 131–55.

Fitzroy, Charles. 1850. *Letters and Documents from Other Sources on Past and Recent Events in The Ionian Islands Shewing the Anomalous Political and Financial Positions of those States*. London: James Ridgway.

Fletcher, Jonathan. 1997. *Violence and Civilization*. Cambridge: Polity Press.

Forsythe, William. 1860. Process of Legal Reform. *The Edinburgh Review* CXI: 189–203.

Foster, George M. 1965. Peasant Society and the Image of the Limited Good. *American Anthropologist* 67: 293–315.

Fox-Genovese, Elizabeth, and Eugene D. Genovese. 1976. The Political Crisis of Social History: A Marxist Perspective. *Journal of Social History* 10: 205–20.

Fox, Robin. 1967. *Marriage and Kinship*. Harmondsworth: Penguin.

Frader, Linda Levine. 1991. *Peasants and Protest: Agricultural Workers, Politics and Unions in the Aude, 1850–1914*. Berkeley: University of California Press.

Franks, Matthew E. 1998. Cadastral Kerkyra: The World System in Eighteenth Century Venetian Commodity Production. *Journal of the Hellenic Diaspora* 24, no. 2: 41–68.

Frazee, Charles. 1969. *The Orthodox Church and Independent Greece 1821–1852*. Cambridge: Cambridge University Press.

————. 1979. The Greek Catholic Islanders and the Revolution of 1821. *East European Quarterly* 13: 315–26.

Freeman, Edward Augustus. 1881. *Sketches from the Subject and Neighbour Lands of Venice*. London: Macmillan and Co.

Frevert, Ute. 1991. *Ehrenmänner: das Duell in der bürgerlichen Gesellschaft.* München: C. H. Beck.

———. 1993. Honour and Middle-class Cultures: The History of the Duel in England and Germany. In *Bourgeois Society in Nineteenth-century Europe,* ed. Jürgen Kocka and Alan Mitchell, 207–40. Providence: Berg.

———. 1995. *Men of Honour: A Social History of the Duel.* New York: Basil Blackwell.

———. 1998. The Taming of the Noble Ruffian: Male Violence and Duelling in Early Modern and Modern Germany. In *Men and Violence: Masculinity, Honor Codes and Violent Rituals in Europe and America, 17th–20th Centuries,* ed. Pieter Spierenburg, 23–47. Columbus: The Ohio State University Press.

Friedl, Ernestine. 1962. *Vasilika: A Village in Modern Greece.* New York: Holt, Rinehart, Winston.

———. 1986. The Position of Women: Appearance and Reality. In *Gender and Power in Rural Greece,* ed. Jill Dubisch, 42–52. Princeton: Princeton University Press.

Friedman, Jonathan. 1989. Culture, Identity and World Process. In *Domination and Resistance,* ed. Daniel Miller, Michael Rowlands, and Christopher Tilley, 246–60. Boston: Unwin Hyman.

———. 1992. The Past in the Future: History and the Politics of Identity. *American Anthropologist* 94, no. 4: 837–59.

Fuchs, Rachel. 1984. *Abandoned Children: Foundlings and Child Welfare in 19th Century France.* Albany: SUNY Press.

———. 1987. Legislation, Poverty and Child-abandonment in Nineteenth-century France. *Journal of Interdisciplinary History* 18 (summer): 55–80.

Fuchs, Rachel, and Leslie Page Moch. 1990. Pregnant, Single, and Far From Home: Migrant Women in Nineteenth-Century Paris. *American Historical Review* 95: 1007–31.

Fuchs, Rachel G., and Paul E. Knepper. 1989. Women in the Paris Maternity Hospital: Public Policy in the Nineteenth-century. *Social Science History* 13: 187–209.

Gallant, Thomas W. 1982. An Examination of Two Island Polities in Antiquity: The Lefkas-Pronnoi Survey. Ph.D. diss., University of Cambridge.

———. 1988. Greek Bandit Gangs: Lone Wolves or a Family Affair? *Journal of Modern Greek Studies* 6: 269–90.

———. 1990. Peasant Ideology and Excommunication for Crime in a Colonial Context: The Ionian Islands (Greece), 1817–1864. *Journal of Social History* 24, no. 3: 485–512.

———. 1991. Agency, Structure and Explanation in Social History: The Case of the Foundling Home on Kephallenia, Greece, during the 1830s. *Social Science History* 15, no. 4: 479–508.

———. 1994. Turning the Horns: Cultural Metaphors, Material Conditions, and the Peasant Language of Resistance in Ionian Islands (Greece) during the Nineteenth Century. *Comparative Studies in Society and History* 36, no. 4: 702–19.

———. 1995. Collective Action and Atomistic Actors: Labor Unions, Strikes, and Crime in Greece in the Post-war Era. In *Greece Toward the 21st Century*, ed. Theofanis Stavrou and Dimitri Constas, 149–90. Baltimore: Johns Hopkins University Press.

———. 1998. Murder in a Mediterranean City: Homicide Trends in Athens, 1850–1936. *Journal of the Hellenic Diaspora* 24, no. 1: 1–27.

———. 2000a. Honor, Masculinity, and Ritual Knife-fighting in Nineteenth Century Greece. *American Historical Review* 105, no. 2: 359–82.

———. 2000b. Crime, Violence, and Reform of the Criminal Justice System during the Era of Trikoupis. In *O Harilaos Trikoupis and I Epochi tou*, ed. K. Aroni-Tsihli and L. Triha, 401–10. Athens: Papazisis.

———. 2001. *Modern Greece*. London: Arnold.

Garrioch, David. 1987. Verbal Insults in Eighteenth-century Paris. In *The Social History of Language*, ed. Peter Burke and Roy Porter, 104–19. New York: Cambridge University Press.

Gatley, Clement. 1967. *Gatley on Libel and Slander*. London: Sweet & Maxwell.

Gay, Peter. 1985. *The Bourgeois Experience from Victoria to Freud. Volume 1: Education of the Senses*. New York: Oxford University Press.

———. 1986. *The Bourgeois Experience from Victoria to Freud. Volume 2: The Tender Passions*. New York: Oxford University Press.

———. 1993. *The Bourgeois Experience from Victoria to Freud. Volume 5: The Cultivation of Hatred*. New York: Oxford University Press.

Gellner, Ernest. 1983. *Nations and Nationalism*. Oxford: Basil Blackwell.

Gibbons, Luke. 1996. Topographies of Terror: Killarney and the Politics of the Sublime. *South Atlantic Quarterly* 95, no. 1: 23–44.

Gibson, Mary. 1986. *Prostitution and the State in Italy, 1860–1915*. New Brunswick: Rutgers University Press.

Giddens, Anthony. 1978. *Central Problems in Social Theory: Action, Structure and Contradictions in Social Analysis*. Berkeley: University of California Press.

———. 1984. *The Constitution of Society: Outline of a Theory of Stucturation*. Berkeley: University of California Press.

Giffard, Edward. 1837. *A Short Visit to the Ionian Islands, Athens and the Morea*. London: John Murray.

Gilmore, David D. 1984. Andalusian Anti-clericalism: An Eroticized Rural Protest. *Anthropology* 8, no. 1: 31–44.

———. 1987a. *Aggression and Community: The Paradoxes of Andalusian Culture*. New Haven: Yale University Press.

————. 1987b. The Shame of Dishonor. In *Honor and Shame and the Unity of the Mediterranean*, ed. David D. Gilmore, 2–21. Washington, D.C.: American Anthropological Association.

————, ed. 1987. *Honor and Shame and the Unity of the Mediterranean*. Washington, D.C.: American Anthropological Association.

————. 1990. *Manhood in the Making: Cultural Concepts of Masculinity*. New Haven: Yale University Press.

Gilsenan, Michael. 1976. Lying, Honor and Contradiction. In *Transaction and Meaning: Directions in the Anthropology of Exchange and Symbolic Behavior*, ed. Bruce Kapferer, 191–219. Philadelphia: Institute for the Study of Human Issues.

Goddard, Victoria A. 1994. From Mediterranean to Europe: Honour, Kinship and Gender. In *The Anthropology of Europe: Identities and Boundaries in Conflict*, ed. Victoria A. Goddard, Jospe R. Llobera, and Cris Chore, 57–92. Providence: Berg Publishers.

Goodison, William A. 1822. *Topographical and Historical Essay upon the Islands of Corfu, Leucadia, Cephalonia, and Zante*. London: Thomas and George Underwood.

Gorky, Maxim. 1987. Peasantry in the Eyes of Others: The Barbarians. In *Peasants and Peasant Society*, ed. Teodor Shanin, 382–84. New York: Basil Blackwell.

Gorn, Elliot J. 1985. "Gouge and Bite, Pull Hair and Scratch": The Social Significance of Fighting in the Southern Backcountry. *American Historical Review* 90, no. 1: 18–43.

Gourgouris, Stathis. 1996. *Dream Nation: Enlightenment, Colonization, and the Institution of Modern Greece*. Stanford: Stanford University Press.

Gowing, Laura. 1995. Language, Power, and the Law: Women's Slander Legislation in Early Modern London. In *Women, Crime, and the Courts in Early Modern England*, ed. Jenny Kermode and Garthine Walker, 26–47. Chapel Hill: University of North Carolina Press.

————. 1996. *Domestic Dangers: Women, Words, and Sex in Early Modern London*. New York: Oxford University Press.

Green, Thomas Andrew. 1985. *Verdict According to Conscience: Perspectives on the English Criminal Trial Jury, 1200–1800*. Chicago: University of Chicago Press.

Greenberg, Kenneth. 1996. *Honor and Slavery: Lies, Duels, Noses, Masks, Dressing as Women, Gifts, Strangers, Humanitarianism, Death, Slave Rebellions, the Proslavery Argument, Baseball, Hunting and Gambling in the Old South*. Princeton: Princeton University Press.

Gregory, Desmond. 1986. A Defence Policy for the Ionian Islands—Some Wrong Conclusions Drawn by Soldiers and Statesmen. *Journal of the Society for Army Historical Research* 64, no. 257: 24–33.

Groebner, Valentin. 1995. Losing Face, Saving Face: Noses and Honour in the Late Medieval Town. *History Workshop* 40: 1–15.

Gullickson, Gay L. 1986. *Spinners and Weavers of Auffay: Rural Industry and Sexual Division of Labor in a French Village, 1750–1850*. Cambridge: Cambridge University Press.

Hall, Sammuel. 1981. In Defence of Theory. In *People's History and Socialist Theory*, ed. Raphael Samuel, 378–85. London: Routledge and Kegan Paul.

Hammel, Eugene, M. Johansson, and S. Ginsberg. 1983. The Value of Childern during Industrialization: Childhood Sex Ratios in Nineteenth-century America. *Journal of Family History* 8: 346–66.

Hannell, David. 1987. A Case of Bad Publicity: Britain and the Ionian Islands. *European History Quarterly* 17, no. 2: 131–43.

———. 1989. The Ionian Islands under the British Protectorate: Social and Economic Problems. *Journal of Modern Greek Studies* 7, no. 1: 105–32.

Harris, Marvin. 1987. Cultural Materialism: Alarums and Excursions. In *Waymarks: The Notre Dame Inaugural Lectures in Anthropology*, ed. Kenneth More, 107–35. Notre Dame: University of Notre Dame Press.

Harsin, Jill. 1985. *Policing Prostitution in Nineteenth-Century Paris*. Princeton: Princeton University Press.

Harwood, Philip. 1843. The Law of Oaths. *The Westminster Review* 39: 80–104.

Hatch, Elvin. 1989. Theories of Social Honor. *American Anthropologist* 91, no. 2: 341–54.

Helmholz, Richard H. 1984. *Juries, Libel & Justice: The Role of English Juries in Seventeenth- and Eighteenth-Century Trials for Libel and Slander: Papers Read at a Clark Library Seminar 28 February 1981*. Los Angeles: William Andrews Clark Memorial Library, University of California.

———. 1987. Damages in Actions for Slander at Common Law. *The Law Quarterly Review* 103 (October): 624–38.

Henderson, G. P. 1988. *The Ionian Academy*. Edinburgh: Scottish Academic Press.

Hennock, E. P. 2000. The Urban Sanitary Movement in England and Germany, 1838–1914: A Comparison. *Continuity and Change* 15, no. 2: 269–96.

Herzfeld, Michael. 1980. Honour and Shame: Problems in the Comparative Analysis of Moral Systems. *Man* 15: 339–51.

———. 1982. *Ours Once More: Folklore, Ideology and the Making of Modern Greece*. Austin: University of Texas Press.

———. 1983. Semantic Slippage and Moral Fall: The Rhetoric of Chastity in Rural Greek Society. *Journal of Modern Greek Studies* 1, no. 1: 161–72.

———. 1984. The Horns of a Mediterraneanist Dilemma. *American Ethnologist* 1115, no. 3: 439–54.

————. 1985. *The Poetics of Manhood: Contest and Identity in a Cretan Mountain Village*. Princeton: Princeton University Press.

————. 1986. Within and Without: The Category of "Female" in the Ethnography of Modern Greece. In *Gender and Power in Rural Greece*, ed. Jill Dubisch, 215–34. Princeton: Princeton University Press.

————. 1987a. *Anthropology Through the Looking Glass: Critical Ethnography in the Margins of Europe*. Cambridge: Cambridge University Press.

————. 1987b. "As in Your Own House": Hospitality, Ethnography, and the Stereotype of Mediterranean Society. In *Honor and Shame and the Unity of the Mediterranean*, ed. David D. Gilmore, 75–89. Washington, D.C.: American Anthropological Association.

————. 1990. Pride and Perjury: Time and the Oath in the Mountain Villages of Crete. *Man* 25: 305–22.

————. 1991. Silence, Submission, and Subversion: Toward a Poetics of Womanhood. In *Contested Identities: Gender and Kinship in Modern Greece*, ed. Peter Loizos and Evthymios Papataxiarchis, 79–97. Princeton: Princeton University Press.

————. 1995. Hellenism and Occidentalism: The Permutations of Performance in Greek Bourgeois Identity. In *Occidentalism: Images of the West*, ed. James G. Carrier, 218–33. Oxford: Clarendon Press.

Hill, Matthew Davenport. 1850–1851. The Duties of Witnesses and Jurymen. *Household Words* II: 100–104.

Hirschon, Renée. 1989. *Heirs of the Catastrophe: The Social Life of Asia Minor Refugees in Piraeus*. Oxford: Clarendon Press.

Hitiris, G. 1981. *To Kerkiraiko Agrotiko Provlima tin Epomeni tis Enoseos kai i Anafores tou anglou Proksenou*. Kerkyra: Dimosievmata Etairia Kerkiraikon Spoudon.

Hobsbawm, Eric. 1960. *Social Bandits and Primitive Rebels: Studies in Archaic Forms of Social Movements in the 19th and 20th Centuries*. Glencoe, Ill.: The Free Press.

Hobsbawm, Eric, and George Rude. 1975. *Captain Swing*. New York: Norton.

Hochstadt, S. L. 1975–1984. Social History and Politics: A Materialist View. *Social History* 7: 1982.

Hoffer, Peter Charles. 1989. Honor and the Roots of American Litigiousness. *American Journal of Legal History* 33, no. 4: 295–319.

Holdsworth, Sir William Searle. 1936–1966. *A History of English Law*. London: Methuen.

Holland, Henry. 1815. *Travels in the Ionian Isles, Albania, Thessaly, Macedonia, etc.* London: Longman, Hurts, Rees, Orme and Brown.

Holmes, Douglas. 1989. *Cultural Disenchantments: Worker Peasantries in Northeast Italy*. Princeton: Princeton University Press.

Hughes, Steven C. 1997. Men of Steel: Duelling, Honor and Politics in Liberal Italy. In *Men and Violence: Masculinity, Honor Codes and Violent Rituals in Europe and America, 17th–20th Centuries,* ed. Pieter Spierenburg, 95–114. Columbus: The Ohio State University Press.

Ignatiev, Noel. 1995. *How the Irish Became White.* New York: Routledge.

Ingram, Martin. 1987. *Church Courts, Sex, and Marriage in England, 1570–1640.* New York: Cambridge University Press.

———. 1995. "Scolding Women Cucked or Washed": A Crisis in Gender Relations in Early Modern England? In *Women, Crime, and the Courts in Early Modern England,* ed. Jenny Kermode and Garthine Walker, 48–80. Chapel Hill: University of North Carolina Press.

Jervis, Henry Jervis-White. 1852. *History of the Island of Corfu, and the Republic of the Ionian Islands.* London: Colburn and Co.

Johnson, Eric A., and Eric H. Monkkonen. 1996. Introduction. In *The Civilization of Crime: Violence in Town and Countryside since the Middle Ages,* ed. Eric A. Johnson and Eric H. Monkkonen, 1–16. Urbana: University of Illinois Press.

Johnson, R. 1981. Against Absolutism. In *People's History and Socialist Theory,* ed. Raphael Samuel, 386–95. London: Routledge and Kegan Paul.

Jones, David J. V. 1985. *The Last Rising: The Newport Insurrection of 1839.* Oxford: Oxford University Press.

———. 1989. *Rebecca's Children: A Study of Rural Society, Crime, and Protest.* Oxford: Clarendon Press.

Jones, Gareth Stedman. 1983. *Language of Class: Studies in English Working Class History 1832–1982.* Cambridge: Cambridge University Press.

Joyce, Patrick. 1989. The Historical Meaning of Work: An Introduction. In *The Historical Meaning of Work,* ed. Patrick Joyce, 1–30. Cambridge: Cambridge University Press.

Judt, Tony. 1979. A Clown in Regal Purple: Social History and the Historians. *History Workshop* 6: 66–94.

Kalligas, Eleni. 1990. *I Pronia yia to Paidi stin Ellada to 19ou Aiona.* Ioannina: Dodoni.

Kaplan, Steven Laurence, and Cynthia J. Koepp, eds. 1986. *Work in France: Representations, Meanings, Organization and Practice.* Ithaca: Cornell University Press.

Kartodirdjo, Sartono. 1973. *Protest Movements in Rural Java: A Study of Agrarian Unrest in the Nineteenth and Twentieth Centuries.* Singapore: Oxford University Press.

Kendrick, Tetius T. C. 1822. *The Ionian Islands. Manners and Customs.* London: James Haldane.

Kertzer, David I. 1993. *Sacrificed for Honor: Italian Infant Abandonment and the Politics of Reproductive Control.* Boston: Beacon Press.

Kiernan, V. G. 1988. *The Duel in European History: Honour and the Reign of Aristocracy*. Oxford: Oxford University Press.

Kimmel, Michael S. 1996. *Manhood in America: A cultural history*. New York: Free Press.

King, Andrew J. 1991. The Law of Slander in Early Antebellum America. *American Journal of Legal History* 35, no. 1: 1–43.

———. 1995. Constructing Gender: Sexual Slander in Nineteenth-century America. *Law and History Review* 13, no. 1: 63–110.

King, Peter. 1996. Punishing Assault: The Transformation of Attitudes in the English Courts. *The Journal of Interdisciplinary History* 26, no. 1: 43–75.

Kirkwall, Viscount. 1864. *Four Years in the Ionian Islands: Their Political and Social Conditions*. London: Chapman and Hill.

Kloos, Peter. 1983. Nothing But the Truth, a Question of Power. *Journal of Northern Luzon* 14: 121–37.

Knodel, John E. 1988. *Demographic Behavior in the Past: A Study of Fourteen German Village Populations in the Eighteenth and Nineteenth Centuries*. Cambridge: Cambridge University Press.

Knox, B. 1984. British Policy and the Ionian Islands, 1847–1864: Nationalism and Imperial Administration. *English Historical Review* 99: 503–29.

Kochman, Thomas. 1972. Toward an Ethnography of Black American Speech Behavior. In *Rappin' and Stylin' Out: Communication in Black America*, ed. Thomas Kochman, 241–56. Urbana: University of Illinois Press.

Kock, Gerald L. 1964. *The French Code of Criminal Procedure*. South Hackensack, N.J.: F. B. Rothman.

Koliopoulos, John S. 1987. *Brigands with a Cause: Brigandage and Irredentism in Modern Greece, 1821–1912*. Oxford: Clarendon Press.

Konczal, Michael A. 1989. *Defamation Law in Louisiana, 1800–1988*. Lanham, Md.: University Press of America.

Kosmetatos, N. 1972. H Kalliergia tis Stafidos en Kefallenia. *Parnassos* 23: 276–284S.

Kotzageorgi, Xanthippi. 1992. British Travellers in the Early Nineteenth Century on Greece and the Greeks. *Balkan Studies* 33, no. 2: 209–21.

Kriger, Norma J. 1992. *Zimbabwe's Guerrilla War: Peasant Voices*. New York: Cambridge University Press.

Kukku, E. E. 1983. *Istoria ton Eptanison apo to 1797 mehri tin anglokratia*. Athens: D. N. Papadima.

Kuper, Adam. 1988. *The Invention of Primitive Society: Transformations of an Illusion*. Boston: Routledge.

Kupferman, Theodore R., ed. 1990. *Defamation—Libel and Slander*. Westport, Conn.: Meckler.

Labov, William. 1972. Rules of Ritual Insults. In *Rappin' and Stylin' Out: Communication in Urban Black America*, first ed., ed. Thomas Kochman, 265–314. Urbana: University of Illinois Press.

Laslett, Peter. 1980. Introduction: Comparing Illegitimacy over Time and Between Cultures. In *Bastardy and Its Comparative History*, ed. Peter Laslett, Karen Oosterven, and Roger M. Smith, 1–65. Cambridge: Harvard University Press.

Lazaridis, Gabriella. 1995. Sexuality and Its Cultural Construction in Rural Greece. *Journal of Gender Studies* 4, no. 3: 281–97.

Lebow, Richard Ned. 1976. *White Britain and Black Ireland: The Influence of Stereotypes on Colonial Policy*. Philadelphia: Institute for the Study of Human Issues.

Lee, W. R. 1980. Bastardy and the Socio-economic Structure of South Germany. In *Marriage and Fertility: Studies in Interdisciplinary History*, ed. Robert I. Rotberg and Theodore K. Rabb, 121–44. Princeton: Princeton University Press.

Lehning, James R. 1982. Family Life and Wet Nursing in a French Village. *Journal of Interdisciplinary History* 12: 645–56.

Lencek, Lena, and Gideon Bosker. 1998. *The Beach: The History of Paradise on Earth*. New York: Viking.

Leontis, Artemis. 1995. *Topographies of Hellenism: Mapping the Homeland*. Ithaca: Cornell University Press.

Leontsinis, George N. 1994. Northwest European Influences on Education in the Ionian Islands 1780–1863. *History of European Ideas* 19, no. 4–6: 575–81.

Levine, David. 1987. *Reproducing Families: The Political Economy of English Population History*. Cambridge: Cambridge University Press.

Litchfield, R. Burr, and D. Gordon. 1980. Closing the "tour": A Close Look at the Marriage Market, Unwed Mothers, and Abandoned Children in Mid-Nineteenth-century Amiens. *Journal of Social History* 13: 458–72.

Llobera, Josep P. 1986. Fieldwork in Southwestern Europe: Anthropological Panacea or Epistemological Straitjacket? *Critique of Anthropology* 6, no. 2: 25–33.

Lloyd, Christopher. 1988. *Explanation in Social History*. Oxford: Basil Blackwell.

Loizos, Peter, and Evthymios Papataxiarchis, eds. 1991. *Contested Identities: Gender and Kinship in Modern Greece*. Princeton: Princeton University Press.

Mackesy, Piers. 1957. *The War in the Mediterranean 1803–1810*. Cambridge: Harvard University Press.

Mahairas, K. 1940. *Lefkas kai Lefkadi epi Anglikis Prostasias (1810–1864)*. Athens: Karavia.

Manchester, Colin. 1991. A History of the Crime of Obscene Libel. *Journal of Legal History* 12, no. 1: 36–57.

Mani, Lati, and Ruth Frankenberg. 1985. The Challenge of *Orientalism*. *Economy and Society* 14, no. 2: 174–92.

Margaritis, Stephen. 1978. *Crete and the Ionian Islands under the Venetians.* Athens: Leontiadis Publishing.

Marshall, P. J. 1995. Imperial Britain. *Journal of Imperial and Commonwealth History* 23, no. 3: 379–94.

Martin, Robert Montgomery. 1856. *The British Colonies. Volume 6: The Mediterranean.* London: The London Printing and Publishing Company.

Matesis, Antonios. 1981. *O Vasilikos.* Fifth ed. Athens: Hermes.

McAleer, Kevin. 1994. *Dueling: The Cult of Honor in Fin-de-Siècle Germany.* Princeton: Princeton University Press.

McClure, Ruth K. 1981. *Coram's Children: The London Foundling Hospital in the Eighteenth Century.* New Haven: Yale University Press.

McDonald, Maryon. 1993. The Construction of Difference: An Anthropological Approach to Stereotypes. In *Inside Mediterranean Identities: Ethnography in Western Europe,* ed. Sharon Macdonald, 219–36. Providence: Berg Publishers.

McEldowney, John F. 1991. Policing and the Administration of Justice in Nineteenth-Century Ireland. In *Policing Western Europe: Politics, Professionalism, and Public Order, 1850–1940,* ed. Clive Emsley and Barbara Weinberger, 18–35. Westport, Conn.: Greenwood Publishing Group, Inc.

McGowen, Randall. 1983. The Image of Justice and Reform of the Criminal Law in Early Nineteenth-century England. *Buffalo Law Review* 32: 91–125.

McLaren, Angus. 1997. *The Trials of Masculinity: Policing Sexual Boundaries, 1870–1930.* Chicago: University of Chicago Press.

Medick, Hans. 1987. "Missionaries in a Row Boat"? Ethnological Ways of Knowing as a Challenge to Social History. *Comparative Studies in Society and History* 29: 76–98.

Memmi, Albert. 1990. *The Colonizer and the Colonized.* London: Earthscan.

Merry, Sally Engle. 1984. Rethinking Gossip and Scandal. In *Toward a General Theory of Social Control. Volume 1: Fundamentals,* ed. Donald Black, 271–302. New York: Academic Press.

———. 1991. Law and Colonialism. *Law and Society Review* 25, no. 4: 879–922.

———. 1995. Resistance and the cultural power of law. *Law and Society Review* 29, no. 1: 11–26.

Meyer, J. 1980. Illegitimates and Foundlings in Pre-industrial France. In *Bastardy and Its Comparative History,* ed. Peter Laslett, Karen Oosterven, and Roger M. Smith, 249–63. Cambridge: Harvard University Press.

Miller, Peter N. 1994. *Defining the Common Good: Empire, Religion, and Philosophy in Eighteenth-Century Britain.* Cambridge: Cambridge University Press.

Miller, William. 1903. The Ionian Islands under Venetian Rule. *The English Historical Review* 70: 209–39.

Mingay, G. E. 1989. "Rural War": The Life and Times of Captain Swing. In *The Unquiet Countryside*, ed. G. E. Mingay, 36–51. Boston: Routledge.

Mintz, Jerome R. 1997. *Carnival Song and Society: Gossip, Sexuality, and Creativity in Andalusia*. New York: Berg Publisher.

Mitchell, Timothy. 1991. *Colonizing Egypt*. Berkeley: University of California Press.

Moogk, Peter N. 1979. "Thieving Buggers" and "Stupid Sluts": Insults and Popular Culture in New France. *William and Mary Quarterly* 36, no. 4: 524–47.

Morgan, Cecilia. 1995. 'In Search of the Phantom Misnamed Honour': Duelling in Upper Canada (Conceptions of Masculine Honour). *Canadian Historical Review* 76, no. 4: 529–63.

Morris, Desmond et al., eds. 1979. *Gestures: Their Origins and Distributions*. London: Jonathan Cape.

Muchembled, Robert. 1989. *La violence au village. Sociabilité et comportements populaires en Artois du 15e au 17e siècle*. Turnhout, Belgium: Editions Brepols.

Muir, Edward. 1997. *Ritual in Early Modern Europe*. New York: Cambridge University Press.

Mure, William. 1852. *Journal of a Tour in Greece and the Ionian Islands*. London: W. Blackwood and Sons.

Murphy, Michael. 1985. Rumors of Identity: Gossip and Rapport in Ethnographic Research. *Ethnology* 44, no. 2: 132–37.

Myrsiades, Linda S. 1992. *Karagiozis: Culture and Comedy in Greek Puppet Theater*. Lexington: University of Kentucky Press.

NA. 1860. *Kanonismos ton Verfon kai Orfanontrofiou*. Argostoli: State Press.

Napier, Charles J. 1833. *The Colonies: Treating of their Value Generally and of the Ionian Islands in Particular*. London: T. & W. Boane.

Napier, Sir W. 1857. *The Life and Opinions of General Sir Charles James Napier*. London: John Murray.

Newton, C. T. 1865. *Travels and Discoveries in the Levant*. London: Day and Son.

Nicol, Donald M. 1984. *The Despotate of Epiros 1267–1479: A Contribution to the History of Greece in the Middle Ages*. Cambridge: Cambridge University Press.

Nikiforou-Testone, Aliki. 1991. *Arhio Ektelestikis Astinomias*. Kerkira: Istoriko Arhio Kerkira.

Nisbett, Richard E., and Dov Cohen. 1996. *Culture of Honor: The Psychology of Violence in the South*. Boulder: Westview Press.

Norton, Mary Beth. 1987. Gender and Defamation in Sevententh-Century Maryland. *William and Mary Quarterly* 44, no. 1: 3–39.

Nye, Robert A. 1990. Fencing, the Duel, and Republican Manhood in the Third Republic. *Journal of Contemporary History* 25, no. 2–3: 365–82.

———. 1991. Honor Codes in Modern France: An Historical Anthropology. *Ethnologia Europea* 21: 5–17.

———. 1993. *Masculinity and Male Codes of Honor in Modern France.* New York: Oxford University Press.

———. 1997. The End of the Modern French Duel. In *Men and Violence: Masculinity, Honor Codes and Violent Rituals in Europe and America, 17th–20th Centuries,* ed. Pieter Spierenburg, 115–28. Columbus: The Ohio State University Press.

O'Hanlon, Rosalind, and David Washbrook. 1992. After Orientalism: Culture, Criticism, and Politics in the Third World. *Comparative Studies in Society and History* 34, no. 1: 141–67.

Orso, Ethelyn G. 1979. *Modern Greek Humor: A Collection of Jokes and Ribald Tales.* Bloomington: University of Indiana Press.

Paine, Robert. 1989. High-wire Culture: Comparing Two Agonistic Systems of Self-esteem (Marri Baluch of Pakistan and Sarakatsani of Highland Greece). *Man* 24, no. 4: 657–73.

Palmer, Bryan D. 1990. *Descent into Discourse: The Reification of Language and the Writing of Social History.* Philadelphia: Temple University Press.

Palmer, Stanley H. 1988. *Police and Protest in England and Ireland, 1780–1850.* Cambridge: Cambridge University Press.

Panikkar, K. N. 1989. *Against Lord and State: Religion and Peasant Uprising in Malabar, 1836–1921.* Delhi: Oxford University Press.

Partsch, Johann. 1982. *Kephallenia kai Ithaka.* Athens: Note Karabia.

Past and Present Society. 1982. *Agrarian Unrest in British and French Africa, British India and French Indo-China during the Nineteenth and Twentieth Centuries.* Oxford: Past and Present Society.

Pavlides, Eleftherios, and Jane Hesser. 1986. Women's Roles and House Form and Decoration in Eressos, Greece. In *Gender and Power in Rural Greece,* ed. Jill Dubisch, 68–96. Princeton: Princeton University Press.

Paximadopoulos-Stavrinou, Maria. 1977. Dimografikii Pinakes ton Eton 1840–1863 yia tin Kefalonia. *Kefalleniaka Hronika* 2: 120–63.

———. 1980a. *I Exeyersis tis Kefallenias kata ta eti 1848 ke 1849.* Athens: Eteria Kefalliniakon Istorikon Erevnon.

———. 1980b. *Some Notes on Britain's Attitude towards the Ionian Protectorate.* Athens: Panteios Graduate School of Political Science.

Peristiany, John G., ed. 1968. *Contributions to Mediterranean Sociology.* The Hague: Mouton.

Perkin, Harold. 1969. *The Origins of Modern English Society.* Toronto: University of Toronto Press.

Pitt-Rivers, Julian Alfred. 1961. *The People of the Sierra*. Chicago: University of Chicago Press.

———. 1977. *The Fate of Schechem*. New York: Cambridge University Press.

Pizanias, P. 1988. *Oikonomiki Istoria tis Ellinikis Stafidas 1851–1921*. Athens: Idryma Erevnas kai Paideias tes Emborikes Trapezas tes Ellados.

Politis, L. 1973. *A History of Modern Greek Literature*. Oxford: Clarendon Press.

Polk, Kenneth. 1994. *When Men Kill: Scenarios of Masculine Violence*. Cambridge: Cambridge University Press.

———. 1998. Masculinity, Honour, and Confrontational Homicide. In *Criminology at the Crossroads: Feminist Readings in Crime and Justice*, ed. Kathleen Daly and Lisa Maher, 188–205. New York: Oxford University Press.

Post, Robert C. 1986. The Social Foundations of Defamation Law: Reputation and the Constitution. *California Law Review* 74: 691–742.

Prakash, Gyan. 1992. Writing Post-orientalist Histories of the Third World: Indian Historiography is Good to Think. In *Colonialism and Culture*, ed. Nicholas B. Dirks, 353–88. Ann Arbor: University of Michigan Press.

———. 1995. Orientalism Now (Forum: The Meaning of Historicism and Its Relevance for Contemporary Theory). *History and Theory* 34, no. 3: 199–211.

Pratt, Michael. 1978. *Britain's Greek Empire*. London: Rex Collings.

Rabb, Theodore K. 1981. Coherence, Synthesis, and Quality in History. *Journal of Interdisciplinary History* 12: 315–32.

Rangabes, L. 1925–1927. *Libra d' Or de la Noblesse Ionienne vols. 1–3*. Athens: Eleftheroudakis.

Ransel, David L. 1978. Abandonment and Fosterage of Unwanted Children: The Women of the Foundling System. In *The Family in Imperial Russia: New Lines of Historical Research*, ed. David L. Ransel, 189–217. Urbana: University of Illinois Press.

———. 1988. *Mothers of Misery: Child Abandonment in Russia*. Princeton: Princeton University Press.

Roeder, Philip G. 1984. Legitimacy and Reasant Revolutions: An Alternative to Moral Economy. *Peasant Studies* 11: 150–68.

Roemer, John. 1982. Methodological Individualism and Deductive Marxism. *Theory and Society* 11: 513–20.

Rosnow, Ralph L. 1976. *Rumor and Gossip: The Social Psychology of Hearsay*. New York: Elsevier.

Rotundo, E. Anthony. 1993. *American Manhood: Transformations in Masculinity from the Revolution to the Modern Era*. New York: Basic Books.

Rouland, Norbert. 1994. *Legal Anthropology*. Stanford: Stanford University Press.

Ruane, Joseph. 1992. Colonialism and the Interpretation of Irish Historical Development. In *Approaching the Past: Historical Anthropology through*

Irish Case Studies, ed. Marilyn Silverman and P. H. Gulliver, 293–323. New York: Columbia University Press.

Runciman, Steven. 1985. *The Great Church in Captivity.* Cambridge: Cambridge University Press.

Sabetti, Filippo. 1984. *Political Authority in a Sicilian Village.* New Brunswick: Rutgers University Press.

Sahlins, Marshall. 1985. *Islands of History.* Chicago: University of Chicago Press.

Said, Edward. 1978. *Orientalism.* New York: Vintage Books.

Salamone, S. D., and J. B. Stanton. 1986. Introducing the Nikokyria: Ideality and Reality in Social Process. In *Gender and Power in Rural Greece,* ed. Jill Dubisch, 97–120. Princeton: Princeton University Press.

Salamone, Stephen D. 1987. Tradition and Gender: The Nikokyrio: The Economics of Sex Role Complementarity in Rural Greece. *Ethnos* 15, no. 2: 203–25.

Sandiford, Keith A. P. 1981. Gladstone and Liberal Nationalist Movements. *Albion* 13: 27–42.

Sant Cassia, Paul, with Constantina Bada. 1992. *The Making of the Modern Greek Family: Marriage and Exchange in Nineteenth-century Athens.* Cambridge: Cambridge University Press.

Sarti, Roland. 1985. *Long Live the Strong: A History of Rural Society in the Apennine Mountains.* Amherst: University of Massachusetts Press.

Schmidhauser, John R. 1989. Power, Legal Imperialism, and Dependency. *Law and Society Review* 23, no. 6: 857–78.

Schwartz, Bill, ed. 1996. *The Expansion of England: Race, Ethnicity and Cultural History.* New York: Routledge.

Scott, James C. 1985. *Weapons of the Weak: Everyday Forms of Peasant Resistance.* New Haven: Yale University Press.

———. 1989. Everyday Forms of Resistance. In *Everyday Forms of Resistance,* ed. Forrest D. Colburn, 3–33. New York: M. E. Sharpe, Inc.

———. 1990. *Domination and the Art of Resistance: Hidden Transcripts.* New Haven: Yale University Press.

———. 1992. Domination, Acting and Fantasy. In *The Paths to Domination, Resistance and Terror,* first ed., ed. Carolyn Nordstrom and JoAnn Martin, 55–84. Berkeley: University of California Press.

Segalen, Martine. 1986. *Historical Anthropology of the Family.* Translated by J. C. Whitehouse and Sarah Matthews. Cambridge: Cambridge University Press.

Seidman, Steven. 1996. Empire and Knowledge: More Troubles, New Opportunities for Sociology. (Edward Said's Book, *Orientalism*). *Contemporary Sociology* 25, no. 3: 313–17.

Sewell Jr., William H. 1980. *Work and Revolution in France: The Language of Labor from the Old Regime to the French Revolution.* Cambridge: Cambridge University Press.

Sharpe, J. A. 1980. *Defamation and Sexual Slander in Early Modern England: The Church Courts at York.* York: Borthwick Papers, 58.

Sherwood, Joan. 1988. *Poverty in Eighteenth-century Spain: The Women and Children of the Inclusa.* Toronto: University of Toronto Press.

Shorter, Edward. 1981a. *Bastardy in South Germany: A Comment.* Princeton: Princeton University Press.

———. 1981b. *Illegitimacy, Sexual Revolution, and Social Change in Modern Europe.* Princeton: Princeton University Press.

Silverman, Sydel. 1975. *Three Bells of Civilization: The Life of an Italian Hilltown.* New York: Columbia University Press.

Simpson, Anthony E. 1988. Dandelions on the Field of Honor: Duelling, The Middle Classes and the Law in Nineteenth-century England. *Criminal Justice History* 9: 99–155.

Sivaramakrishnan, K. 1995. Situating the Subaltern: History and Anthropology in the Subaltern Studies Project. *Journal of Historical Sociology* 8, no. 4: 395–429.

Slaughter, M. M. 1992. The Development of Common Law Defamation Privileges: From Communitarian Society to Market Society. *Cardozo Law Review* 14 (November): 351–406.

Smith, Anthony. 1987. *The Ethnic Origins of Nations.* New York: Basil Blackwell.

Solomos, Dionysios. 1944. *I Gynaika tis Zakynthos.* Third ed. Athens: Ikaros.

Souris, Yiorgos A. 1989. O Gladstone sta Eptanisa: Enotiko Kinima kai Vretanika Aieksoda. *Ta Istorkia* 11: 277–312.

Souyoudzoglou-Haywood, Christina. 1999. *The Ionian Islands in the Bronze Age and early Iron Age, 3000–800 B.C.* Liverpool: Liverpool University Press.

Spencer, Edmund. 1853. *Travels in European Turkey.* London: Hurst and Blackett Publishers.

Spencer, Herbert. 1892. *The Principles of Ethics, vol.1.* London: Williams and Norgate.

Spierenburg, Pieter. 1994. Faces of Violence: Homicide Trends and Cultural Meanings: Amsterdam, 1431–1816. *Journal of Social History* 27, no. 4: 701–16.

———. 1996. Long-term Trends in Homicide: Theoretical Reflections and Dutch Evidence, Fifteenth to Twentieth Centuries. In *The Civilization of Crime: Violence in Town and Countryside since the Middle Ages,* ed. Eric A. Johnson and Eric H. Monkkonen, 63–105. Urbana: University of Illinois Press.

———. 1998a. Masculinity, Violence and Honor: The Long Term. In *Men and Violence: Masculinity, Honor Codes and Violent Rituals in Europe and America, 17th–20th Centuries,* ed. Pieter Spierenburg, 3–22. Columbus: The Ohio State University Press.

———. 1998b. Knife Fighting and Popular Codes of Honor in Early Modern Amsterdam. In *Men and Violence: Masculinity, Honor Codes and Violent Rituals in Europe and America, 17th–20th Centuries*, ed. Pieter Spierenburg, 48–72. Columbus: The Ohio State University Press.

Spindel, Donna J. 1995. The Law of Words: Verbal Abuse in North Carolina to 1730. *American Journal of Legal History* 39, no. 1: 25–42.

Spivak, Gayatri Chakravorty. 1988. Can the Subaltern Speak? In *Marxism and the Interpretation of Culture*, ed. Cary Nelson and Lawrence Grossberg, 271–313. Urbana: University of Illinois Press.

St. Clair, William. 1972. *That Greece Might Still Be Free: The Philhellenes in the War of Independence*. Oxford: Oxford University Press.

Starkie, Thomas. 1843. *A treatise on the law of slander and libel, and incidentally of malicious prosecutions. From the 2d English ed. of 1830, with notes and references to American cases and to English decisions since 1830. By John L. Wendell*. Albany: C. Van Benthuysen and Co.

Starr, June. 1978. *Dispute and Settlement in Rural Turkey: An Ethnography of Law*. Leiden: Brill.

Stavrinos, Miranda. 1985. The Reformist Party in Ionian Islands (1848–1852): Internal Conflicts and Nationalist Aspirations. *Balkan Studies* 26: 351–61.

Stearns, Carol Zistowitz, and Peter N. Stearns. 1986. *Anger: The Struggle for Emotional Control in America's History*. Chicago: University of Chicago Press.

Stearns, Peter N. 1990. *Be A Man! Males in Modern Society*. New York: Holmes & Meier.

Stewart, Charles. 1991. *Demons and the Devil: Moral Imagination in Modern Greek Culture*. Princeton: Princeton University Press.

Stewart, Frank Henderson. 1994. *Honor*. Chicago: University of Chicago Press.

Stocking, George. 1988. *Victorian Anthropology*. New York: The Free Press.

Stoianovich, Traian. 1949. The Ionian Islands in the Time of Napoleon. New York University Library, unpublished typescript.

Stone, Lawrence. 1979. The Revival of Narrative: Reflections on a New Old History. *Past & Present* 86: 3–24.

Sturtevant, David Reeves. 1976. *Popular Uprisings in the Philippines, 1840–1940*. Ithaca: Cornell University Press.

Sussman, George. 1977. The End of the Wet-nursing Business in France. *Journal of Interdisciplinary History* 2: 304–28.

———. 1981. *Parisian Infants and Norman Wet Nurses in the Early Nineteenth Century: A Statistical Study*. Princeton: Princeton University Press.

———. 1982. *Selling Mothers' Milk: The Wet-nursing Business in France*. Urbana: University of Illinois Press.

Taylor, Lawrence J. 1990. Stories of Power, Powerful Stories: The Drunken Priest in Donegal. In *Religious Orthodoxy and Popular Faith in European Society*, ed. Ellen Badone, 163–84. Princeton: Princeton University Press.

———. 1996. "There are two things that people do not like to hear about themselves": The Anthropology of Ireland and the Irish Views of Anthropology. *South Atlantic Quarterly* 95, no. 1: 213–26.

Tebbutt, Melanie. 1995. *Women's Talk?: A Social History of "Gossip" in Working-class Neighbourhoods, 1880–1960*. Aldershot, England: Scolar Press.

Temperley, H. 1937. Documents Illustrating the Cession of the Ionian Islands to Greece, 1848–1870. *Journal of Modern History* 9, no. 1: 49–65.

Thomas, David Hurst. 1986. *Refiguring Anthropology*. Prospect Heights, N.J.: Waveland Press, Inc.

Thomas, Ella Cooper. 1963. *Libel and Slander and Related Actions*. Dobbs Ferry, N.Y.: Oceana Publications.

Thomas, Nicholas. 1989. *Out of Time: History and Evolution in Anthropological Discourse*. Cambridge: Cambridge University Press.

———. 1990. Sanitation and Seeing: The Creation of State Power in Early Colonial Fiji. *Comparative Studies in Society and History* 32: 149–70.

———. 1991. *Entangled Objects: Exchange, Material Culture, and Colonialism in the Pacific*. Cambridge: Harvard University Press.

———. 1994. *Colonialism's Culture: Anthropology, Travel and Government*. Princeton: Princeton University Press.

Thompson, E. P. 1978. *The Poverty of Theory and Other Essays*. New York: W. W. Norton.

———. 1991. Rough Music. *Customs in Common: Studies in Traditional Popular Culture*, 467–538. New York: W. W. Norton.

Thompson, John B. 1989. The Theory of Structuration. In *Social Theory of Modern Societies: Anthony Giddens and His Critics*, ed. D. Held and J. B. Thompson, 56–76. Cambridge: Cambridge University Press.

Thompson, Neville, and Thomas C. Sosnowski. 1994. The British Protectorate of the Ionian Islands and the Greek War of Independence, 1815–1827. *Consortium on Revolutionary Europe 1750–1850: Proceedings* 23: 302–11.

Tilly, Charles. 1985. Retrieving European Lives. *Reliving the Past: The Worlds of Social history*. ed. Olivier Zunz, 11–52. Chapel Hill: University of North Carolina Press.

———. 1986. *The Contentious French: Four Centuries of Popular Struggle*. Cambridge: Harvard University Press.

Todorova, Maria. 1994. The Balkans: From Discovery to Invention. *Slavic Review* 53, no. 2: 453–82.

———. 1997. *Imagining the Balkans*. New York: Oxford University Press.

Tosh, John. 1994. What Should Historians Do About Masculinity? Reflections on Nineteenth Century Britain. *History Workshop Journal* 38: 179–202.

———. 1996. New Men? The Bourgeois Cult of Home (in the 19th century). *History Today* 46, no. 12: 9–16.

Tsigakou, Fani-Maria. 1981. *The Rediscovery of Greece: Travellers and Painters of the Romantic Era.* New York: Caratzas.

Tsotsoros, S. 1989. *Oikonomikoi kai Koinonikoi Mexanismoi ston Oreino Xoro.* Athens: Istroiko Arxeio, Emporike Trapeza tesEllados.

Tsouganatos, D. 1976. I Epanastasis tis Skalas (16.8.1849) kai o Papa Listis. *Kefalleniaka Hronika* 1: 46–69.

Tuckerman, Charles K. 1872. *The Greeks of To-Day.* London: Sampson & Low Co.

Tumelty, J. J. 1953. *The Ionian Islands under British Administration, 1815–1864.* Cambridge: Ph.D. dissertation, University of Cambridge.

Turner, Frank M. 1981. *The Greek Heritage in Victorian Britain.* New Haven: Yale University Press.

Tutino, John. 1986. *From Insurrection to Revolution in Mexico: Social Bases of Agrarian Violence, 1750–1940.* Princeton: Princeton University Press.

Typaldos, Ioannis. 1846. *Statistica penale, ossia, Rendi-conto generale dell'amministrazione della giustizia penale in Corfu.* Kerkyra: State Press.

von Bar, Carl Ludwig. 1916. *A History of the Continental Criminal Law.* Chicago: Studies in Criminal Law.

Walvin, J. 1982. Black Caricature: The Roots of Racialism. In *Race in Britain: Continuity and Change,* ed. C. Husband, 60. London: Hutchinson.

Waters, John Paul. 1996. Introduction: Ireland and Irish Cultural Studies. *South Atlantic Quarterly* 95, no. 1: 1–5.

Weber, Max. 1958. *The Protestant Ethic and the Spirit of Capitalism.* New York: Charles Scribner's Sons.

Wiener, Martin. 1997. The Victorian Criminalization of Men. In *Men and Violence: Masculinity, Honor Codes and Violent Rituals in Europe and America, 17th–20th Centuries,* ed. Pieter Spierenburg, 149–63. Columbus: The Ohio State University Press.

Wikan, Unni. 1984. Shame and Honor: A Contestable Pair. *Man* 19: 635–52.

Wilson, Adrian. 1989. Illegitimacy and Its Implications in Mid-eighteenth-century London: The Evidence of the Foundling Hospital. *Change and Continuity* 4: 103–64.

Wilson, Samuel Sheridan. 1839. *A Narrative of the Greek Mission; or, Sixteen Years in Malta and Greece: Including Tours in the Peloponnesus, in the Aegean and Ionian isles.* London: John Snow.

Wilson, Stephen. 1988a. *Feuding, Conflict and Banditry in Nineteenth-century Corsica.* Cambridge: Cambridge University Press.

———. 1988b. Infanticide, Child Abandonment, and Female Honor in Nineteenth-century Corsica. *Comparative Studies in Society and History* 30: 762–83.

Wolfe, John. 1994. *God and Greater Britain: Religion and National Life in Britain and Ireland, 1843–1945*. New York: Routledge.

Wolfgang, Marvin E. 1958. *Patterns in Criminal Homicide*. New York: John Wiley and Sons, Inc.

Wrigley, W. David. 1978. The Ionian Islands and the Advent of the Greek State (1827–1833). *Balkan Studies* 19: 413–26.

———. 1987a. The British Enforcement of Ionian Neutrality against Greek and Turkish Refugees, 1821–1828: A Study in Selectivity. *Südost-Forschungen* 56: 95–112.

———. 1987b. The Neutrality of Ionian Shipping and Its Enforcement during the Greek Revolution (1821–1831). *The Mariner's Mirror* 73: 245–60.

———. 1988a. *The Diplomatic Significance of Ionian Neutrality 1821–1831*. New York: Lang Highlights.

———. 1988b. The Issue of Ionian Neutrality in Anglo-Ottoman Relations, 1821–1830. *Südost-Forschungen* 47: 109–43.

Wyatt-Brown, Bertram. 1982. *Southern Honor: Ethics and Behavior in the Old South*. New York: Oxford University Press.

———. 1988. The Mask of Obedience: Male Slave Psychology in the Old South. *American Historical Review* 93, no. 4: 1228–52.

Zeno-Zencovich, Vincenzo. 1991. Damage Awards in Defamation Cases: An Italian View. *The International & Comparative Law Quarterly* 40 (July): 691–99.

Zinovieff, Sofka. 1991. Inside and Outside In: Gossip, Hospitality and the Greek Character. *Journal of Mediterranean Studies* 1, no. 1: 120–34.

Zunz, Olivier, ed. 1985. *Reliving the Past: The Worlds of Social History*. Chapel Hill: University of North Carolina Press.

INDEX

The use of *f* with a page number indicates a photograph or drawing, and the use of *t* indicates a table.